Culture and Customs
of Namibia

Culture and Customs of Namibia

ANENE EJIKEME

Culture and Customs of Africa
Toyin Falola, Series Editor

 GREENWOOD

AN IMPRINT OF ABC-CLIO, LLC
Santa Barbara, California • Denver, Colorado • Oxford, England

Library of Congress Cataloging-in-Publication Data

Ejikeme, Anene.
  Culture and customs of Namibia / Anene Ejikeme.
    p. cm. — (Culture and customs of Africa)
  ISBN 978-0-313-35891-3 (hardcopy : alk. paper) —
  ISBN 978-0-313-35892-0 (ebook)
  1. Namibia—Civilization. 2. Namibia—Social life and customs. I. Title. II. Series: Culture and customs of Africa.
  DT1552.E38 2011
  968.81—dc22   2011010009

ISBN: 978-0-313-35891-3
EISBN: 978-0-313-35892-0

15 14 13 12 11   1 2 3 4 5

This book is also available on the World Wide Web as an eBook.
Visit www.abc-clio.com for details.

Greenwood
An Imprint of ABC-CLIO, LLC

ABC-CLIO, LLC
130 Cremona Drive, P.O. Box 1911
Santa Barbara, California 93116-1911

This book is printed on acid-free paper ∞

Manufactured in the United States of America

Contents

Series Foreword

AFRICA IS A vast continent, the second largest, after Asia. It is four times the size of the United States, excluding Alaska. It is the cradle of human civilization. A diverse continent, Africa has more than fifty countries with a population of over 700 million people who speak over 1,000 languages. Ecological and cultural differences vary from one region to another. As an old continent, Africa is one of the richest in culture and customs, and its contributions to world civilization are impressive indeed.

Africans regard culture as essential to their lives and future development. Culture embodies their philosophy, worldview, behavior patterns, arts, and institutions. The books in this series intend to capture the comprehensiveness of African culture and customs, dwelling on such important aspects as religion, worldview, literature, media, art, housing, architecture, cuisine, traditional dress, gender, marriage, family, lifestyles, social customs, music, and dance.

The uses and definitions of "culture" vary, reflecting its prestigious association with civilization and social status, its restriction to attitude and behavior, its globalization, and the debates surrounding issues of tradition, modernity, and postmodernity. The participating authors have chosen a comprehensive meaning of culture while not ignoring the alternative uses of the term.

Each volume in the series focuses on a single country, and the format is uniform. The first chapter presents a historical overview, in addition to information on geography, economy, and politics. Each volume then proceeds to examine the various aspects of culture and customs. The series highlights the mechanisms for the transmission of tradition and culture across generations: the significance of orality, traditions, kinship rites, and family property distribution; the rise of print culture; and the impact of educational institutions. The series also explores the intersections between local, regional, national, and global bases for identity and social relations. While the volumes are organized nationally, they pay attention to ethnicity and language groups and the links between Africa and the wider world.

The books in the series capture the elements of continuity and change in culture and customs. Custom is represented not as static or as a museum artifact but as a dynamic phenomenon. Furthermore, the authors recognize the current challenges to traditional wisdom, which include gender relations, the negotiation of local identities in relation to the state, the significance of struggles for power at national and local levels and their impact on cultural traditions and community-based forms of authority, and the tensions between agrarian and industrial/manufacturing/oil-based economic modes of production.

Africa is a continent of great changes, instigated mainly by Africans but also through influences from other continents. The rise of youth culture, the penetration of the global media, and the challenges to generational stability are some of the components of modern changes explored in the series. The ways in which traditional (non-Western and nonimitative) African cultural forms continue to survive and thrive—that is, how they have taken advantage of the market system to enhance their influence and reproductions—also receive attention.

Through the books in this series, readers can see their own cultures in a different perspective, understand the habits of Africans, and educate themselves about the customs and cultures of other countries and people. The hope is that the readers will come to respect the cultures of others and see them not as inferior or superior to theirs but merely as different. Africa has always been important to Europe and the United States, essentially as a source of labor, raw materials, and markets. Blacks are in Europe and the Americas as part of the African diaspora, a migration that took place primarily because of the slave trade. Recent African migrants increasingly swell their number and visibility. It is important to understand the history of the diaspora and the newer migrants as well as the roots of the culture and customs of the places from where they come. It is equally important to understand others in order to be able to interact successfully in a world that keeps shrinking. The accessible nature of the books in this series will contribute to this understanding and enhance the quality of human interaction in a new millennium.

Toyin Falola
Frances Higginbothom Nalle Centennial Professor in History
The University of Texas at Austin

Author's Note

Bantu languages use prefixes to denote, for instance, reference to a single person, to many persons, or to a language. For example, the language is Ru-Kwangali, a single individual is a MuKwangali, and the community members are VaKwangali (or WaKwangali). An OmuHerero speaks OtjiHerero and belongs to the OvaHerero community, while a MoTswana speaks SeTswana and belongs to the BaTswana community. I have used prefixes here only in reference to languages.

Another note on language: In Namibia spellings sometimes vary a great deal. This is in large part a result of Namibia's multiple European-language heritage (mainly British/English, German, and Afrikaans). So, for example, the name of Namibia's most celebrated anti-apartheid leader is usually written Toivo *ja* Toivo but sometimes Toivo *ya* Toivo. The country's first president is Sam Nujoma, but many who share the same last name spell theirs Nuyoma. Cassinga is also Kassinga, and *tackies* are also *takkies;* Bethanie is also Bethany, or even Bethanien.

Preface

NAMIBIA, IN THE top 20 percent of the world's largest countries, is an enormous country dominated by two deserts. The country is named after the world's oldest desert, more than 55 million years old. Namibia is a land of vast open spaces; yet although more than half of the country's landmass is covered by desert (or semidesert), its landscape, wildlife, and plant life are startlingly rich. Even plants and animals found elsewhere have made unique adaptations to survive in an often-harsh natural environment; a significant number of other plants and animals are found nowhere else on earth. Apart from flora and fauna, Namibia offers other particularities: Some scientists and laypersons are eager, for example, to see the largest known meteorites in the world.

It is impossible to speak about contemporary Namibia without discussing its recent history, one that is marked by painful episodes. Namibia was the site of the first genocide in the 20th century; indeed, many of the ideas and policies pursued by the Nazis in Germany were first executed in Namibia. One of only a handful of German colonies, Namibia was one of the last countries in Africa to gain its independence. Namibia is the only modern African country to have been colonized by another African country. The country has been politically stable since independence, but there is discontent in many quarters about the continuing extreme inequity in wealth, joblessness, and what some consider to be, in effect, one-party rule.

Namibia is a country of rich cultural traditions and with a diverse heritage, and I have tried to capture this, without, as is so often the case when Africa is being discussed, giving the impression that there is a Tradition (with a capital *t*) that every member of the particular ethnic group in question follows in specifically the same unchanging and fixed way. This book attempts to capture some of the diversity of Namibia's peoples and their customs, without resorting to idealized accounts of supposedly traditional ways. As in the United States, individuals in Namibia often modify tradition to suit their purposes—for example, in celebrating their marriages or Christmas. I have tried to focus on what people do rather than what they say should be done.

The key aim of this work is to provide an accessible introduction to contemporary Namibia. Like all the other books in the series, this one is organized along thematic lines, with chapters devoted to topics such as religion and worldview, gender roles, and marriage and family. In this volume I have included a chapter on the environment and tourism. Namibia was the first country in the world to include environmental protection in its constitution; this is a significant event. Given the extreme aridity in much of the country and concerns about the effects of climate change, Namibia may have to lead the way in finding solutions to the environmental problems that seem likely to challenge many parts of the world in the years and decades ahead.

Acknowledgments

I OWE SO many people a huge debt of gratitude. First, I wish to thank Professor Toyin Falola for inviting me to contribute this volume to the Culture and Customs of Africa series. I am enormously indebted to the many scholars whose works on various aspects of Namibian society, from history and politics to gender relations and poverty, have molded my understanding of Namibia. My debt to these scholars is evident in the bibliography.

My deepest gratitude goes to the many Namibians who were so generous in giving of their time to speak to me about their lives and to answer, with the greatest patience and grace, my sometimes, no doubt, tedious questions. I am indebted to the unnamed informants I met through friends and acquaintances, and the many more that I approached without any prior introduction—on buses, in taxis, in markets and offices, on school campuses, on street corners, in bookshops and in shopping malls, and in cafés and restaurants. Unfortunately, I cannot thank all of these generous, gracious individuals by name.

However, I am happy that I can thank some individuals by name. First, I wish to thank the Greytons (Christi, Jovan, and Whitney) for introducing me to the joys of *kapana* and in other ways too numerous to list, Beauty Jacobs of Gibeon for so readily giving her time, time and time again, and Mathilda Isaacs for making me so welcome and introducing me to her friends and family. I am also grateful to Honurable Hansina Christian for making the time to answer my questions, Chanel Frey for being herself and showing me aspects of Katutura I would never have found, Claudia and Dirk Haarmann for expediting necessary documentation, Henning Melber for his assistance in tracking down poets, Priscilla Kamati for always being ready to make introductions, Sheena Magenya and the staff at Sister Namibia for their collegiality as well as the leaflets, pamphlets, and magazines, Ambassador Patrick Nandago for answering emails, Vasco for the conversations, Sarala Krishnamurthy for her willingness to help, Helen Vale for sharing her work on Namibian poetry, and Bishop Dr. Zephania Kameeta and Gerson Uaripi Tjihenuna for permission to quote from their poetry. I am also grateful to the staff at the Konrad Adenauer Foundation who gave me several publications to which I would otherwise not have had access.

I am delighted to acknowledge my deep gratitude to Maria G. McWilliams and all the staff at the interlibrary loan office at Trinity University in San Antonio, Texas, and the wonderful student workers in the History Department. Ms. McWilliams was ever ready to assist and always with good cheer. I thank Albright College, Reading, Pennsylvania, for hosting me during the time I was completing this book. Also in the United States, I wish to thank the following: Ada Ejikeme, Ruqayya Khan, Alida Metcalf, Linda Salvucci, and Kaitlin Ciarmiello at ABC-CLIO/Greenwood Press for her patience. Finally, I thank my family for their unflagging support.

List of Acronyms

AFM	Apostolic Faith Mission
AME	African Methodist Episcopal Church
CCN	Council of Churches in Namibia
COTA	College of the Arts
DELK	Deutsche Evangelisch-Lutherische Kirche (German Evangelical Lutheran Church)
DRC	Dutch Reformed Church
DRN	Democratic Republic of Namibia
DTA	Democratic Turnhalle Alliance
ELC	Evangelical Lutheran Church
ELCIN	Evangelical Lutheran Church in Namibia
ELCIN-GELC	German-speaking Evangelical Lutheran Church in Namibia (also DELK)
ELCRN	Evangelical Lutheran Church in the Republic of Namibia
ELOC	Evangelical Lutheran Ovambo-Kavango Church (formerly Finnish Missionary Society)
FELM	Finnish Evangelical Lutheran Mission (also Finnish Missionary Society, FMS)
FNCC	Franco-Namibian Cultural Centre
JMAC	John Muafangejo Art Centre

KCAC	Katutura Community Arts Centre
LMS	London Missionary Society
LWF	Lutheran World Federation
MET	Ministry of Environment and Tourism
NAMCOL	Namibian College of Open Learning
NBC	Namibia Broadcasting Corporation
NFC	Namibia Film Commission
NNC	Namibia National Convention
OMI	Missionary Oblates of Mary Immaculate (Catholic religious order)
OPC	Ovambo People's Congress
OPO	Ovambo People's Organisation
OSFS	Oblates of St. Francis of Sales (Catholic religious order)
OYO	Ombetja Yehinga Organisation
PLAN	People's Liberation Army of Namibia (military wing of SWAPO)
RMS	Rhenish Missionary Society
SABC	South African Broadcasting Corporation
SADF	South African Defence Force
SPWC	SWAPO Party Women's Council
SWANLA	South West African Native Labour Agency
SWANU	South West Africa National Union
SWAPO	South West Africa People's Organisation
SWBC	South West Africa Broadcasting Corporation
TRP	The Rainbow Project
UCC-NELC	United Church Council of the Namibian Evangelical Lutheran Churches
UNAM	University of Namibia
UNFPA	United Nations Population Fund
UNIN	United Nations Institute for Namibia (in Lusaka, Zambia)
WAD	Women's Actions for Development (advocacy group)
WIMSA	Working Group of Indigenous Minorities in Southern Africa
WMMS	Wesleyan Methodist Missionary Society

Chronology

450,000,000 B.C.E.	Extraterrestrial rocks fall down on site of Hoba Farm near Grootfontein, leaving behind the largest known meteorite in the world (Hoba meteorite, over 60 tons).
25,000 B.C.E.	Beginning of production of rock art.
1st centuries C.E.	Bantu-speaking migrants, widely considered ancestors of the Nama and Damara, begin to arrive in areas of modern-day Namibia.
14th–17th centuries	New waves of Bantu migrants, considered ancestors of the Ovambo and Herero, settle in Namibia.
1486	Adventurer Diego Cão and his group reach Namibian waters.
1488	Bartholomeu Diaz erects a stone cross in area of present-day Luderitz.
1793	Dutch settlers from Cape Colony seize Walvis Bay.
Late 18th century	Orlam Afrikaners, migrants from Cape Colony, settle in Namibia.
1806	First Christian mission station is established in Namibia by the Albrecht brothers (London Missionary Society, or LMS).
1814	Johann Heinrich Schmelen establishes first LMS mission station in Bethanie (Bethanien).
1838	Orlam Afrikaner migrants under their leader Jonker Afrikaner establish a community in area of the modern suburb of Klein Windhoek.

1842	Rhenish Mission Society (RMS) establishes a mission station in Windhoek but is soon forced to withdraw.
1858	Treaty of Hoachanas signed by more than a dozen Nama and Herero leaders.
1861	Death of Jonker Afrikaner.
1868	Baster group from present-day South Africa establishes a community in Rehoboth.
1878	Britain annexes Walvis Bay to Cape Colony.
1883	German merchant Adolf Luderitz purchases land on the coast from Nama chief Joseph Fredericks; historians continue to debate if the two sides understood the transaction in the same way, or, indeed, whether Fredericks actually had the authority to make such a sale.
1884	Germany declares protectorate of South West Africa.
1890	Germany builds a fort in Windhoek, the Alte Feste.
1894	Hendrik Witbooi, Nama chief, finally agrees to a truce (or protection treaty) with German forces.
1896–1897	Outbreak of rinderpest in southern Africa decimates cattle.
1904–1908	War of Herero and Namas against Germans.
August 1904	Battle of Waterberg, turning point in German-Herero war.
October 1904	German General Lothar von Trotha issues infamous extermination order.
1905	Nama chief Hendrik Witbooi dies from injury sustained while fighting the Germans.
1908	Diamond discovered by a Namibian who had worked in South African mines. Rush of new settlers from Germany, seeking to make their fortune.
1915	South Africa invades and occupies Namibia, and large numbers of South African whites begin to settle in Namibia.
1920	South Africa is authorized to govern South West Africa under a Class C Mandate from the League of Nations.
1926	Creation of the two forerunners of SWANLA (or South West African Native Labour Agency). The two organizations are amalgamated to create a single one in 1943, and from then until 1972 SWANLA is responsible for all labor recruitment in Namibia, recruiting predominantly Ovambo men, all on a contract basis.

1946	United Nations rejects South Africa's application to be allowed to incorporate Namibia (South West Africa); Chief Hosea Kutako and other leading chiefs, denied passports by the South African government and thus unable to travel to the United Nations, lead a petition drive calling for an end to South African occupation.
1948	The new South African apartheid government declares it will no longer send annual reports on Namibia to the United Nations.
1950	The International Court of Justice at The Hague rules that South Africa is still required to send these annual reports, although its mandate to govern Namibia had been established under the League of Nations, because the United Nations is the successor body.
1957	Ovambo People's Congress (OPC) founded by Andimba Toivo ya Toivo and others in Cape Town, South Africa.
1958	OPC is renamed the Ovambo People's Organisation (OPO).
September 1959	Herero activists, chiefs, and intellectuals establish the South West Africa National Union (SWANU).
December 1959	Forced removals of Africans from Old Location to Katutura result in at least one dozen dead and many injured. The police fire on peaceful demonstrators, many of whom are children.
1960	OPO becomes the South West Africa People's Organisation (SWAPO).
November 1960	Ethiopia and Liberia bring separate suits to the International Court contesting South African rule over Namibia and asking the court to give a ruling on South African rule over Namibia.
1961	United Nations establishes UN Special Committee for South West Africa (Brazil, Mexico, Norway, Philippines, Somalia, and Togo); in its first report the commission calls for South West African independence.
1964	The South African government-appointed Odendaal Commission releases its report. The report recommends the division of the country into native reserves (39%), white territories (40%), and government reserves (16%). The Odendaal Plan essentially makes Namibia a province of South Africa and institutes a Bantustan policy.
1965	United Nations rejects the Odendaal Plan.

1966	In July the International Court of Justice rules that Ethiopia and Liberia do not have any standing to bring a suit concerning South Africa's actions in Namibia; in October the UN General Assembly issues Resolution 2145 terminating South Africa's mandate for failure to meet its trusteeship obligations in Namibia. SWAPO announces an end to pacifism, and on August 26, SWAPO and South African soldiers engage in their first open military encounter—armed struggle begins.
1967	UN Council for Namibia (initially called UN Council for South West Africa) created; the council recognizes Namibia as the country's legitimate name. The council was intended to take over the administration of the country, but South Africa refuses to relinquish control.
1968	South Africa tries and sentences several Namibians in Pretoria; they serve long prison sentences on Robben Island.
1969	UN Security Council ratifies UN General Assembly Resolution 2145 (1966), which calls on South Africa to leave Namibia (Britain and France abstain from the vote); UN Security Council passes Resolution 269 condemning South Africa's continued presence in Namibia.
1970	UN Security Council passes Resolution 276, which declares South Africa's presence in Namibia an illegal occupation.
1971	The International Court of Justice, in response to a suit brought by the UN Security Council, rules that South African presence in Namibia is illegal. Two of the judges—one British and one French—dissent from the majority opinion.
	General strike involving thousands of workers including miners, students at teacher training colleges, and other students also plays a significant role; bishops Auala and Paulus //Gowaseb write an "Open Letter" to the South African Prime Minister Vorster condemning the contract labor and the apartheid systems in Namibia.
1973	UN General Assembly resolution recognizes SWAPO as the sole and authentic representative of Namibia.
August 1975	Angola achieves independence.
September 1975	Turnhalle Constitutional Conference begins, bringing together conservative white and black leaders to discuss Namibia's future, but SWAPO and several other groups refuse to participate, insisting they would do so only if the meetings are held under UN auspices.

1976	United Nations Institute for Namibia (UNIN) is established in Lusaka, Zambia, to train young Namibians for future work and service in an independent Namibia.
	UN Security Council Resolution 385 affirms its commitment to Namibian independence and calls on South Africa to begin this process.
1977	Turnhalle Conference issues its draft constitution, which calls for Namibia to be divided into ethnically based administrative units; UN and SWAPO denounce this constitution, insisting instead on the principles of universal adult suffrage and a parliamentary system.
May 4, 1978	Cassinga (Kassinga) massacre: South African troops cross the border into Angola and attack the Cassinga refugee camp, killing 600 and wounding hundreds; the dead and wounded consist mostly of women and children.
September 1978	UN Security Council Resolution 435 ("the UN Plan") is passed, calling for UN-supervised elections to be held.
1983	UN Security Council passes Resolution 532, which "condemns South Africa's continued illegal occupation of Namibia in flagrant defiance of resolutions of the General Assembly and decisions of the Security Council." (Altogether, the Security Council issued 26 resolutions on South African rule in Namibia, and the General Assembly issued 18.)
1984	Andimba Toivo ya Toivo is released from Robben Island prison after 16 years.
June 1988	Major strikes take place throughout the country to protest apartheid violence and repression; more than 80,000 students boycott school, and more than 60,000 workers, in solidarity with the students, stay away from work.
December 1988	South Africa finally agrees to Namibian independence to be implemented according to UN Resolution 435, in exchange for withdrawal of Cuban troops from Angola.
1989	United Nations supervises voter registration and elections to elect a Namibian assembly. SWAPO gets 57 percent of the vote.
1990	On March 21, the new constitution goes into effect; Sam Nujoma is elected president by the Constituent Assembly. Two days after its independence, Namibia joins the United Nations.
1992	Namibia is ravaged by severe drought. Food production plummets by as much as two-thirds in some cases.

1991	Frankie Fredericks wins the Olympic silver medal in the men's 100-meter race. Fredericks has a total of four Olympic silver medals.
1992	Michelle McLean, Miss Namibia, becomes Miss Universe.
February 1994	South Africa returns Walvis Bay and 12 nearby islands to Namibia; the celebrations to mark this event are attended by major international figures, including South African anti-apartheid heroes Walter Sisuslu and Thabo Mbeki, Sonia Gandhi of India, and Robert Mugabe of Zimbabwe.
December 1994	Nujoma wins second term, with SWAPO winning more than 75 percent of the popular vote.
1995	Landmark Land Reform Act of 1995 authorizes the government to acquire land for redistribution under strict but not so clearly defined guidelines.
1998	Namibian constitution amended to allow President Nujoma to run for a third term.
1998–1999	Secessionist tensions and violence in Caprivi Strip.
2001	The autobiography of Namibia's first president, Sam Nujoma's *Where Others Wavered,* is published. The book is later made into a film.
2004	Hifikepunye Pohamba, of SWAPO, is elected president of Namibia and succeeds Nujoma, the country's first president.
2007	Chinese President Hu Jintao visits Namibia as part of a tour of several African countries.
March 2009	Floods of biblical proportions leave over 100 dead.
December 2009	SWAPO gets 75 percent of the votes in the elections, and Pohamba is returned to power.
March 2010	20th anniversary of independence; major celebrations and commemorative events take place throughout the country, attended by South Africa's Jacob Zuma, Zimbabwe's Robert Mugabe, Democratic Republic of Congo's Joseph Kabila, and the former president of Finland and Nobel Peace Laureate Maartti Ahtisaari.
December 2010	According to leaked diplomatic cables (*WikiLeaks*), in exchange for defaulting on loans from China, the Namibian government allowed 5,000 Chinese to settle in Namibia. This report leads to a tremendous outcry in the country, denials by the government, and calls for greater transparency and accountability.

1

Introduction

THE REPUBLIC OF Namibia is a country of enormous size relative to its population. With a population of just over two million people in a country almost as big as France and Germany combined, Namibia has one of the lowest population densities in the world. With 318,260 square miles (824,292 square kilometers), Namibia is about 40,000 square miles smaller than Nigeria and about 10,000 square miles larger than Mozambique.[1] Nigeria has an estimated population of some 130 million, while Mozambique has a population of some 22 million. Namibia is divided into 13 administrative regions (Caprivi, Erongo, Hardap, Karas, Khomas, Kunene, Ohangwena, Okavango, Omaheke, Omusati, Oshana, Oshikoto, and Otjozondjupa). Windhoek, the capital, occupies a central place in the country, not only because it is the administrative center and seat of government, but also because it is the home of more than 10 percent of the country's population.

Namibia, formerly known as German South West Africa, was a German colony until World War I. During the war, Germany's African possessions were taken over by the Allied forces and their collaborators. South Africa invaded German South West Africa, defeating the German forces, and after the war, the Allies decided South Africa should administer the colony as a League of Nations mandate. After World War II, South Africa annexed the country and began to impose its segregationist apartheid policies.

Today, English is the official language, but Afrikaans, German, and Oshivambo, all recognized as national languages, are widely spoken. The Ovambo

Namib desert. (Corel)

make up about half of the total population, followed by the Kavango with close to 10 percent, and then the Herero, who constitute about 7 percent of the country's population. The Herero population never recovered fully from the brutal decimation it suffered as a result of a genocide waged against it by Germany at the beginning of the 20th century. Prior to the war of 1904–1908 in which the Herero, Nama, and Damara fought against the Germans, the Herero were the largest ethnic group in central Namibia.[2]

As in other former settler colonies in Africa to which significant numbers of Europeans migrated and established themselves, Namibia's road to independence was long and bloody. While most African countries proclaimed their independence in the 1960s, Namibia did not win its independence until 1990. The South West Africa People's Organisation (SWAPO), the most important of the liberation groups that brought the country to independence, remains at the helm of political power. Led by Sam Nujoma, SWAPO fought a guerrilla war against the white minority government from 1966 until 1990. Nujoma ruled the country for 14 years until 2004, then stepped down; SWAPO again was victorious at the polls, taking 76 percent of the votes, and SWAPO member Hifikepunye Pohamba took over the reins of power. In December 2009 Pohamba won 75 percent of the votes in the presidential election. Ten candidates competed for the presidency; the closest challenger carried less than 11 percent of the votes.

Namibia. (ABC-CLIO)

Following independence, the government prioritized education, and Namibia currently enjoys an enviable literacy rate. More than 85 percent of adults are literate. Despite this signal achievement, Namibia remains a country of enormous disparities. There is a huge gulf between, for example, the life of the casual laborer living in Katutura and that of the business executive in Klein Windhoek, an exclusive suburb of Windhoek. According to the United Nations Development Programme (UNDP), in 2005 about 35 percent of the Namibian population lived on $1 a day. Unemployment is a huge problem: In late 2010 the government revealed that the official level of unemployment stood at 52.2 percent. Almost half of the labor force is engaged in agriculture, even though very little of the land is arable.

LAND

The most striking feature of the landscape is its aridity. Water scarcity is a huge problem of long standing in most of the country, and any traveler to Namibia will be made aware of this by signs encouraging water-conservation measures in hotels and elsewhere. The topography of Namibia is often strikingly dramatic, much of the land inhospitable. Namibia is about half the size of Alaska, or the size of Texas and Louisiana combined, but less than 1 percent of its land is arable. Sandwiched between two deserts, the Namib and the Kalahari, Namibia lies in the southwestern portion of the African continent, bordered on the west by the Atlantic Ocean. Namibia has just under 1,000 miles (over 1,500 kilometers) of coastline, and the sea plays an important role in the country's economic life. Its neighbors are South Africa to the south, Angola and Zambia to the north, and Botswana to the east. Topographically, Namibia is typically considered to consist of five zones: the Namib Desert in the west; the Kalahari Desert in the east; the bushveld (sometimes styled Caprivi Bushveld) in the northeast; the Central Plateau, which dominates the landscape; and the Escarpment, wedged between the Namib and the Central Plateau. The highest elevations in the country, the Brandberg Mountains, are in the Central Plateau, also the location of the nation's capital, Windhoek.

The Namib is considered the world's oldest desert; it has some of the tallest sand dunes in the world, some rising to a height of about 1,000 feet (300 meters). The second-largest desert in Africa, the Namib lies on the country's western border, along the South Atlantic Ocean. While recognizing it as a challenging landscape, some do not consider the Namib a true desert because of its proximity to the ocean. The Namib Desert has a varying topography, its red-orange sand dunes sometimes forming into crescent shapes, sometimes rising into high, flat-topped mountains. Covering about one-fifth of the total land area of the country, the Namib is home to a natural life enriched by its wide variety of flora and fauna, which draws scientists as well as tourists. Some of Namibia's best-known tourist destinations are located along the coast in the Namib Desert. The list of sites along the coastal desert includes Skeleton Coast Park and Sandwich Harbour as well as the country's two major ports, Walvis Bay and Luderitz. Walvis Bay is the country's only deepwater harbor. A center for scientific research, the Namib Desert Station, is located in the desert.

There are only two permanent rivers in the country, the Kunene in the north, forming part of the border with Angola, and the Orange in the south, which constitutes the border with the Republic of South Africa. A severely dry and drought-prone country, Namibia has limited access to natural freshwater, and desertification is a challenge. Washing a car using a hose is illegal in Namibia; only buckets of water may be used.[3] At all tourist points, visitors are advised on ways to conserve water, for example, by not leaving the water running while brushing one's teeth. Given its unique environmental situation, it is perhaps no surprise that Namibia was the first country in the world to include environmental protection in its constitution. Article 95 of the Constitution of Namibia states that the government is responsible for the "maintenance of ecosystems, essential ecological processes and biological diversity of Namibia and the utilization of living natural resources on a sustainable basis for the benefit of all Namibians, both present and future; in particular, the Government shall provide measures against the dumping of recycling of foreign nuclear and toxic waste on Namibian territory."[4]

Another distinguishing feature is the high number of airports in Namibia relative to its population. Namibia has 132 airports for its two million citizens! Lesotho, which has roughly the same population of about two million (and a challenging terrain of its own), has 28 airports. Macedonia, in the same population league, has just 17 airports. Italy, with a much larger population, has exactly the same number of airports as Namibia. The large number of airports in a country with Namibia's population profile speaks to the size of the country, the difficulties of the terrain, and disparities in wealth. It also reflects the presence of high-value industries that can and do cater to their own transportation needs; only a handful of the country's airports are available to commercial airline carriers. Namibia has over 26,000 miles (42,000 kilometers) of roads and almost 1,500 miles (more than 2,300 kilometers) of railroad.

Looking at a map, one is struck by how straight most of Namibia's borders are. Then, in the northeastern corner, there appears an odd, thin strip of land that juts into central Africa: the Caprivi Strip. This tiny piece of land was for many years clamed by Namibia, Angola, Botswana, Zimbabwe, and Zambia, as well as Caprivi nationalists. In 1992 Caprivi became the 13th region in Namibia, following a decision by the United Nations to acknowledge Namibian claims. Tensions over the status of Caprivi remain, as some groups continue to agitate for greater autonomy or outright independence.

Just two years after the Caprivi Strip became integrated into a newly independent Namibia, the country gained another valuable territory, one that had been in contention between it and South Africa: Walvis Bay. Most of the coastline of Namibia is forbidding, without any deep natural harbors. Walvis Bay is the one exception. For years South Africa and Namibia disputed ownership of Walvis Bay, a significant port with its deep natural harbor and valuable fishing. Walvis Bay is famous for its flamingos, pelicans, and a host of other waterbirds. While the South African government ruled South-West Africa, it had, with an eye on the future, incorporated Walvis Bay into its

Cape Province, hoping that this maneuver would allow it to retain the port in the event of Namibian independence. This strategy succeeded for a while, but in 1994, South Africa was forced to return Walvis Bay to the now-independent Namibia.

The Kalahari, which covers most of Botswana and extends into Zimbabwe as well as eastern Namibia, is considered by specialists a semidesert (and not a true desert). Although it is dry and sandy, the Kalahari sustains savanna grasses, shrubs, and trees. Fruits and other edible plants grow in the Kalahari, which, for centuries, was the home of the San people. The Fish River Canyon in the southern Kalahari is the second-largest canyon in the world. Nowadays the river is mostly dry.

Namibia's striking landscapes attract tourists from all around the world: The great red sand dunes of the Namib Desert have enormous dramatic appeal. Namibia's plant and animal life is also alluring, with some species unique to the country. The odd-looking *Welwitschia mirabilis,* for example, is an extremely unusual plant, the oldest of which are thought to be as old as 2,000 years. The sole plant in its genus, the *Welwitschia* has just two leaves and is found only in the Namib Desert in northern Namibia and southern Angola. The so-called quiver tree (*kokerboom*), a type of aloe, is also striking. Acacia and baobab trees, widespread elsewhere in Africa, also grow in Namibia. The baobab is a wonderfully useful tree as every part of the tree can be for food, fuel, or medicine and cosmetics or in the construction of shelter. The leadwood tree (known locally as the Omumborombonga tree), which produces the heaviest wood in the world, may be seen in Etosha National Park and parts of the Central Plateau. Like the *mopane* tree, another hardy tree and one endemic to southern Africa, it is resistant to termites and very good for fuel.

CLIMATE AND WATER

Typically, the weather is hot and sunny, but there are changes in season, and evenings can be quite cool. There are two seasons in Namibia: winter and summer. Winter lasts from April/May until September/October. During the day the weather is generally seasonable (64–77 degrees Fahrenheit, or 18–25 degrees Celsius), but in the evening and at night temperatures may drop dramatically, and frost is not uncommon. In summer (October–April), average temperatures in most of the country range between 68 and 94 degrees Fahrenheit (20–34 degrees Celsius). The extreme north and south of the country experience much hotter weather than the Central Plateau region, with temperatures above 104 degrees Fahrenheit (40 degrees Celsius) not

Quiver tree, Fish River Canyon, Namibia. (Travel Pictures Gallery)

uncommon. Much of central Namibia, including the capital, is at a high elevation, where the temperature is generally a little less hot. The rains fall during the summer months, with average annual rainfall ranging from two to four inches (50 to 350 millimeters); the rains are usually short and heavy, and floods are common during the rainy season. Most of Namibia's rivers remain dry, except when enough rain falls to fill their beds. The rainfalls turn dry riverbeds into rivers for a period of time, allowing residents to pursue a number of seasonal activities that are dependent on rain, such as shallow-water fishing (often using specially constructed fishing baskets) and gathering the enormous termite-hill mushrooms and the Kalahari truffles (!nabas in Khoisan) that appear in some parts of Namibia following the rains. Termite-hill mushrooms are white in color and can weigh as much as two pounds. Namibia is also windy, a potential boon for alternative energy endeavors; in the coastal areas it is often foggy, a result of the cold Benguela current off the Atlantic coast. The Caprivi Strip is extremely green, in sharp contrast with much of the rest of the country; it receives significant amounts of rain, which enables it to sustain a verdant tropical vegetation. In the last few years,

Namibia has experienced devastating floods during the rainy season, resulting in loss of life, government relocation of thousands, and severe damage to farms, pastures, businesses, schools, and hospitals. Changes in weather pattern are widely attributed to climate change.

Namibia has always been a country where water is scarce, but with increasing concerns about global climate change, environmentalists and conservationists disagree about the impact of pastoralism on the environment and government attempts to settle these pastoral communities. Some scholars believe that pastoralists such as the Himba have evolved strategies that contribute to the preservation of the land and have retained its sustainability over the centuries. Others argue that pastoralism is unsustainable in the modern world.[5]

PEOPLE

Namibia, like other African countries, is multiethnic, with about a dozen different ethnic groups. The vast majority of Namibians—more than 85 percent of the total population—are black, while white and mixed-race groups make up the rest. Given the country's history, it is not surprising that the black/white divide often draws the most attention. But the reality is that there are great differences between the different black African ethnic groups too, as well as between whites.[6]

More than 90 percent of the population identifies as Christian, with at least half of those belonging to Lutheran churches. The Ovambo make up about half of the population; the rest of the black Namibian population is mostly Kavango, Herero, Damara, and Nama. There are also Caprivians, San, Himba, Coloureds, and Tswana. White Namibians are mostly of German or Afrikaner descent. Many scholars place the Nama and Damara into a single group; some list the Herero and Himba as a single group. Most consider the diverse residents of the Caprivi Strip as a single category, Caprivian, even though the area is markedly heterogeneous in language and culture.[7]

Namibian scholars typically identify 11 to 14 different ethnic groups, depending on how the groups are delineated. It is important to keep in mind that ethnic identities are not primordial markers that remain fixed throughout time. There is a tendency to imagine African so-called tribes as constant; however, Africanist scholars continue to point out that many ethnic markers in Africa are relatively recent creations. The Ovambo, who today constitute the single largest ethnic group in Namibia, are a case in point. Before European colonial rule, the various groups that are today considered Ovambo did not identify themselves by a single name. Some groups that live in both Namibia and Angola are classified as Ovambo in one country and not in the other.

The Ovambo are matrilineal, and today most Ovambo are Christian (largely Lutheran, Roman Catholic, Anglican, and increasingly Pentecostal). The pre-Christian religion of the Ovambo included belief in a supreme deity and veneration of ancestors. The Ovambo are divided into as many as 12 or as few as 7 subgroups, most of which correspond to distinct pre-colonial kingdoms. The nine main groups into which the Ovambo are most often divided are the Kwanyama, Ndonga, Kwambi, Ngandjera, Mbalantu, Kwaluudhi, Nkolonkaadhi, Eunda, and Mbadja. Linguists divide the Ovambo into two broad groups; the two main languages spoken by the Ovambo are OshiNdonga and OshiKwanyama. According to some, the Ovambo and the Herero are descended from two brothers; thus some consider these two communities as siblings. The area in northern Namibia that the Ovambo consider their ancestral home was formerly known as Ovamboland. The area is known today by the names of the districts into which it is divided: Omusati, Ohangwena, Oshana, and Oshikoto, popularly known as the four O's.

Many of the Ovambo who live in the north of the country are farmers and also raise a variety of animals, including cattle and goats. While they do not get as much rain as the Caprivi Strip, the predominantly Ovambo areas of northern Namibia receive greater rainfall than much of the rest of the country, allowing for agriculture and cattle rearing. Christianity is deeply rooted in Ovambo contemporary life, as is the case for most Namibians today. The national dress worn today by Ovambo women is based on the dress style of 19th-century Finnish missionaries; it is a loose-fitting maxi-length dress, usually worn with a headscarf, which is not necessarily made from the same fabric. While Christian missionary activity achieved great success, some pre-Christian practices and beliefs remain important, for example, the ritual importance of the sacred fire. This should be no surprise: Christianity must always embed itself in an already-existing, dynamic cultural milieu, and it does not encounter any society as a *tabula rasa*.

The Kavango, the second-largest ethnic group, live mainly along the Kavango River in northeastern Namibia. In the past the Kavango lived in multifamily homesteads, and this practice continues today; however, some couples now choose to set up a home independently in a nuclear family style. Like the Ovambo, to whom they are considered to be related, many Kavango farm and raise cattle and follow a matrilineal system of descent. The Kavango are divided into subgroups, each under the leadership of a chief. Kavango also live in Angola. They are known throughout Namibia for their great tradition of wood carving.

The Herero, the third-largest group in Namibia, were the targets of the first genocide of the 20th century (1904–1908). The Battle of Waterberg in August 1904 was the turning point in the struggle of the Herero, Nama, and others against German colonial rule. After the Germans forced a major Herero retreat, the German commander issued an order that all Herero who were not killed in battle should be driven into the desert to die. Recent estimates place the number of dead at between 70 and 90 percent of the total Herero population at the time. After the genocide all Herero land was seized. Today, many Herero engage in wage labor, in towns and on farms. Most Herero maintain links to communities in central Namibia; however, there are Herero communities of long standing all over Namibia.

The Herero, who are believed to have migrated into the region from central or eastern Africa beginning about 1550, also live in Botswana and Angola. Cattle played an important role in the life of the early Hereros, who were nomadic and seminomadic pastoralists, and to this day cattle remain crucial in Herero cultural life. Notwithstanding the centrality of cattle to the Herero, a portion of Herero society formed urban-based communities in the late 19th century, according to historian Jan-Bart Gewald (1999). In the 19th century (i.e., prior to the genocide), a large number of Herero lived in central Namibia, in and around the town of Okahandja, which is about 45 miles (75 kilometers) north of Windhoek. Today, Okahandja is considered the capital of the major branch of the Herero; it is the site of the graves of Herero national heroes who fought against the Germans. The annual commemoration of the heroes' valor, which takes place annually toward the end of August, begins at the cemetery in Okahandja. Other branches of the Herero celebrate their deceased leaders at festivals in Omaruru and Gobabis.

The Herero leader Samuel Maharero, who fought valiantly against the German genocidal war, is considered a Namibian national hero. On the Sunday closest to the 23rd of August, the Herero celebrate the life of Maharero at a festival in Okahandja. The highlight of Maharero Day is a parade involving various groups, including paramilitary ones, whose costumes are reminiscent of the 19th-century German military uniforms. Prior to the genocide, the Herero were the dominant population in the region. The issue of a "return" to this area, which many claim as a Herero homeland, continues to arouse intense debate and emotion in Namibia, not least of all because it is hard to see who will determine which persons or groups are allowed to return, and to where precisely, and to assure the solution is one that satisfies all, Herero and non-Herero. The Herero national dress worn by women is a modified form of the clothing worn by German missionary women in the 19th century, with full-bodied skirts and a twin-peaked headdress designed to recall cattle horns.

The Himba, especially their women, are much photographed by foreigners; as Namibia scholars Wolfram Hartmann, Jeremy Silvester, and Patricia Hayes note in the introduction to their fascinating book on colonial photography in

Namibia, "those catching the eye of the national and international media are the Himba," who are presented as icons of the traditional.[8] The Himba have been much less willing than their compatriots to adopt (and adapt) European forms of dress. Himba women go topless, wear intricate hairstyles, and color their skin with red ochre and an oil-based protectant. The Himba live mostly in the extreme northwest of the country, in the Kunene region. The Herero and Himba share the same language, OtjiHerero, and lay claim to a common ancestry. Most scholars consider the Himba one of the subcategories of the Herero; others, while recognizing the historical linkages, consider the Himba distinct now.

Scholars believe that the Damara are the descendants of Bantu-speaking people who migrated to southern Africa from West Africa, even though they speak Nama, which is not a Bantu language. In the turbulent 19th century, the Damara struggled over land with other groups, such as the Herero and Europeans. Under South African rule, in keeping with its apartheid policies, the government created a territory known as Damaraland, carved out of European-held land that was not suitable for grazing or agriculture. Some scholars class the Nama and Damara, with other linguistically related groups, under the general category Khoisan.

The Nama (or Namaqua) are still sometimes referred to as Hottentot, but this term is widely considered derogatory and is not found often in contemporary scholarly works.[9] Some scholars believe that the Nama moved into Namibia from the area of the southern Cape in South Africa as a result of European seizure of land. Other scholars, however, maintain that the Nama's primordial home is in the area of Namaland in southern Namibia. Some of the movements of Nama groups are recorded in written historical documents: Some did move into southern Namibia from the Cape in South Africa, driven by the activities of white settlers; other Nama groups moved into Namibia earlier, in their own search for land and water. However, the question of original homelands may reveal more about contemporary obsessions than anything else. Like other ethnic groups in Namibia, the Nama are in fact a heterogeneous people, speaking variants of their language and with subgroups tracing distinct histories. Yet the tendency to conceptualize Africans first and foremost along tribal categories that ignore nuance and essentialize Africans persists. Some Nama, though by no means all, do have a distinctive appearance, with a light skin complexion, high cheekbones, and the epicanthic (or Asian) fold over the upper eyelid. Along with the San, the Nama speak a Khoisan (click) language, and in the past they lived throughout southern Namibia. Some Nama groups were pastoralists and some agriculturalists. As with the Ovambo, Herero, and Namibia's other ethnic groups, there are several subgroups of Nama. There are, for example, the Orlam Nama, the

Bondelswaart Nama, the Topnaar Nama, and the !Aman Nama; these are best understood as clan groups. The historical literature in particular, however, can be confusing because different authors refer to the same Nama clan or community by different names: For example, depending on the speaker, the descendants and followers of Jager Afrikaner are labeled Afrikaner, Afrikaner Nama, Orlam Afrikaner, or Orlam Nama.[10] Nama communities live mostly in southern Namibia, with the Karas and Hardap regions being most commonly associated with the Nama.

With the Maasai of East Africa, the San of southern Africa are probably one of the two most photographed African groups. The San live throughout southern Africa. About 40,000 San live in Namibia; the vast majority of San live in Botswana. In the past and sometimes still today, the San are referred to as *Bushmen*, a term that most scholars reject today as offensive. Some scholars now also reject the term *San* as derogatory, claiming it originates from the Nama word for slave, and prefer to refer to each subgroup by its own name. San public figures also participate in the nomenclature debate, but there is no consensus; some are willing to accept the term *San* as a way (especially for outsiders) to refer to the various branches of their community but insist that each community should be referred to by its proper name, such as !Kung (also !Xu), Hai//om, and Jo/Hoansi.[11] The San have been a favorite of photographers to show "exotic Africa" as well as of anthropologists. In the past the San lived a nomadic existence as gatherer-hunters, traveling in small family groups. The portrayal of the San in the hugely successful South African film *The Gods Must Be Crazy* has been the subject of much negative comment by scholars, who take the filmmakers to task for creating a romanticized portrayal of the San as living a timeless, ahistorical, primitive, and idyllic existence. The film portrays a San existence that bore little resemblance to the living realities of the majority of the San in Namibia at the time the film was made.

The San are considered the "first people" of southern Africa.[12] Under the rubric San are in fact several communities, with distinct identities. The best-known San group are the !Kung. Originally published in 1981, *Nisa: The Life and Words of a !Kung Woman* by the anthropologist Majorie Shostak remains popular and widely available. (The exclamation mark is used in English to denote one of the click sounds in Khoisan languages.) Shostak wrote an update in 2000. With their traditions of foraging and migration, which involved settling for periods of time at different locations, with access to water a prime consideration, San communities have found themselves victims of European and African land grabbing. European settlers and African agriculturalists had very different ideas about landownership from the San, who saw land as inalienable. San life revolved around securing water, access to food for

San man, Namibia. Considered the earliest inhabitants of southern Africa, the San communities can be found in South Africa, Botswana, Angola, as well as Namibia. (Travel Pictures Gallery)

gathering, and the hunt. Agriculturalists, black and especially white settlers, restricted hunting and closed off lands from those they considered poachers.

The San are sometimes grouped together with the Nama (sometimes Khoi Khoi) and Damara as Khoisan. Khoisan people are considered non-Bantu linguistically, and some also classify the Nama and the San as nonblack. Today, the San find themselves still extremely marginalized and with little ability to shape policies affecting them, or even public perceptions about them. In Botswana, where more than 60 percent of the San live, the government has allowed mining in the Kalahari Game Reserve, where many San live, thus either expelling entire communities from the area or forcing them to abandon their homes and lifestyle and to seek work elsewhere. In Namibia, the situation of the San is no better. In 1907 when Namibia's Etosha National Park was established, the San living there were forcibly removed.

Under South African rule, the system of apartheid was imported to Namibia, with the state attempting to establish separate reserves for each government-identified tribe. In 1952 the Schoeman Commission recommended that two San reserves be established, one at Etosha National Park and the second in Nyae Nyae for the !Kung. The latter reserve was established but not the former. When Etosha National Park was established, all the San who could not prove that they were working as warders in the newly created park were deemed persona non grata and required to move out.

In 1996 San groups from Namibia, Botswana, Zambia, and Zimbabwe founded the Working Group of Indigenous Minorities in Southern Africa (WIMSA) in an effort to advocate for and protect San rights. The San continue to be extremely marginalized, landless, and poor. In school, San children describe frequent taunting by their peers, who label them Bushmen and liken them to wild animals.

South African troops took Namibia (then called German South West Africa) from Germany during World War I, and the Allies placed the country under South African rule. Many of the Afrikaners in Namibia are the descendants of the South African settlers and rulers of this period, and they make up the single largest European group in Namibia, about 70 percent of the total European population.[13] Some Namibian Afrikaners have Lusophone ancestry as they trace descent to Afrikaners who settled in Namibia from Angola, also a settler colony; a small percentage of Namibian whites trace their roots to Portuguese settlers (or their offspring) from Angola. The descendants of German settlers make up over 25 percent of the white population. There is a small population of Europeans who speak English as a first language. Although they are the mother tongues of small minorities, German, Afrikaans, and English are widely spoken in Namibia. German was, of course, the language of the first colonizers, and Afrikaans the language of the second colonizers. Today, English is the official language, but Afrikaans and German remain important and are officially recognized as national languages.

The Rehoboth Basters are the descendants of mixed marriages between Nama and Dutch in what is today South Africa. Their name stems from their origins as offspring of mixed heritage in a colonial context characterized by slavery and racism. They migrated from their homeland in the area of the Cape Colony in the turbulent days of the second half of the 19th century when various groups—Africans as well as Europeans—were vying for access to and control over land and water. The original group settled at Rehoboth. Rehoboth Basters speak a distinct Afrikaans dialect of their own; their traditional dress recalls the clothing worn by 19th-century Boertrekkers, from which it is descended. While they share a mixed heritage with other Coloured Namibians, the Rehoboth Basters are recognized as a distinct group.

Coloureds are of mixed descent, and many of them trace their heritage to South Africa's Cape Colony. This category is a reminder of the apartheid policies of an earlier era. There is also a small number of Tswana, who are related to the Tswana of Botswana. Most Caprivians are categorized as Subiya or Fwe; however, the Caprivi Strip is a heterogeneous area, with communities maintaining distinct ethnic identities. SiLozi is widely spoken as a lingua franca in Caprivi, especially in Katima Mulilo, the regional capital, and in marketplaces and other places of business. There are Lozi communities in Zambia, Botswana, Angola, Mozambique, and Zimbabwe as well, some of them clamoring for an independent Lozi state. SiLozi-speaking peoples established an empire in the 17th century in this region, bringing under imperial rule a diverse group of distinct ethnic communities. Some of those who were formerly tributary to the Lozi empire today speak SiLozi but maintain a distinct identity; others may be fluent in SiLozi but retain a distinct maternal language and also maintain a separate ethnic identity.[14] Other communities in the Caprivi include the Kololo (a Sotho-speaking people who conquered the Lozi state in the 19th century, following their migration from the area of modern-day South Africa), the Yeyi, and the Totela.

LANGUAGES

Just 30 years ago, Afrikaans was considered the most widely spoken language in Namibia.[15] Only a very small minority of the population speaks English as a first language, but as the language of instruction in many instances, English is the lingua franca of the young. English became an official language in 1915, following the South African invasion of German South West Africa; German and Afrikaans were also official languages. At independence in 1990 English was declared the sole official language rather than Afrikaans, which although widely spoken was associated with the apartheid rule of South Africa, or German, the language of the German colonizers. English was also seen as appealing because it is the language of international commerce, and so, for a country with a keen sense of the need to catch up with the rest of the world, this was thought to be a far-sighted choice.[16] Afrikaans and German are recognized as national languages, along with other languages such as Oshivambo and OtjiHerero. Indigenous languages fall into two broad categories: Bantu or Khoisan. Khoisan, sometimes referred to as click languages, include San, Nama, and Damara. Oshivambo is spoken at home by the ethnic Ovambo, about half of the population. Afrikaans remains a widely spoken second language, especially for older generations; in many Nama as well as Coloured families, Afrikaans is the language spoken at home exclusively or alongside Nama (in the case of the Nama). English is the more popular second language for the younger generations. "Namlish" is also popular with the youth and is used by musicians; this is a variant of English in which the syntax deviates from that of standard English and there are words from a host of other languages spoken in Namibia, including Ovambo and Afrikaans. German remains disproportionately important given that it is the first language of only about 10 percent of the population. There are many

German-language schools in Namibia and a number of German-language newspapers.

As the official language, English is the language of instruction in secondary and tertiary schools. In primary schools, instruction is often not in English; private elementary schools offer instruction in Afrikaans, German, and a host of African languages, and government schools provide instruction in the mother language for the first few years of primary school. Portuguese is spoken in some quarters, especially among those from the extreme north, and Angolan radio and television stations broadcasting in Portuguese can be heard and seen in Windhoek and elsewhere in the country.

The Herero, Ovambo, Kavango, Damara/Nama, Lozi, and San all include numerous subgroups, each of which speaks sometimes very different dialects. For example, although the San constitute only about 3 percent of the total population, there are at least half a dozen distinct San subgroups who each have their own language. For example, the Hai//om are a San group living in northern Namibia; they consider what is now Etosha National Park their homeland. The most well-known—as well as the largest—San group are the !Kung, who fall into three smaller subgroups. In 2004, when the government announced its "Vision 2030" initiative, plans were made to have the document translated into the following languages: OshiKwanyama, OshiNdonga, OtjiHerero, RuKwangali, SiLozi, ThiMbukushu, Rumanyo, Khoekhoegowab (Damara-Nama), SeTswana, Afrikaans, German, and Ju/'Hoansi.[17] One possible outcome of such government production of written documents may be to foster greater standardization in these languages. The question of language use is often an emotionally charged issue; for example, in the Caprivi, which is home to a linguistically diverse population, SiLozi is the dominant language, used in schools and on the radio. Some of those who speak another language as their first language resent this and would like to see their language on par with SiLozi.[18]

WINDHOEK AND KATUTURA

Apart from the capital, the principal urban centers in Namibia are Oshakati, Rundu, Walvis Bay, Swakopmund, Katima Mulilo, Rehoboth, Keetmanshoop, Tsumeb, and Luderitz, Okahandja, and Otjwarongo, which are all relatively small towns. Although a majority of Namibians (although probably fewer than 65%) live in rural areas, Windhoek, the capital, plays a central role in the life of the country. Windhoek consists of more than a dozen distinct neighborhoods, such as City Centre, the chief financial district; Khomasdal; Hochland Park; Eros Park; Suiderhof; and Klein Windhoek, the capital's most exclusive suburb. Katutura, which is also a suburb of Windhoek, is in

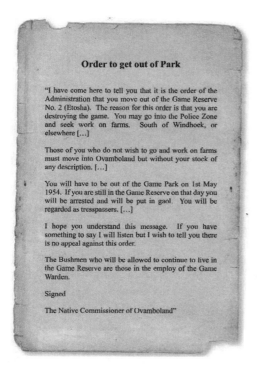

Order to get out of Park

"I have come here to tell you that it is the order of the Administration that you move out of the Game Reserve No. 2 (Etosha). The reason for this order is that you are destroying the game. You may go into the Police Zone and seek work on farms. South of Windhoek, or elsewhere [...]

Those of you who do not wish to go and work on farms must move into Ovamboland but without your stock of any description. [...]

You will have to be out of the Game Park on 1st May 1954. If you are still in the Game Reserve on that day you will be arrested and will be put in gaol. You will be regarded as tresspassers. [...]

I hope you understand this message. If you have something to say I will listen but I wish to tell you there is no appeal against this order.

The Bushmen who will be allowed to continue to live in the Game Reserve are those in the employ of the Game Warden.

Signed

The Native Commissioner of Ovamboland"

Eviction order issued by the South African government, ordering thousands of Hai//om San residents out of Etosha, 1954. Today, Etosha National Park is a major tourist attraction; former residents remain bitter about their eviction. (Courtesy of the National Archives of Namibia)

reality a city in its own right. In Namibian parlance, Katutura is a *township,* a term from the country's segregationist history, reserved for black urban sites. About one-tenth of the Namibia's total population resides in Windhoek, and about one-fifth of the city's population is of European descent. About two-thirds of Windhoek's inhabitants live in the formerly black-only settlement of Katutura. Blacks still constitute the overwhelming majority of the population in Katutura, but the township is now quite diverse, both ethnically and economically. While Windhoek is widely seen as a quintessentially colonial town, its earliest inhabitants were African and settled in the area long before the German colonial period. Although Herero and Nama communities lived in Windhoek before the arrival of the first European settlers, the town has a distinctly German vibe, from the names on streets and buildings, to the beer in restaurants and pastries in the cafés, to, most notably, of course, the architecture and even the sound of German on the streets.

In 1912 the German colonial government embarked on a policy of racial segregation, removing blacks from Windhoek to a new location, Main Location, also known as Old Location. In the 1950s the government decided to move blacks again, from the Old Location to a new area, about eight miles northwest of the city center. Most residents of the Old Location opposed the forced relocation, but the government prevailed, forcibly removing black residents from the area in December 1959. The forced removals resulted in 13 casualties, and this moment is widely acknowledged as the final push that led to the formation of SWAPO. Africans named the new location Katutura, which means "a place where we do not want to reside." With this move, Windhoek was officially divided into three distinct areas: the city for whites, Khomasdal for Coloureds, and Katutura for blacks. Within Katutura distinct areas were set aside for each ethnic group, and individuals were supposed to live only in the area designated for their particular group. Today, residents of Katutura have a new nickname for their town, Matutura, or "the place where we wish to live."[19]

Windhoek is located in the heart of the country, in a valley surrounded by hills. Noted historically for its warm mineral springs, Windhoek is over 5,000 feet (1,650 meters) above sea level. Windhoek was founded by the Nama, Damara, and Herero, who were drawn by the ready availability of water. Later, in the mid-19th century the celebrated Cape Colony–born Nama leader Jonker Afrikaner brought his followers to settle in the area. Jonker is often credited as being the founder of Windhoek; in fact, others

Street corner, Windhoek. This signage shows how the different strands of Namibia's recent history remain quite evident in language. (Courtesy of Anene Ejikeme)

were already living there before Jonker's mixed group of Nama and others arrived, but until his death in 1861, Jonker was the dominant power in central Namibia. The origins of the name Windhoek are unclear, some suggesting it is derived from a name given by Jonker and others suggesting the German settlers coined the name by which the capital is known today.[20] The first Europeans to settle in Windhoek were missionaries of the Rhenish Missionary Society (Rheinische Missionsgesellschaft, or RMS), invited there by Jonker Afrikaner. Missionaries and European traders lived and worked in Windhoek for decades before the coming of German colonial rule. It was not until the end of the 19th century that Germany laid claim to what it called German South West Africa. The construction of a railway line from the coast to Windhoek (completed in 1902) played a significant role in the development of Windhoek as the country's central lifeline. Windhoek's population was about 200,000 at independence in 1990, but it has been growing at the rate of about 5 percent per annum, with much of the growth due to migration. This rapid rate of growth is, unsurprisingly, a source of great concern as it puts pressure on the infrastructure and services. The country's only international airport is in Windhoek, as is its only public university.[21]

EDUCATION

Namibia has a relatively high literacy rate, with at least 85 percent of the total adult population able to read and write. Education was a top priority for the government at independence, and the quality of schooling is the subject of widespread public commentary and discussion. Under South African apartheid rule, the official policy was one of substandard education for non-whites. One of the remarkable successes of the liberation movement was the attention to education; schools, including tertiary institutions, were set up in exile in Zambia, Angola, and Congo. Tens of thousands of Namibians—some born in exile—were educated in these SWAPO-administered schools in neighboring countries or even farther away, in East Germany, Canada, Finland, and other places, with the help of groups and governments that supported the goal of ending the South African occupation. Today, education remains a priority, and schooling is compulsory for children from the age of 6 until 16; however, a majority of schoolchildren do not complete all grades. In 2007 409,500 children were receiving primary education and 158,000 secondary education. Enrollment at the primary level is close to 95 percent, and a huge chunk of the government's annual budget (about 20% in 2009) goes to education. These numbers are impressive, even though concerns about the quality of education and questions about equity are entirely valid and still need to be resolved.

There is one state-sponsored university, the University of Namibia (UNAM). The university was established in Windhoek in 1992, just two years after independence, and it continues to expand, adding new programs as well as satellite campuses. Currently, UNAM has eight faculties (or schools): Agriculture, Economics and Management Science, Education, Engineering and Information Technology, Humanities and Social Sciences, Law, Health Sciences, and Science. Many Namibian students travel to neighboring countries to pursue tertiary education, especially to South Africa; some travel further afield, to Germany, the United States, and, more recently, China. Students go from other African countries to study at UNAM and other schools in Namibia. UNAM is not the only school for tertiary education in the country; there is also the Polytechnic of Namibia and the private International University of Management. The latter offers courses leading to certificates, diplomas, and bachelor's and master's degrees in business administration; travel, tourism, and hospitality; business information systems; HIV/AIDS management; finance management; human resource management; information technology; and marketing management. Namibia has two colleges of agriculture. In December 2009 Namibia's colleges of education (located in different parts of the country) were merged into a single Faculty of Education and brought into the UNAM system.

NATURAL RESOURCES AND THE ECONOMY

Mining remains an important part of the Namibian economy, even though in 2008, following the world economic crisis, diamond exports dropped by 30 percent. In 2008 Namdeb Diamond Corporation, owned equally by the South African juggernaut De Beers and the government of the Republic of Namibia, mined more than two million carats of diamonds but was able to export just over one-and-a-half (1.6) million carats. The previous year the company had mined and successfully sold over 2.2 million carats. Diamond mining is a dangerous and strictly controlled business; access to the diamond-mining areas is tightly restricted, with stringent controls to assure that workers do not carry diamonds out on their bodies or clothing, intentionally or otherwise. A good deal of the diamond mining in Namibia involves moving huge mountains of beach sand before the actual mining for diamonds from the sand and the rocks buried underneath can begin.

Diamonds, which were first discovered in Kolmanskop (Kolmanskuppe), near Luderitz, in 1908 by Zacharias Lewala, are mined on- and offshore in Namibia. Diamonds have been the main source of export earnings in Namibia for several years. According to the government, more than 50 percent of the country's foreign income earnings come from mined minerals, with diamonds making up 70 percent of that. Besides diamonds, uranium, copper, silver, gold, zinc, lead, and tin are also mined in Namibia. It must be added, however, that only about 3 percent of the population is employed in the mining sector, and mining accounts for only 8 percent of the gross domestic product (GDP). Half of the Namibian population depends on subsistence agriculture. Millet, sorghum, and peanuts are among the chief agricultural products of Namibia.

The coastal waters around Namibia used to hold some of the richest stocks of fish to be found anywhere in the world. Unfortunately, this made the area a major target for fish pirates from countries as far away as Japan, China, Spain, and other European countries. Mackerel, anchovies, and hake are the main fish in Namibian coastal waters. Fish and fish products account for about one-fifth of the economy, although there are continuing concerns about the overfishing of already severely depleted fish stocks by legal as well as pirate trawlers. Foreign fishing trawlers from Europe and the United States began fishing in Namibian waters as early as the 18th century.

Another important export is the pelt from the karakul sheep. Not indigenous to Namibia, the karakul sheep appears to have been introduced into the country by German settlers in the early 20th century. The karakul sheep is indigenous to Central Asia. Namibia's karakul pelts are known as *swakara,* and they are used by internationally known designers. In Namibia swakara is referred to as "black gold." The breeding of karakul sheep for their pelts has attracted the attention of antifur and animal rights protesters. Supporters, on the other hand, often point to the high unemployment rate in Namibia and insist that karakul breeding and harvesting in Namibia meet strict ethical guidelines.

Leather goods (from cows, goats, springbok, and other animals), basketry and woven goods, masks and carvings, pottery, and shell and other jewelry are some of the items visitors to Namibia are most likely to purchase. One unusual product from Namibia is paper, made either from pearl millet or from elephant dung. This is made into cards, diaries, and sheets of paper. White gold is another unusual Namibian product, this one "mined" chiefly for export. *White gold* is the term often used to describe bird guano, which is harvested on the offshore islands and along the coast and then shipped overseas to be used as fertilizer.[22]

The Namibian dollar is pegged to and equal with the South African rand. The rand, which was the official currency until 1993, is accepted everywhere in Namibia. Namibia is a member of the Southern African Customs Union, along with South Africa, Swaziland, Botswana, and Lesotho. South Africa is Namibia's main trade partner, with about 80 percent of all Namibian

Weaver making a carpet from karakul wool, Swakopmund. (Steve
Estvanik | Dreamstime.com)

imports coming from that country. As the regional superpower, South African economic clout is visible throughout the country, with most chains
(for example, Shoprite and Pick 'n' Pay) having South African owners. In
2008 China became Africa's second-largest trade partner, after the European Union, pushing the United States to third place. The Chinese presence in Namibia is readily visible; by the end of 2010 international news
reports were announcing that China had become Africa's chief trade partner, providing more loans to so-called emerging (or developing) countries,
including Africa, than the World Bank.[23] Some Chinese firms provide job
and training opportunities; however, other Chinese companies import their
own workers from China, leading to popular discontent in a country with
a huge unemployment problem. The Chinese presence is also visible in the
explosion of Chinese-owned businesses from Katima Mulilo, in the extreme
northeast corner of the country, to the capital, Windhoek, which now has
a significant Chinatown. In recent years the government has undertaken
major projects to increase transportation capabilities in the country. This
effort has targeted road networks as well as sea and air routes. Port facilities
at Walvis Bay were improved in the last decade of the 20th century, and the
Namibian Airports Company has targeted Walvis Bay Airport for major

improvements in order to transform it into the country's second international airport.

TOURISM AND THE NATURAL ENVIRONMENT

In 2008 tourism contributed almost 20 percent to the country's gross national product (GNP); the previous year almost a million tourists visited Namibia, with the vast majority (almost 700,000) coming from other countries of southern Africa. European visitors numbered almost 200,000, with just under 20,000 American visitors. A major concern for the future is how to sustain the environment while developing tourism. The issue of water highlights some of the tensions involving economic development, natural resources, and the needs of local communities.

Namibia's dramatic landscape and abundance of exotic flora and fauna draw large numbers of tourists to the country. Namibia has over 20 national parks and the country is a popular destination for hikers, fishers, sand surfers, and ecotourists. Some tourists are drawn by game hunting, and Namibia has a range from big game to smaller prey. Big game include lions, leopards, zebras, elephants, rhinos, and giraffes. Namibia has a number of animals and plants that are found only in the country. For example, the Namib Desert, dry and forbidding as it appears (and is to humans), supports a variety of animal and plant life. There are species of beetles, for example, that are found only in the Namib Desert. The Namib is also noted for its Cape fur seals.

One unfortunate aspect of some of the tourism to Namibia is the tendency to see some Namibian groups as objects to be observed in much the same way as one observes the flora and fauna. Tourist brochures, including those made by Namibian tour groups, often invite tourists to visit communities of "primitive tribes" and "stone-age people" who are living lives "unchanged for centuries." Such inaccurate and ahistorical claims are often put forward about the San and Himba.

HISTORICAL OVERVIEW

In general histories of Africa, one still finds too often that the story begins with the arrival of Europeans—missionaries, traders, adventurers, plunderers, and others. There are two reasons for this. First, there remains a remarkably persistent view that African peoples had lived in an unchanging, static manner until the arrival of Europeans and thus have no history as such prior to European contact. Second, for much of Africa, the sources familiar to Europeans as the basis for writing history are sparse. Not only is it absolutely incorrect that Africans lived "outside history" before European missionaries and

Sesriem Canyon, Namib Naukluft National Park. (Travel Pictures Gallery)

colonizers arrived, but African communities have typically been extremely interested in the preservation of their histories. How were these histories preserved if they were not written down? Often, they were passed on orally—in songs, praise poetry, stories, and epic accounts.

Until relatively recently, Western academic historians were extremely suspicious of oral documents or dismissed them entirely. However, since the 1960s oral histories have been used to write down the pasts of groups—in and out of Africa—that had been largely left out of the history books up to then. Even before the 1960s, academically trained historians of Africa had begun to make use of oral data to write histories of certain regions or communities. Nevertheless, the histories of large parts of Africa remain unknown to outsiders, not least because the process of translating oral histories into written forms is laborious and often contentious. In southern Africa, the development of academic study of the histories of African communities was often thwarted by the apartheid policies of white settler governments that promoted their own falsified official accounts of the region.

Historians and archaeologists believe that the earliest settlers in the area of present-day Namibia were gatherers and hunters. These early residents left a remarkable record of their existence in the famed petroglyphs of Namibia; their engravings and paintings depict animals as well as humans engaged in a wide variety of pursuits. From this pictographic evidence, scholars have speculated about the lifestyle of these earliest Namibians. Some images clearly show individuals engaged in hunting; other images are open to a range of interpretations.

Cave paintings provide evidence of human habitation in the area going back more than 25,000 years. Following the gatherer-hunters, Bantu-speaking pastoralists were next on the scene. Like gatherer-hunter groups, the pastoralists were peripatetic, moving from one watering hole to the next. The first agriculturalists were Bantu-speaking migrants. Then as now, much of Namibia was not suited to agriculture, so this no doubt restricted the numbers of agriculturalists drawn to the area. The natural habitat of Namibia is best suited to pastoral and hunting-and-gathering lifestyles. Given the mobile lifestyles of the early citizens of what was to become Namibia and the scarcity of water throughout much of the region, conflict sometimes erupted between groups. At the same time, the mobility of these communities also meant that one group was able to move easily to a new location in the event of conflict, potential or real.

The earliest Europeans to reach the area of modern-day Namibia were the Portuguese. The Portuguese were also the first people to enter this area by ocean, sailing down the African coast. In 1486 a Portuguese expedition led by Diego Cão erected a stone cross in the area known today as Cape Cross, north of modern-day Swakopmund. In 1487–1488, another Portuguese expedition sailed down the Namibian coastline, led by Bartholomeu Dias, who was the first European to reach the Cape of Good Hope. Dias's circumnavigation of the Cape of Good Hope facilitated Vasco da Gama's more famous voyage around the Cape and on to India a decade later. Although the Portuguese established a presence in various parts of Africa, Namibia was not one of those. The waters off the coast of Namibia were, as they remain, extremely treacherous, with almost no natural harbors suitable for oceangoing vessels. Indeed, many of the earliest Europeans to settle in Namibia (who came much later than these early explorers) traveled by land, coming from the areas of modern-day South Africa and Angola.

In the late 19th century, groups of migrants began to move into areas of present-day Namibia from areas further south. Throughout southern Africa, the 19th century was a period of great ferment, often referred to as the *difaqane* or *mfecane*. This tumultuous period saw large population movements, as well as the rise and decline of various new states and leaders, the most famous being the Zulu ruler Shaka of modern-day South Africa. In the case of Namibia, various groups of Africans and Europeans, including Nama, Rehoboth Basters, Sotho (who established the Kololo Empire in Caprivi), Afrikaners, and Germans, moved into the area from what is today South Africa in this period. Some of the groups that we group into a single

ethnic category (including the Herero, Nama, and Ovambo) were consti-
tuted into distinct communities, which sometimes forged alliances and at
other times battled one another for control over cattle, land, and water.

European Settlers: From White Minority to Majority Rule

As elsewhere in Africa, missionaries and traders were usually the first European settlers to arrive, followed by official representatives of European imperial rule. The latter often came after much campaigning on the part of those
on the ground, namely, the traders and missionaries. An early example of
the latter was Dr. Fabri, an agent of the Rhenish Mission who co-authored a
book entitled *Does Germany Need Colonies?* Fabri argued that for economic
reasons Germany did indeed need colonies. German merchants were eager
to have colonies of their own, and merchants figure highly in German colonial history. The name Adolf Luderitz is central to the history of modern
Namibia. In 1884, the merchant Luderitz declared the area around the town
that now bears his name a German possession.[24] In the quest to acquire raw
materials, merchants without colonial territories and the protections these
provided—namely, military ones—were clearly at a disadvantage vis-à-vis
merchants from countries whose governments had a military presence and
claims over territories. The German public also came to show an interest in
being a world power, and all kinds of associations were created that vigor-
ously promoted the idea of a German colonial empire.

The first Christian mission in Namibia was established in 1806 in southern Namibia by two German brothers working for the London Missionary
Society (LMS). In 1814 another German LMS missionary, Johann Heinrich
Schmelen, founded a mission station at a place he christened Bethanien.
Later, Schmelen married a Nama woman, and thanks to her efforts he was
able to translate several Gospels of the New Testament into Nama. Schmelen's
house, completed in 1815, has been converted into a museum and is considered the oldest building in Namibia.

The LMS missionaries were soon joined by the Wesleyans. Then came
Lutherans belonging to the RMS, who established a mission in 1842. Carl
Hugo Hahn, one of the best-known figures in Namibian mission history, and
three fellow missionaries were the first RMS workers in Namibia. Although
the RMS was interdenominational, the missionaries in Namibia were mostly
Lutheran, and most came from the area around the Wupper River in Germany, where the mission was based. While missionaries and colonial officials
sometimes came into conflict and did not always see eye to eye, there were
frequent contacts and connections between the two groups. Many colonial
officials were former missionaries, and missionaries married into colonial
families, and vice versa.

By the time Germany began to acquire colonial territories in Africa, it was already far behind the French and the British, who, between them, had carved up much of Africa. Historians have long debated why the German state appeared to have little interest in acquiring colonies in Africa (and elsewhere) as the French and British were doing rapidly throughout the 19th century. Many historians have insisted that Otto Bismarck (later Count von Bismarck), the powerful German chancellor, was focused on consolidating Germany's power in Europe and had little interest in foreign adventures, which he deemed, unimportant, and expensive. It must be remembered that Germany did not come into existence until 1871. Prior to this time, what would become Germany consisted of distinct and separate principalities and dukedoms. A new country in the late 19th century, Germany confronted the task of consolidating a sense of national identity and was eager to be on equal footing with more established European states.

To some, one avenue to parity was to emulate those European countries that were not only national states but also global powers. This required an empire. Acquiring overseas possessions, many historians argue, became a key goal for European states anxious to maintain the balance of power within Europe. While historians will no doubt continue to debate whether Bismarck was pushed by German merchants to enter into "colonial adventures" or whether in the end he too came to the conclusion that colonies were necessary, what is indisputable is that in the last quarter of the 19th century Germany rapidly acquired large tracts of territory in Africa (and elsewhere), in what appeared to be a mad scramble to catch up with other European imperial powers.

Germany's road to empire was a rapid one. Between 1884 and 1899 Germany acquired numerous territories in Africa and the Pacific. In the space of just two months in 1884, from July to August, Germany declared possession of Namibia, Togo, and Cameroon, and shortly thereafter of Tanzania, Rwanda, and Burundi. Later that year, in November, the powers of Europe gathered in Berlin to divide up Africa. Describing Germany's role in the carving up of Africa that occurred at the Berlin Conference, the preeminent African political scientist and public intellectual Ali Mazrui has noted that Bismarck "set the stage for the partition of Africa." Bismarck himself described his role in bringing the various European states together to discuss Africa as that of an "honest broker."[25]

Bismarck's successor as chancellor was Count Georg Leo von Caprivi di Caprara di Montecuccoli. He managed to negotiate successfully for the transfer from Britain to Germany of the piece of land in northeastern Namibia that today bears his name. The Caprivi Strip has been at the center of claims and counterclaims ever since. Count Caprivi was trying to find a means to link Germany's eastern and southwestern African possessions; in the end, the river on which he had pinned his hopes, the Zambezi, turned out to be quite unnavigable because of numerous rapids and sandbars and its insurmountable shallowness in many places. Historians often point to this Caprivi adventure as a prime example of the ways in which the Scramble for Africa created unnatural boundaries that would long remain a source of conflict.

As well as merchants, the public, and missionaries, another group was interested in German possessions overseas: advocates of settler colonialism. This latter group included not only those who sought opportunities to make a new (and better) life but also those who advocated the need for the German people to spread their culture. The British had felt a duty to take up the "white man's burden," and the French spoke about their *mission civilisatrice*. German pro-empire theorists advocated a controlled emigration policy aimed at creating a German state in which German culture and economic interests would hold the far-flung parts together. Karl Peters was a major figure advocating the benefits of a German colonial empire. Peters and a group of like-minded compatriots founded the commercial company the German East Africa Corporation (Deutsch-Ostafrikanische Gesellschaft, or DOAG). The DOAG entered into agreements with a number of chiefs in East Africa. Namibia received more German settlers than all the other colonies (Cameroon, Tanganyika or German East Africa, and Togo) combined. Other groups and individuals were active in pushing the cause of empire, including the novelist Frieda von Bulow. For example, the German Colonial Society (Deutsche Kolonialgesellschaft), which came into being in 1884 when two previous pro-empire organizations were amalgamated, published a bimonthly periodical that contained stories about life in the colonies.[26]

German traders were not the first Europeans interested in Namibia as a source of economic opportunities. Already in the 18th century, fishing trawlers were traveling from North America as well as Europe to fish in Namibian waters; guano, the excrement of seabirds, which is a rich fertilizer, was also a draw for Western countries. In the 17th and 18th centuries, vessels of various nationalities, especially Dutch and British, explored Namibian waters, interested in the possibilities of new economic opportunities. By the late 18th century, fishing vessels from North America and Europe were regularly fishing off the coast of Namibia; by early in the next century, the rich guano deposits were being exploited. In the late 19th century Britain established a formal presence with its annexation of Walvis Bay; thereafter, Germany formally declared the surrounding area its colonial possession. But even before the German state began sending officials and settlers from Germany to South West Africa, whites and Coloureds from the Cape area were moving into the area of present-day Namibia. Groups of migrants, black and white, were moving up from the area of present-day South Africa in a search for new lands. Jonker Afrikaner, now generally celebrated as a Namibian national hero, emerged as the leader of an ethnically diverse group made up of African migrants from the Cape, local Herero, and others. Jonker's people lived in the Windhoek area and dominated much of central Namibia. The 19th century saw a great deal of shifting alliances as chiefs and communities tried to protect their interests or to expand their reach. German agents sought and secured so-called protection treaties with African rulers; with powerful military backing, the Germans were often successful in persuading even the most reluctant to sign. By the end of the century, two of the most formidable rulers in central Namibia, Nama leader Hendrik Witbooi and Herero chief Samuel Maharero, had a history of checkered dealings with each other and with the Germans.

In 1904 the Herero declared war against the German colonial state. The Battle of Waterberg, in August of that year, was the climax of the war, with the retreat of the Herero forces delivering a major tactical victory to Germany. Yet, two months later, the German general Lothar von Trotha issued his famous extermination order calling for the death of every Herero man, woman, and child. Of those Hereros who were not killed in the fighting, a great number died as they tried to make their way across the Kalahari into Botswana.[27] Before the year was out, the Namas under Hendrik Witbooi had taken up arms against the Germans, and the German policy of extermination was extended to include them. Following their defeat, the greatly reduced numbers of Hereros and Namas who remained in Namibia were herded into concentration camps where conditions were so abysmal that some historians insist that the conditions at the camps were part of the strategy of annihilation. Land and cattle were seized from the defeated rebels and given to German settlers. In the decade between the end of the war and the outbreak of World War I, the population of German settlers increased to well over 12,000.

Although Namibia received far more German settlers than either Cameroon or German East Africa (Tanganyika), the numbers remained very slight for quite some time. For example, in 1902 there were only about 2,500 German settlers, almost 1,500 Boers, and about 500 British. Like Luderitz, other German businessmen were attracted by the prospects of making their fortunes in diamond and copper mining. Once Germany declared South West Africa its colonial property, Germans were encouraged to settle there. In the 19th century many Germans were emigrating to the United States and other parts of the Americas; many advocated that German migrants should be encouraged to remain within the German political and economic sphere. Settlers were promised land and opportunities. Significant numbers of German troops and settlers began to arrive in the last decade of the 19th century, and many missionaries of the RMS wore two hats: one as missionaries to the Africans and another as pastors to congregations of German settlers. During World War I, the South African forces incarcerated German pastors, including those of the RMS. By 1914, when the war broke out, there were about 12,000 German settlers in Namibia. In the official and unofficial (for example, in letters to friends and relatives back home) settler historiography, settlers claimed that prior to the Europeans' arrival the Africans in Namibia lived in "deepest ignorance" and without any morality, essentially existing outside historical time. A few German officials were more clear-eyed and honest. For example, Theodor Leutwein, governor of German South West Africa from 1894 to 1904, wrote that "the final aim of each and every colonization is—stripped of all its idealistic and humanitarian accessories—finally just a simple business."[28]

Genocide

The year 2004 was the centennial of the first holocaust in modern history, one with deep but little-known links to the most famous genocide of our times. As the somber date approached, historians and activists shed light on this episode in German colonial history that had been completely erased from official German history. According to Joachim Zeller and other German historians, even 100 years after this murderous plan was signed, no German textbooks or general histories made reference to this episode in the country's history.[29] For decades no German chancellor had ever agreed to apologize for the genocide, fearful of possible legal ramifications. In 2004, however, on a visit to Namibia during events to mark the 100th anniversary of the incident, the German Minister for Development Aid acknowledged that a genocide had taken place and apologized. It was the first time a representative of the German government had apologized, something for which many had long campaigned.

South African Rule

Germany lost its African empire even more quickly than it had acquired it. In 1919, at the Treaty of Versailles, Germany was officially stripped of its colonial possessions. South West Africa was declared a League of Nations mandated territory, and South Africa was put in charge of the country. In fact, German South West Africa had been under South African occupation since 1915 when the latter country successfully invaded its neighbor. This was the beginning of South African rule in Namibia, which would last until the armed resistance struggle achieved victory in 1990.

Over the decades South Africa took steps to bring Namibia closer, administratively, to South Africa, intent on the eventual amalgamation of the two countries. Several attempts by the United Nations, which had replaced the League of Nations, to revise the basis of South African overrule were rebuffed by South Africa. In 1946, for example, the United Nations sought to regularize the South African presence in Namibia and asked South Africa to sign a trusteeship agreement since the agreement under the League of Nations was no longer operative. South Africa refused to sign the agreement, intent on its desire to make Namibia part of South Africa. Two years later, in 1948, the Nationalist Party came to power in South Africa and began to pass laws enshrining the policy of apartheid ("apartness"). The following year South Africa passed a constitutional amendment that gave parliamentary representation to Namibia, thus effectively making Namibia a quasi-province of South Africa. Black Namibians, unsurprisingly, did not welcome the South African occupation, nor the steps taken by the government to replicate apartheid policies in Namibia. In 1946, Chief Hosea Kutako, who fought in the 1904–1908 war, spearheaded a petition to the United Nations calling for an end to the South African occupation. Today, in recognition of his numerous efforts on behalf of his country, there is a statue of Kutako in front of the Tintenpalast, the seat of government in Namibia, and the country's main airport is named after him. International outrage was widely expressed over the South African occupation, but, for decades, no meaningful action was taken. Meetings were held and attempts were made to bring the South African government to negotiations, but these were all unsuccessful. South Africa continued to occupy Namibia, even if it did so illegally in the eyes of most of the world.

In 1960 Ethiopia and Liberia, the only two African countries that were members of the United Nations, brought a case before the International Court of Justice challenging South Africa's right to rule Namibia. It was not until 1966 that the court issued a verdict on the suit brought by the two African countries: It ruled that Liberia and Ethiopia did not have the right to bring a suit about Namibia before the court. While Liberia and Ethiopia protested the violent suppression of civil disobedience by the South African regime, the British and the United States insisted on the need for slow and deliberate action in South West Africa. The Central Intelligence Agency (CIA) insisted that sanctions, which Liberia and Ethiopia were calling for, were ineffective. It should be noted that this was about the same time that sanctions were being adopted by the United States against Cuba.[30]

In 1964, the Odendaal Commission, which had been appointed by the South African government, issued its report, which called for the creation of supposedly independent homelands in which each community would live separately and independently. Following the report's recommendations, South Africa created 12 homelands (Bantustans) where each people was to dwell and develop. The different groups of whites were deemed one people, and they retained about 60 percent of the land, while the rest of the population received 40 percent of the land. The best lands were reserved for whites. Apartheid policies extended beyond politics and land to the economy, religious worship, education, and all aspects of public and private life. As in South Africa, marriage across racial lines was deemed illegal. In the public sector, the lowliest jobs were reserved for blacks, with black waged employment being concentrated in the mining industry and farming. In 1964, the same year that the Odendaal Commission issued its recommendations, African political leaders announced they were abandoning nonviolent tactics and would embark on an armed struggle against the South African white minority rule. The leaders of SWAPO, the main resistance movement, charged that the United Nations' failure to take action against South Africa's blatant infringement of the terms of its trusteeship had left them no choice. For years they had exercised patience and waited for a positive outcome, but once apartheid became a fait accompli in Namibia, they lost hope in the nonviolent option.

South Africa's mandate over Namibia was revoked by the United Nations in 1966. By then, at the same time as the International Court dismissed the case brought by Ethiopia and Liberia, the complexion of the United Nations had changed greatly from the time when these two countries had first brought the case to the court. There were now many African member states in the UN General Assembly, and with other newly emerged states they formed an anticolonial bloc that consistently pushed for votes in the General Assembly condemning South African rule over Namibia. In 1971, following a request from the UN Security Council for an opinion, the International Court of Justice finally declared South African occupation of Namibia illegal. Despite resolutions and international condemnation, South Africa held fast to Namibia.

Throughout the 1960s and 1970s, Western governments, invested heavily economically in South Africa and Namibia, insisted on a policy of "constructive engagement" in southern Africa. Mining was then, as now, Namibia's main industry. Of the three companies that then accounted for 90 percent of Namibia's mining production, two were owned mostly by the United States and Britain. The third was a subsidiary of De Beers, South Africa's mining giant. Mining profits accounted for about half of the country's income at the time. Namibian blacks, with SWAPO leading the charge, organized strikes and protest actions and also maintained an all-out guerrilla war. Strike action was one of the main forms of protest, and these strikes sometimes involved huge numbers of people. The 1971 strike, for example, is estimated to have involved about 70 percent of all those who worked in the mining sector and other nonfarm occupations. In 1973 Africans boycotted the elections organized by South Africa in the Ovambo Bantustan (or homeland).

Nationalism and Independence

It is impossible to understand Namibia's recent history without attention to regional and international developments. The modern histories of the countries of southern Africa are intimately tied together, not just by European settler minority rule nor by South Africa's decades-long direct rule over Namibia. As already noted, Western governments were eager to safeguard the business links and opportunities with South Africa and thus were loath to take any action that could jeopardize these. At the same time, there was the important issue of the Cold War. Western governments, especially the United States, feared that if vigilance was not maintained, Communism would triumph in places such as Namibia. It is certainly true that African nationalist leaders sometimes had links with the Soviets or the Chinese, but scholars continue to debate to what extent these links were due to ideological commitments and to what extent they were pragmatic choices, indeed sometimes the only option available. In the context of the Cold War, nationalist conflicts were never strictly at the state level alone. This was true of developments in southern Africa as well as in other parts of Africa, most notably the Horn of Africa, where the Soviets and the United States battled each other for friendships and influence in the region. South Africa, and many supporters in the West, most notably President Nixon and his National Security Adviser, Henry Kissinger, insisted that South African rule over Namibia provided a protective layer ensuring that the country did not fall into Communist hands. Across the border in Angola, Cubans were assisting the nationalists in their war to bring an end to Portuguese colonial rule. The United States and South Africa insisted that there could be no independence for Namibia if Cuban troops remained in Angola.

In 1973 the UN General Assembly acknowledged SWAPO to be the sole and authentic representative of the Namibian people. Three years later, SWAPO was granted observer status at the United Nations. When a new government came to power in Portugal in 1974 and signed a peace treaty with the Angolan rebels the following year, bringing to an end a war that had lasted 13 years, the dynamics in the region changed. Many hardened their position on the need to preserve Namibia and the rest of the region from Communism. For South Africa, the independence of Angola (and Mozambique) hardened its resolve, and the government embarked on a huge program of torture and intimidation in Namibia.

At the same time, the fall of Angola and Mozambique also strengthened the position of SWAPO by providing it access to allies nearby. The victory of the nationalists in Angola meant SWAPO now had the opportunity to have bases right across the border from Namibia. South Africa, which for years had managed to maintain its tight grip on Namibia, tried a new approach in the 1970s as calls for change, often perfunctory, were coming from even its most reliable international supporters. Between 1975 and 1977 the Turnhalle Constitutional Conference met, supposedly to discuss how to provide for ethnically based development. Many saw the effort as simply an attempt to undermine SWAPO's influence; SWAPO leaders and many in the international community denounced Turnhalle as little more than a political charade.

Finally, in 1988 the United Nations, South Africa, Angola, and SWAPO reached an agreement that Cuban forces would withdraw from Angola and the South Africans would follow suit and withdraw from Namibia after elections had been held there. In September 1989, after 30 years in exile, SWAPO leader Sam Nujoma returned home. Two months later, polls were held to elect members to the Constituent Assembly. SWAPO won 57 percent of the votes, while the Democratic Turnhalle Alliance (which materialized from the Turnhalle Conference) won 28 percent. The Constituent Assembly adopted a new constitution and declared that Namibian independence would be formally inaugurated on March 21, 1990. Nujoma, the veteran war leader, was elected president. The following month, Namibia joined the United Nations, an organization which had so often debated the fate of the country.

Today, SWAPO remains in power, 20 years after winning the first democratic elections in the country. There are concerns about the absence of viable political challengers to SWAPO's dominance. There are numerous political parties in Namibia, but none has been able to attain anything near the popularity of SWAPO. The Rally for Democracy and Progress (RDP), founded by former SWAPO members, is currently emerging as possibly the first significant challenger to SWAPO. In 2008 President Hifikepunye Pohamba, who was returned to office in December 2009, called the members of RDP "traitors like Judas Iscariot." Church leaders were so concerned about the tense relations between RDP and SWAPO leaders that the Lutheran bishops issued an open letter that was read in all Lutheran churches on Sunday, April 1, 2009, calling on leaders, political, religious, and traditional, to do more to promote greater civil discourse and to discourage the intolerance and violence that were becoming a feature of political debates and elections.

Some accuse SWAPO of being too much of an Ovambo party. It is true that the precursor of SWAPO was the Ovambo People's Party (OPO). It is also true that the Ovambo have voted overwhelmingly for SWAPO in all three of Namibia's democratic elections (1989, 2004, and 2009). While the complaints that the Ovambo dominate the government and government-appointed offices are true, it is also true that the Ovambo constitute about half of the population. The next-largest group, the Kavango, make up only

Sam Nujoma was an important nationalist leader within the colony of South West Africa and achieved international recognition as a diplomat for his country's independence. He led the South West African People's Organization (SWAPO) and became the first president of independent Namibia. (UPI-Bettmann/Corbis)

about 10 percent. There are also complaints that government funds go overwhelmingly to the areas of northern Namibia where the Ovambo live. This is true. However, it is also true that the population of Namibia is concentrated in the northern half of the country, and in the early years of independence, the north required more rehabilitation than other areas because the fighting during the liberation period had been concentrated there. Having said all that, it should be noted that even some SWAPO supporters express concern that the failure of any effective political challenge to SWAPO is a threat to democracy. However, only time will tell what the future holds for SWAPO and for Namibia.

Another source of conflict that can be traced back to the independence struggle is the tension between those who went into exile and those who remained in the country, and their respective offspring. Many of those who remained in the country throughout the struggle feel that a disproportionate amount of resources are reserved for those who went into or were born in exile. At the same time many of those who fought as guerillas feel their contributions to the country are not adequately recognized. One major issue that is unlikely to be unresolved any time soon is the question of land. As Namibia was a settler colony, a small minority of European settlers claimed large amounts of land, leaving the vast majority of Africans with little or no land. At independence, less than 1 percent of the population controlled more than 70 percent of the arable land. This was a result of the policies of the apartheid South African regime, which had declared 52 percent of the land for commercial purposes and 48 percent communal, as well as general apartheid policies that favored white settlers. Prior to independence, SWAPO promised that there would be no seizure of white-owned lands; instead, after independence, the government pursued a policy of "willing buyer, willing seller," whereby landowners who intended to sell had to offer the land for sale first to the government before it could go on sale to the public. This policy has not satisfied everyone because most of the productive land remains in the hands of white commercial farmers and ranchers. In 2005, for example, there were 4,422 white commercial farms, 324 black commercial farms, 240 foreign commercial farms, and 34 government-owned commercial farms. Between 2005 and 2010 the government seized half a dozen white-owned farms that were deemed to be underutilized or part of excessive holdings. Naturally, this had led to anxiety on the part of some white landowners; three other such subsequent seizures were successfully challenged in court. The question for Namibia remains how to assure continued productivity while providing a measure of justice and equity: Commercial farms are responsible for most of the beef and other farm exports, which altogether contribute about 10 percent of the gross domestic product.

In 2008, the government began to map the communal lands from which most Africans with access to land drew their subsistence. The plan is to make small parcels of these lands available to individual land seekers, who will be granted certificates of ownership. The whole issue of land is a complicated one; even when black farmers are given land or allowed to buy it, other problems remain, for example, the issue of securing access to finance and how to compete with large commercial farms. In the 20 years since independence, the government has been able to buy fewer than 350 farms and resettle some 2,000 families.

Although Namibia continues to have one of the lowest population densities in the world, it has one of the fastest population growth rates. With its limited supplies of water and arable land, it can be expected that population stresses will be of major concern in the future. Water availability has long been an issue of great importance to Namibians, and if projections by scientists prove accurate, the future will present even greater challenges. Added to the challenges of water and land scarcity is the AIDS scourge, which has hit the countries of southern Africa, including Namibia, particularly hard. Some estimates project that in some parts of the country as many as one in three Namibians is infected with the HIV virus; because it is impossible to get accurate numbers, estimates vary widely.[31] In such a severely dry and drought-prone country, the HIV/AIDS epidemic is likely to be eclipsed by ecological transformations being wrought by climate change. Climate change, AIDS and HIV, income inequities, and the growing discontent with Ovambo domination are among the major challenges facing Namibia. In September 2010, the government announced that 51.2 percent of the Namibian work-force was unemployed; in some places the figure is above 70 percent. The employment situation, combined with an inflation rate of about 10 percent and the other challenges facing the country, make for a highly combustible situation. Some hope can be found in the long as well as the more recent history of Namibians, which has shown them to be a people who are survivors and who no doubt will rise to whatever challenges the future presents.

NOTES

1. Different sources give slightly different numbers for Namibia's total size. These figures are taken from the United Nations Environment Programme (UNEP), *Africa: Atlas of Our Changing Environment* (Nairobi, Kenya: UNEP, 2008).

2. This is the widely held view among scholars, notwithstanding the recognition that many of the groups (such as the Herero, but also other groups including Nama and Ovambo) who today are considered part of a single ethnic community did not have a common group identity in the tumultuous 19th century. Today, of course, making an ethnic map of Namibia is perhaps no less problematic: as we have noted, one often refers to the Kavango and even Caprivians, but in both of these cases it is also recognized that each of these identity markers may (or should) be further broken down.

3. The apprehension and prosecution of offenders are rare. In the last few years, Namibia has endured massive flooding during the rainy season, especially in the north. The rain brings water; unfortunately, the severity of the rains leads to destructive flooding, destroying fields and crops and submerging homes and buildings. In 2011, for example, more than 250 schools were closed down due to severe flooding and thousands of people had to be relocated. Tragically, scores lost their lives.

4. The Namibian Constitution may be accessed online at either of the two sites provided here: http://www.namibia-1on1.com/namibiaconstitution-1.html or http://www.servat.unibe.ch/icl/wa00000_.html.

5. See, for example, Brian T. B. Jones, Moses Makonjio Okello, and Bobby E. L. Wishitemi, "Pastoralists, Conservation and Livelihoods in East and Southern Africa: Reconciling Continuity and Change through the Protected Landscape Approach,"

in *The Protected Landscape Approach: Linking Nature, Culture and Community,* ed. Jessica Brown, Nora Mitchell, and Michael Beresford (Gland, Switzerland: World Conservation Union, 2005), p. 114.

6. In local Namibian parlance, the San are not classed as black. Neither black nor white, they are classified—and often refer to themselves—as red people. This may be a little confusing, as there are some Nama who refer to themselves, and are known, as the Red Nation.

7. The same can also be said for Kavango. Kavango is one of the 12 districts of the country, and residents are also known as Kavango. However, Kavango speak different languages and maintain distinct cultural identities. Kavango ethnic identities are, most typically, based on the traditional kingdoms recognized in the Namibian Constitution.

8. Wolfram Hartmann, Jeremy Silvester, and Patricia Hayes, eds., *The Colonising Camera: Photographs in the Making of Namibian History* (Athens: Ohio University Press, 1999), 18.

9. More recently, other scholars insist that the term *Nama* is offensive, arguing that the belief that *Hottentot* is offensive is in error. An incident that almost turned deadly illustrates the gulf that sometimes exists between the views of scholars and those of the people they describe. In 2011, a fight between two men almost ended in a fatality; the fight broke out, according to the assailant, because the other man referred to him as Hottentot. See Luqman Cloete, "Gochas Businessman's Son Arrested on Attempted Murder Charge," *Namibian,* January 14, 2011, available at http://www.namibian.com.na/news/full-story/archive/2011/january/article/gochas-businessmans-son-arrested-on-attempted-murder-charge/.

10. Orlam is also spelled Oorlam. The debate over Nama origins is sometimes reflected in the labels assigned to Nama groups: Some authors reserve the term *Nama* for so-called indigenous communities while labeling those groups that migrated from South Africa *Orlam*. To add further to the confusion, each Nama community has *at least* one Nama name and an Afrikaner name.

11. The exclamation mark and the slash represent different types of clicks in Khoisan languages.

12. The historian Gregory Maddox cautions against this type of thinking. He writes, "This tendency toward assigning a special place to such foragers, whether romanticized as 'original people' or dehumanized as closer to other animals . . . is false on several levels. First, historic San (Bushmen) and Khoi herders are no closer to our common ancestors than anyone else alive. More importantly, from the moment iron-using agriculturalists appeared, foragers began to change their lifeways in response to new conditions." *Sub-Saharan Africa: An Environmental History* (Santa Barbara, CA: ABC-CLIO, 2006), pp. 58–59.

13. Afrikaners are the descendants of Dutch settlers to South Africa, who began to arrive there in the 17th century. Over time, small numbers of other Europeans (most notably French Huguenots) were absorbed into the Afrikaner community. For much of the 19th century and into the 20th, groups of Afrikaners migrated from South Africa and established new communities in other parts of southern Africa.

14. In January 2011, a secessionist group based in Zambia, the Black Bulls, ordered all non-SiLozi-speaking peoples in Zambia's Western Province (formerly Barotse Province) to leave Barotseland or else face death. It is interesting to note that in Lozi oral history as well as academic history, the foundations of the Lozi empire are often traced to the arrival in the area of migrants from what is today the Democratic Republic of Congo.

15. The question of what is the most widely spoken language in Namibia continues to be a matter of disagreement. On the difficulties of plotting language use in Namibia, see Jan Knappert, *Namibia: Land and Peoples, Myths and Fables* (Leiden: Brill, 1981), pp. 4–6.

16. It is interesting to note the case of Rwanda, a country that was the site of a major genocide in 1994. In 2008 the government of Rwanda declared English the official language alongside Kinyarwanda and French. Since then the government has actively promoted English as the medium of instruction in state schools, arguing that English is the language of international commerce. French was the language of Belgian colonial rule in Rwanda, and the postgenocide government of Rwanda (and some international commentators) continues to insist that the French government was complicit in the genocide.

17. These languages are often given without the prefix. In other words, OtjiHerero may appear as simply Herero and SiLozi as Lozi, while OshiNdonga and OshiKwanyama become, respectively, Ndonga and Kwanyama.

18. On March 16, 2009, at his farewell appearance at the National Assembly prior to his retirement, Namibian politician and former Minister of Veterans Affairs Dr. Ngarikutuke Tjiriange delivered an impassioned speech in Herero, reminding his colleagues that "the revolution had not yet been won." Tjiriange called on Namibians to take pride in their own languages rather than communicate in second languages they have not yet mastered.

19. Other meanings have been given for the word *Katutura,* including "we do not have a permanent dwelling place." One of the most well-known incidents in the annals of South African rule was the destruction of black and Coloured neighborhoods in Namibia. It is worth noting that the forced removals from Old Location happened at the same time as the forcible removal of blacks (including a large number of black middle-class intelligentsia and artists) from Sophiatown in South Africa. Sophiatown was famously heterogeneous, with blacks, whites, Coloureds, and Indians. After the removal of the nonwhites, Sophiatown was renamed Triomph ("triumph").

20. The Damara-Nama name for Windhoek is /Ae//Gams ("hot springs"; literally, "fire water"); the Herero name is Otjomuise ("place of stream").

21. The University of Namibia (UNAM) has several satellite campuses.

22. The use of guano as fertilizer is not recent: the Incas are known to have harvested and used guano as fertilizer in pre-Columbian times.

23. The important point is that in a relatively short amount of time China has emerged as a critical player in Africa. In some African countries, including Namibia, vibrant Chinatowns are emerging. Chinese clout is evident in factories, building, and road and rail construction. Chinese loans are hard to tally as the Chinese banks do

not release their figures, so there is a great deal of speculation and disagreement about total Chinese investments in Africa. All agree, however, that the total—whatever it is—is huge and is impacting African politics. As Deborah Brautigam notes, comparing Chinese and World Bank investments in Africa is akin to comparing apples to lychees. Brautigam, *The Dragon's Gift: The Real Story of China in Africa* (Oxford: Oxford University Press, 2009), p. 182.

24. W. O. Henderson, "Germany's Trade with Her Colonies, 1884–1914," *Economic History Review* 9, no. 1 (November 1938). While Luderitz is not mentioned by name in this essay, written just before World War II, it offers a very interesting look at German colonial history.

25. Ali Mazrui, "African Security: The Erosion of the State and the Decline of Race as a Basis for Human Relations," in *Globalization, Human Security and the African Experience,* ed. Caroline Thomas and Peter Wilkin (Boulder, CO: Lynne Rienner, 1999), p. 163.

26. Historian Woodruff Smith categorizes 19th-century pro-empire German groups into "migrationist colonialists" and "economic colonialists" and traces how these tendencies evolve to become central philosophical tenets at the core of the Nazi regime. See Woodruff D. Smith, *The Ideological Origins of Nazi Imperialism* (Oxford: Oxford University Press, 1989).

27. To this day there is a sizable Herero population in Botswana that traces its roots to the 1904 defeat.

28. Quoted in Henning Melber, "Colonialism, Culture and Resistance: The Case of Namibia," in *It Is No More a Cry: Namibian Poetry in Exile,* ed. Henning Melber (Basel, Switzerland: Basler Afrika Bibliographien, 2004), p. 22.

29. Zeller is interviewed in the documentary, *Le Malentendu Colonial* (Jean-Marie Téno, 2004).

30. The United States adopted sanctions against Cuba in 1962, following their unsuccessful attempt the previous year to overthrow the Marxist Castro regime.

31. The incidence of HIV/AIDS can vary enormously across the country from community to community. Reports for the last decade of the 20th century suggested that the Caprivi region had by far the highest incidence of HIV/AIDS in Namibia.

2

Religion and Worldview

INTRODUCTION

Religion is very much in evidence in public life in Namibia. For students, for example, whether in public or private school, the day typically begins with an assembly at which prayers are said. Public functions, including government events, often begin and end with prayer. An overwhelming majority (more than 90%) of Namibians are Christians, belonging to a variety of different denominations. Estimates of the numbers of Catholics in Namibia range from just over 10 percent to about 20 percent. Similarly, the number of Namibian Muslims is a matter of dispute, with estimates varying between 1 and 3 percent. There are also small numbers of Jews and Bah'ai who sometimes gather to hold regular prayer services, in Windhoek at least.

Pentecostal churches are rapidly gaining ground in Namibia, and all over Namibia the signs of this are evident; however, it is still widely accepted that at least half of all Namibians are Lutherans. In 2007, the United Church Council of the Namibian Evangelical Lutheran Churches (UCC-NELC) was established in Windhoek. This was the culmination of efforts to bring greater cooperation to the Lutheran community in Namibia. With the creation of this new organization, the three main Lutheran churches agreed to hold common meetings, with the aim of working toward greater unity and ultimately union. Both lay members and pastoral leaders have expressed concerns about the need to be sensitive to issues of identity, especially with regard to language.

Even before the creation of the UCC-NELC, the three Lutheran congregations were all members of the Lutheran World Federation—Namibian National Committee (LWF-NNC), an earlier organization that recognized their shared Lutheran heritage and theology and worked to achieve greater unity.

The largest church in Namibia is the Evangelical Lutheran Church in Namibia (ELCIN), whose membership is roughly double that of the next-largest church in the country. The second-largest church in Namibia in terms of membership is the Evangelical Lutheran Church in the Republic of Namibia (ELCRN). The smallest of the three Lutheran groups is the German Evangelical Lutheran Church—Evangelical Lutheran Church in Namibia (GELC-ELCIN; also known as the Deutsche Evangelisch-Lutherische Kirche in Namibia, or DELK). In 2006, for example, the ELCIN had 625,000 members, the ELCRN had 350,000, and the GELC-ELCIN had a roster of just 5,200 members. The ELCIN is found extensively in northern Namibia, and it is the denomination to which most Ovambo belong. The ELCIN traces its root to the Finnish missionaries, members of the Finnish Evangelical Lutheran Mission (FELM), which opened its first mission station in Ovamboland in July 1870. Known initially as FELM, the church was rechristened the Evangelical Lutheran Ovambo-Kavango Church (ELOC) in 1954 in recognition

Lutheran Evangelical Church in Swakopmund, the second-oldest church in Namibia, dating from 1912. (Choups/StockphotoPro)

of its target audience, which was primarily Ovambo and Kavango, and it became known by its current name and acronym, ELCIN, in 1984.

Christianity has had an astounding success in Namibia; the first Christian missionaries to set up a permanent station in Namibia arrived only in the early 19th century. For the most part, Christianity was introduced to Namibians by missionaries working for European-based mission societies. Namibia's long history under the rule of a racially segregated, racist South Africa greatly influenced church theology and life in Namibia. While many churches did not embrace the apartheid theology of the Dutch Reformed Church (DRC), the church most closely associated with the South African ruling elite, most mainline churches practiced de facto segregation. Perhaps ironically, the churches later assumed a pivotal role in the liberation struggle, with church leaders speaking up in support of human dignity in the face of the brutal repression perpetrated by the South African apartheid regime.

Christianity has deeply affected all strata of contemporary Namibian life, whether in rural or urban areas, in elite suburbs or poor neighborhoods. While most Namibians are Christian, their faith and practices, as should be expected, are rooted in their particular cultural heritage. Scholars, commentators, and practitioners rarely agree on where to draw the line between religion and culture. What some deem an aspect of a cultural tradition, others may label religion. For example, ancestor reverence is widespread in Namibia; for some this is an aspect of pre-Christian religious beliefs, while for others it is simply a cultural tradition. Ancestors are often invoked at special occasions, including weddings, disputes, and festivals. Among the Herero, rituals involving cattle continue to occupy an important place at major occasions such as weddings and funerals, and many of these rituals predate Christianity. The sacred fire remains an important aspect of ritual and ceremonial life in many communities. The use and function of these rituals are not static, and they have undergone, and continue to undergo, transformations.

Frequently, missionaries failed to distinguish between what, properly speaking, was Christian theology and what were elements of European cultural tradition. Christian missionaries to Namibia often railed against African forms of marriage, in particular polygyny and indigenous forms of sex education. Many missionaries did not seek to transform Africans into Christians only; they sought to remake African cultures. The missionaries' objectives were broad and far-reaching, and they wrote and spoke about their duty to change African culture. The school was often the site where the work of social engineering took place, but it was not the only one. African societies were frequently seen as quite putrid, and Africans as lazy, backward, and licentious.

Missionaries not only sought to transform the domestic life of Africans but also became involved in politics and public life, frequently attempting to play the role of intermediaries between different political entities. Famously, in the 1904–1908 war between the Nama and Herero and the Germans, the missionaries positioned themselves as intermediaries between Europeans and Africans. Critics often point to this and attempts to remake the daily lives of Namibians as evidence of missionary overreaching. In particular, the role of the missionaries during the Herero genocide is a subject that arouses great emotion. Some charge the missionaries with having betrayed their African flocks. In surveying the Namibian past, however, we must be careful not to paint all missionaries in a simplistic fashion; some missionaries saw themselves and were seen by Africans as their friends and defenders. In addition, in times of crises, such as drought or military defeat, Africans sometimes flocked to the church. Of course, African conversion to Christianity did not occur only at times of crises.[1]

INDIGENOUS BELIEFS ABOUT THE SUPERNATURAL

In order to talk about the indigenous religious views of African communities, it is useful to keep in mind that the notion of what constitutes religion and how this shapes daily life is not the same everywhere. Worldviews differ from place to place, and a people's worldview shapes how they understand the supernatural and natural worlds and how they live in the latter. There is great ethnic diversity in Namibia, and there is a correspondingly diverse variety of religious expressions and views. There is a tendency to speak about African religious beliefs prior to Christianity exclusively in the present tense, even when one is referring to beliefs and practices that existed only in the past. This is, in part, due to the mistaken but widespread belief that indigenous African religious traditions are unchanging and have remained static through time. This idea is, of course, false. Beliefs and practices change over time, whether in adaptation to outside forces or to internal dynamism.

In contemporary life, the Ovambo, the largest ethnic group in Namibia, invoke Kalunga quite freely, but views diverge on the role the supreme god played in people's lives in the past. (Kalunga is the word used by the Ovambo and some other southern African groups—such as the Pende and Chokwe—to describe the supreme god.) According to Ovambo traditions, Kalunga created the first man and first woman, and this first couple had two sons and a daughter. The daughter of the first couple is considered the founder of the Ovambo. Kalunga is described by most scholars as the supreme god of the Ovambo. The Ovambo also had other names for Kalunga.

Religious scholars continue to argue about the extent to which African religions were focused on the here and now rather than the afterlife, and what role a supreme deity played in the daily lives of individuals. Did Africans ever pray to the supreme god, or did they approach him only through intercessors? All agree, however, that ancestors played a big role in Namibian lives. Ancestors served as mediators between the living and the supreme deity, and people on earth often made appeals to the ancestors, offering sacrifices and incantations. This demonstrates how life and death were not seen as opposites, but intimately connected. Not everyone who died could become an ancestor; death was a transition between worlds, as one went from this world to the next. In the past scholars wrote about ancestor worship as a component of African belief; today, one speaks about ancestor reverence. The ancestors were often referred to as the "living dead" because, although they had passed on from this life, they continued to play an important part in it.

Ancestors continue to be called upon to assist their relatives in this world. They are believed to have the power to intercede on the behalf of their descendants. Some infractions are considered crimes against ancestors. Some believe that a crime against the ancestors can result in the sickness of the culprit or even in group punishment. This is why a sick person may seek the services of a diviner. Typically, when a person falls ill, the first specialist to be consulted will be a herbalist. Only if the herbalist is unable to help, will the sick person—or his/her family, as is more likely to be the case—seek out a diviner to find out whether the sickness has supernatural causes. Ovambo medical practitioners, or healers, include herbalists, midwives, and a variety of diviners. There are diviners who use ash, for example, to divine. Others are spirit mediums and consult the spirits to diagnose. Healers wear distinctive clothes and amulets, and their rank and specialization can be seen in their apparel.

It is important to note that in the past religious beliefs and practices all over Africa were inherently bound up with notions of health and wellness. This remains true today to varying degrees. Indigenous knowledge about plants was often dismissed by Europeans as witchcraft or superstition; today, scientific research is supplying evidence that the belief that plants could have healing properties is far from wrongheaded. The bark of the African bloodwood tree (*Pterocarpus angolensis*), for example, has long been used by rural Namibians to treat conditions such as diarrhea, sores, and other skin conditions. Modern science today recognizes the astringent properties of the bloodwood's bark. The branches of the *Euclea divinorum* (also known as the magic *gwarri*) are used as a toothbrush; the bark has been shown to have antiseptic properties.

Namibians, whether Christian (as is the majority of the population) or not, tend to see the body in a holistic manner, understanding the spirit and the body to be intertwined. So it is impossible to speak of traditional or indigenous African religious beliefs without saying something about healers and other spiritual specialists. Healers heal the body, but to do so they must be spiritual adepts. Healers who heal the body and specialists who heal the spirit both must be ritual adepts who focus on the whole person. Healing of body and healing of mind go together.

In the modern Western world, there is a new embrace of alternative medicines by scientifically trained doctors, and even health insurance companies now cover such healing practices. This is related to an increasing acceptance of the belief that the person must be treated as a whole. In the worldview of many African communities, it is not only the individual that must be seen holistically but the community itself. In Damara society, *gama-aob* (*khoma-aob*) are healers who attend to both mind and body. *Gama-aob* can be translated as "men of God." When a person falls sick, the first line of treatment is to seek out a herbalist. If the herbalist's medicines fail to restore health, then a patient may turn to a spirit medium. Modern-day Namibians readily consult different ritual specialists. For example, a young Ovambo man who goes to a Lutheran church every Sunday will not necessarily see any reason not to visit a spirit medium if his daughter falls ill and is not responding to biomedical treatment. Indeed, in many instances biomedicine is not an option as parents and guardians cannot afford it, and they instead seek out a medium or a herbalist, or someone who combines both offices.

It is impossible to separate the physical and the supernatural world in talking about health and disease in Ovambo society, just as it is impossible to try to separate these worlds in daily life. We have just noted that when confronted with a severe and protracted illness an Ovambo may bring in a ritual specialist to assist in the diagnosis. It is worth noting, however, that even in the case of more mundane illnesses that respond to plant or other remedies, incantations may accompany the preparation or administration of the medicine. While we can say that the Ovambo see a clear link between observing good relations with the spirit world and physical well-being in this world, it would be incorrect to say that the Ovambo see all illnesses and diseases as attributable to spiritual sources. If the latter were the case, there would be little need for healers with knowledge of herbal remedies or biomedical specialists in clinics and hospitals, but the Ovambo do seek out herbal and biomedical specialists when loved ones fall ill. However, when illness does not respond to the usual therapies, explanations beyond this world will be sought. Specialists in the supernatural world are brought in at this point.

As well as linking physical well-being with spiritual well-being, another feature of the worldview of many Namibian communities is the idea of the holy fire. In the past, the holy fire played an important role in the life of the Nama, Damara, Herero, Ovambo, and San, and the holy fire continues to be an aspect of life for many Namibians, especially at major occasions such as chiefly installations and funerals, weddings, and even naming ceremonies. However, the holy fire no longer occupies the central place it formerly did. In the past, the holy fire was kept burning in honor of the ancestors, who were consulted by the living on important matters, and occasionally also on mundane issues. Today, one rarely finds families that maintain the holy fire continuously; more commonly, the fire is lit for special occasions, such as the funeral of an important person. During the Maharero Day celebrations in Okahandja, the keeper of the holy fire for the Maharero clan plays an important role, receiving ceremonial visits from important dignitaries who arrive from all over the country to take part in the festivities.

Throughout Africa, funerary rites are of capital importance. Indeed, it could be said that one's entire life is a preparation for death. The ultimate goal in death is to become an ancestor. But not everyone can be an ancestor. Indeed, not everyone receives a ceremonial burial. Proper burial is essential to making the transition from this world to the next. Those who die an ignominious death are not accorded proper burial, and this category would include those who commit suicide or murder and those believed to be witches or sorcerers. The Ovambo have a strong belief in the spirit world—in the ancestors who become living dead, in bad spirits, in witchcraft. The Ovambo refer to the ancestors or living dead as *ovakwamungu*. These are the dead to whom one may appeal for assistance and to intercede with God. Not all who die become ovakwamungu; some become *oilulu,* or "bad dead." The means by which a dead person becomes ovakwamungu are complex, but proper burial is a critical component. If one is denied proper burial—for whatever reason—it appears impossible for one to become a living dead. African beliefs in spirits and ancestor veneration are often described as superstitious. However, it is worth noting that all religious beliefs are founded on intangibles; for example, the concept of the Holy Spirit in Christian theology is just as abstract as Ovambo spirits.

How does one communicate with the living dead? One consults a ritual specialist. Ancestors may also send signs. Sometimes a person becomes possessed and messages are relayed in this manner. The sacred and mundane are linked. The Ovambo monarchies reign on earth, but they also have important spiritual functions. The ruler acts as a mediator between the people on earth and the royal ancestors. There are lineage ancestors and royal ancestors. It is the monarch's duty to communicate with and reverence the latter to assure the well-being of the people. If the monarch does not perform this task appropriately, the population is liable to face drought or epidemics.

An individual may be possessed by an ancestral or other spirit that wishes to convey a message to that individual or some other person. Spirit possession is also the means by which spirits make it known they have called someone to be their medium. In the latter case, the individual falls ill, responding to no treatment whatsoever. It is usually a diviner, brought in when all other treatment has failed, who diagnoses the illness as a sign of a calling to be a healer. In the 1971 classic, *Ecstatic Religion,* I. M. Lewis makes a distinction between what he calls "peripheral" possession and "central" possession. Peripheral possession is possession of those in society who are disadvantaged, such as women and lower-status men. Those familiar with the *zar* in West Africa will note that this recalls the long-standing debate about whether spirit possession is a way for those of low status to participate in a community in which they can achieve a higher status, an aspiration not open to them in the larger society. According to Lewis's schema, central possession is part of the apparatus of the status quo; in the case of monarchical institutions, for example, this would be possession of the representatives of the court. While Lewis's thesis that peripheral possession is often a means for those who are otherwise excluded from social and political power to gain prominence, even if only fleetingly, has been rejected by some, many of Lewis's insights remain important.

CHRISTIANITY IN NAMIBIA: A BRIEF HISTORY

Most Namibians today are Christian, and numerous denominations are represented in the country. The majority of Namibians belong to one of three Lutheran congregations; however, there is also a host of other denominations including Anglicans, Seventh-Day Adventists, Methodists, African Methodist Episcopalians, Baptists, United Congregationists, and Jehovah's Witnesses, as well as Catholics. The three different Lutheran churches are a reminder of the multiple missions that came to Namibia from different parts of Europe in the 19th century. Beginning in the late 18th century, a missionary fervor swept across Europe and North America, resulting in the establishment of dozens of missionary bodies on both sides of the Atlantic, some dedicated to winning the souls of fellow citizens at home (typically the poor) and others focused on "taking the Good News to the heathens" in Africa, Asia, and elsewhere. A number of names stand out in the annals of Christian missionary activity in Namibia: Johann Heinrich Schmelen (1777–1848), Carl Hugo Hahn (1818–1895), Heinrich Vedder (1876–1972), and the Albrecht brothers. Although the latter did not remain in Namibia long, they were the first to open a Christian mission station in the country. Christian evangelization in Namibia was a transnational affair, with mission groups and individuals coming from a variety of countries, including Germany, Finland, Sweden, and Switzerland.

The first Christian mission station was established in 1806 in southern Namibia, close to the border with South Africa, by Abraham and Christian Albrecht, two German brothers, members of the London Missionary Society (LMS), one of many such groups that were formed in Europe and North America in the late 18th and early 19th centuries to take the Christian message to the poor and downtrodden at home as well as pagans in faraway places. After spending some time in South Africa, the Albrecht brothers opened a mission station in Warmbad in present-day Namibia. Five years later, Abraham was dead, leaving Christian to run the mission station, along with Abraham's widow and Jan Magerman, a "Cape Coloured" from South Africa. Men and women such as Magerman, who served as African catechists, lay assistants to European missionaries, and teachers, played a pivotal role in the spread of Christianity in Namibia. African men and women assisted in the work of translating documents into local languages. The Nama wife of LMS missionary Heinrich Schmelen worked with him to translate the New Testament into Nama.

Schmelen, another German also in the employ of the LMS, was to become one of the most famous missionaries in the annals of Namibian history. Schmelen was fluent in German, Dutch, and English and spent many years studying the Nama language. He was credited with translating the four Gospels into the Nama language. However, recent research has revealed that while Schmelen was a devoted student of Nama and a gifted linguist, his skills in that language never approached native fluency. The chief translator of the Gospels appears, then, to have been Schmelen's Nama wife, Zara, who has typically been either ignored in the literature or credited only as an assistant. Zara Schmelen has been described by her biographer as "the invisible woman."[2] The names of the Africans who worked alongside European missionaries, as catechists, lay preachers, and teachers are mostly excluded from history books today. The Schmelenhaus (or Schmelen's house), built in 1814 in Bethany, is the oldest building in Namibia.

In 1825, Wesleyan Methodists established a mission, making the Wesleyans the second missionary group to establish a presence in Namibia, but this Wesleyan effort proved short-lived. In 1842 the German Rhenish Missionary Society (RMS) entered into Namibia, reopening the former LMS mission in Bethany and established a new mission in Windhoek. Two years later, members of the Wesleyan Methodist Missionary Society (WMMS) arrived in Windhoek. This led to tensions between the two missionary groups; this was resolved only when Jonker Afrikaner, the most powerful chief in the region, sent away the RMS so that only the WMMS remained in Windhoek. By 1850, however, the WMMS too had departed from Windhoek; the Rhenish missionaries did not return to Windhoek until 1878.

Rhenish Mission church, built 1895, now a museum, Keetmanshoop, Namibia. (Bildagentur/Stockphotopro)

While the LMS established the first mission station in Namibia, the missionary society most often associated with Namibia is the RMS, founded in Bremen, Germany, in 1828. Before the end of the 19th century, the LMS had handed over their missions in Namibia to the RMS. Carl Hugo Hahn of the RMS founded the first Christian mission among the Herero in Namibia in 1842. The first Herero person to be baptized was a woman, the polyglot Uerieta Kazahendike,[3] who in 1858 became Johanna Maria Gertze. Key to the story of missionary success in Namibia were the African agents of the missionaries, acting as assistants, interpreters, and fellow missionaries. European Christian missions deeply influenced aspects of life beyond the strictly ritual. For example, what is today considered the national dress of Herero women was adapted from the costumes of German missionary women and wives.

Evangelical Lutheran Church in Namibia (ELCIN)

With an estimated 625,000 members, the ELCIN is almost double the size of the next-largest Christian denomination in Namibia. Membership is concentrated in the northern regions of the country, among the Ovambo and other groups living in those areas. However, there are members and congregations throughout the country. Although the ELCIN is the largest denomination in Namibia, it was not the first Christian group in the country.

The ELCIN traces its origins to missionaries from the FELM, which began work in 1870, almost three-quarters of a century after the LMS had set up shop in southern Namibia in 1806.

The establishment in 1870 of a FELM station in Namibia was not the first time missionaries had preached to the Ovambo in northern Namibia. Hahn, of the RMS, had traveled to the area in 1857 and 1866. However, with his own commitments already elsewhere, Hahn was unable to pursue his missionary endeavors in the north, and he sent a letter to the newly established FELM, telling of his adventures among the Ovambo and imploring them to "Come and help us!" In addition, it must be remembered that the Portuguese were the first Europeans to land in the area of modern-day Namibia. Indeed, the Portuguese colony in Angola included what are today parts of northern Ovamboland in Namibia. In the late 19th century Germany declared its control of what it called German South West Africa; in the 20th century, the border between Angola and South West Africa was redrawn a number of times.

The first Finnish missionaries arrived in Namibia in 1870, after spending a year at the Cape in South Africa. The first decades were difficult ones, with little success to report. The target population showed little interest in the theological message of the missionaries, but they did welcome the medical treatments and were also willing to avail themselves of the technical skills of the two artisans among this group of eight missionaries. While some chiefs welcomed the missionaries, others were actively opposed. The ascension to the throne in 1883 of a new chief as the ruler of the Ndonga was a turning point in the fortunes of the FELM because Chief Kambonde Mpingana welcomed the missionaries, making ordinary people who may have been interested in associating with the missionaries less hesitant to do so. The year 1883 is considered the anniversary of the first Finnish Mission Church in Namibia because, although the mission started its work in 1870, it was not until 1883 that the first congregation was established. The first person to be baptized by the Finnish missionaries was a woman, Eva Nanguloshi. She was baptized in 1876 in Finland by the director of the mission; she later returned to Namibia and she was married to another Christian convert. The next people to be baptized, four men, also were baptized not in their Ovambo home area but in Omaruru, an area under Chief Maharero, a powerful chief who was considered a patron of the missionaries, more than 200 miles south of their Ovambo homeland.

After the difficult early years, the Finnish Mission Church began to see more success in the 20th century. By 1910 the mission church had 2,000 adherents. Just 10 years later, in 1920, the number on its membership rosters had jumped to almost 8,000. In 1940 the church had a membership of

37,000, and in 1957 the number stood at 85,000. The role of indigenous Namibians in the history of Christian evangelization is often overlooked, and attention has focused on the European missionaries who traveled from their various countries of origin. However, from the earliest days, local individuals played an active role in spreading the gospel in Namibia, whether as evangelizers in their own right or as translators and assistants in a wide variety of capacities. The most celebrated African in the annals of the Finnish Mission is Dr. Leonard Auala (1908–1983), the first African bishop in the history of Namibia, a man often referred to as "father of the people."

Born in 1908, Dr. Auala studied at the ELCIN pastoral training center in Oniipa, which was established in 1922. Dr. Auala trained for many years as a teacher and an evangelist before he was ordained in 1942. When he was invited to study theology in Finland, the South African government refused to allow Auala to go. Subsequently, he was granted permission to study in South Africa. In 1951 Aula was appointed secretary to the ELCIN Church Board, and in 1960 he was elected moderator of the ELCIN synod; in 1963 he was appointed bishop. This was six years after 1957, which Namibian church historians have termed the "year of the churches" because it was a turning point when the local churches achieved greater autonomy, severing many of the lines of authority formerly held by the mother churches in Europe. Ovamboland experienced a "Great Revival" in the 1950s: Groups of mostly young people traveled from congregation to congregation and village to village, singing, preaching, and extolling people to dedicate their lives to God. Occasionally, highly enthusiastic revivalists destroyed items they believed were pagan such as traditional clothing. Although one can argue that the revival of the 1950s was apolitical, it is also possible to draw a line from the revival of the 1950s to the liberation theology of the 1970s and beyond and to the greater autonomy of the local church hierarchies.

With the ELCIN the largest church in Namibia and the Ovambo the largest ethnic group in the country, Dr. Auala was thrust into a prominent position in Namibian public life. Once he was appointed bishop, Dr. Auala immediately came to be seen as the natural spokesperson for the Ovambo. The South African government attempted unsuccessfully to co-opt Auala. In 1971, just weeks after the International Court had ruled that South Africa's occupation of Namibia was illegal, Dr. Auala, along with Pastor Paulus //Gowaseb of the ELCRN, wrote an open letter to the South African prime minister condemning the South African occupation of Namibia and the abusive system of apartheid.

The 1970s saw liberation theology take root in Namibia. While some churches rejected liberation theology, a few actively supported apartheid theology. Most churches simply chose not to take a position, arguing that they did not want to become involved in politics; the attitude of the latter may be characterized as "Render unto Caesar what is Caesar's!" Some commentators insist that the development of liberation theology took quite a different trajectory, in leadership and in scope, from the earlier theological explosion that began almost a generation previously. This view holds that the earlier movement, in the 1950s, was spearheaded by lay youth and not focused on the national political issues of the day. However, it is worth recalling that it was in the 1950s that the independent Oruuano church was founded.

While the history of Christianity in Namibia has been marked at times by great sectarian divides, there is also a tradition of ecumenism. The open letter is one example; another very remarkable and more recent example of this ecumenism was the 1986 Corpus Christi march in Windhoek. Traditionally, Corpus Christi is a Catholic holiday, celebrated on the first Thursday following Trinity Sunday. Corpus Christi is a feast day commemorating the transformation of bread and wine into the body and blood of Jesus at Mass. Corpus Christi is celebrated by Catholics around the world. In 1986 in Namibia the celebration was entirely unusual in that members of other Christian churches, including bishops, took part in the feast of Corpus Christi.

Evangelical Lutheran Church in the Republic of Namibia (ELCRN)

The ELCRN, with a membership roster of about 350,000 (2006 estimate), is the second-largest denomination in Namibia. Membership in the ELCRN is strongest in the southern and central parts of Namibia, among the Herero and Nama, as well as the Afrikaans- and English-speaking populations.

The ELCRN's roots stem from the Rhenish Mission, which was established in Namibia in 1842. The work of the RMS in Namibia cannot be disassociated from South Africa or from the LMS. The German missionary Johann Heinrich Schmelen of the LMS wrote, in 1838, to the German-based RMS to ask them to come and assist the LMS in its work in southern Namibia. The first RMS missionaries in Africa had arrived in Cape Colony in 1829, just one year after the RMS was established following the merger of two smaller missionary societies. In 1842 a group of missionaries, including Carl Hugo Hahn, traveled to Nama territory in modern-day Namibia. The RMS exemplifies the international tone of Christian missionary endeavor in Namibia: While the society was based in Germany, its workers came from diverse backgrounds. For example, accompanying Hahn was the Norwegian Hans Heinrich Knudsen.

The establishment of a RMS station in Windhoek coincided with hostilities between Nama and Herero groups in the area. Nevertheless, the mission station in Windhoek remained the headquarters of RMS activity, and from Windhoek missionaries sought to spread their message to Nama groups in the south and to Herero groups in the north. Hahn eagerly cultivated Jonker Afrikaner, one of the most powerful rulers in southern Africa at the time, whose community consisted of a heterogeneous group of mostly Orlam, who had migrated from South Africa, and local Nama. Relations between Jonker and Hahn/RMS were not always good. In 1844, following conflicts between the Wesleyan missionaries who had just arrived in Windhoek and the longer-established RMS, Jonker made the decision that the Wesleyan missionaries should remain in Windhoek and not the RMS. The RMS was forced to depart, and it would be many years before the RMS would return to Windhoek.

The history of the RMS in Namibia is marked by periods of progress and of retreats. In many instances mission stations would be founded, only to be abandoned a short time or several years later. This happened most famously in Windhoek, but this also occurred in other stations, for example, Bethanie (Bethanien), Hoachanas, and Gobabis. Between 1844 and 1850 RMS missions were established in a number of Herero locations in the vicinity of Windhoek, at places such as Otjikango (1844), Otjimbingwe (1849), and Okahandja (1850). While the RMS was primarily interested in converting Africans to Lutheranism, they also ministered to German settlers.

The war of 1904–1908 had devastating consequences for the RMS. First, since its efforts were focused on the Herero, the German genocide against the Herero decimated the lists of church members. The role played by the RMS missionaries in the war with the Germans led to distrust on the part of some of the few Herero who survived the slaughter. The missionary Heinrich Vedder, who was a gifted linguist and spoke Herero, considered the Herero "his people." It is for these reasons that the role of the RMS missionaries in the German genocide against the Herero has been seen by some as such a great betrayal. Following the war, many who were disenchanted with the role of the missionaries in the war abandoned the church or returned to the practices that had been condemned by missionaries. Some retained faith in their Christianity, embracing the church; still others remained Christian but sought greater African control.

German Evangelical Lutheran Church (GELC) or Deutsche Evangelisch-Lutherische Kirche (DELK)

With about 6,000 members, the GELC (also known as the DELK) is by far the smallest of the Lutheran churches in Namibia. The history of this church resonates with the country's racist past. Like the ELCRN, the GELC has its roots in the RMS, which first began operations in Namibia in the mid-19th century. When the majority of RMS mission churches elected for more local control in 1957 during the South African occupation, some congregations elected to retain German as their liturgical language and also become independent of the rest of the Rhenish Lutheran community. The GELC conducts services in German, and published its literature almost entirely in German.

Dutch Reformed Church (DRC)

The DRC has a strong presence in Namibia, and its history dates from the founding of a church in 1850 at Springbok by a group of Boers who had trekked from the Cape Colony into the area of modern-day Namibia. As more and more Boers/Afrikaners settled in Namibia, they established congregations throughout the country, especially in the southern parts. Most of the congregations did not have a resident pastor, and thus they relied on itinerant pastors from South Africa or from the RMS. Church elders and teachers played a major role in the life of these congregations without permanent pastors. After South Africa invaded Namibia in 1915 and began its occupation of Namibia (then South West Africa), large numbers of Afrikaner troops and others settled in Namibia and swelled the membership rosters of DRC congregations.

Catholicism

An estimated 10–20 percent of Namibians are members of the Roman Catholic Church. The first Catholic missionaries in Namibia were a group of Holy Ghost Congregation missionaries who traveled from Angola and established a mission at Omaruru in 1879. The decision to establish a station in Omaruru was made in large part because there were Catholic settlers there. However, by 1881, that effort had proved unsuccessful, and the missionary endeavor came to an end. A permanent Catholic presence was successfully established in Namibia in 1896 when the Oblates of Mary Immaculate (OMI) began their career in northern Namibia. Two years later Father Simon of the Oblates of St. Francis of Sales (OSFS) launched another successful Catholic mission in Namibia, in what is today the Prefecture of Pella in the south of the country. Other Catholic missionary groups that have operated or currently operate in Namibia include the Holy Cross Sisters and Benedictine Sisters. Catholic missionaries were frequently denied permission by the government to expand the geographic boundaries of their activities. For a long time Roman Catholic efforts were hampered, first, by the stated government claim that it sought to minimize competition among missionary societies, and, second, by the wariness on the part of the different missionary groups to compete for the same souls. Thus, as latecomers, the Catholics found themselves excluded from many potential mission fields.

AFRICAN INDEPENDENT CHURCHES

Some commentators point to disillusionment with South African rule as the motor behind the move toward independence on the part of Namibian parishioners and churches. However, it is important to recognize that such independence movements typically have multiple motives. In addition, it must be noted that independent African churches were already a source of concern to German settlers and other Europeans in the late 19th century. The borders between South Africa and Namibia were quite porous then, and South Africa has a long and well-known history of African independent churches. In Namibia, one of the earliest cases of Ethiopianism (a term used to refer to the emergence in colonial Africa of African-led churches independent of European control) involved a black prophet, Shepherd Stuurman, who was active in both South Africa and Namibia at about the time of the Herero and Nama war with the Germans (1904–1908).[4]

African independent churches in Namibia, as elsewhere, are typically classed as either Ethiopian or Zionist. The latter supposedly appeal to the emotional needs of African congregations by their focus on healing and the spirit. Ethiopian churches, on the other hand, are seen as focused on the issue of political leadership in the churches, rejecting European control. These stark dichotomies, however, have their limits: For one thing, a church can combine both tendencies, and over time, even the mission churches have become more locally oriented, with Namibians playing a bigger role than in the past. It is widely believed that the Finnish Mission Church was the first of the three major churches to promote a policy of greater African participation. In 1925, the first ELCIN synod was held in Namibia, a moment many see as a critical stage on the road to self-rule.

For the Herero, 1923 was a pivotal moment in terms of the development of greater autonomy in the church. When Chief Samuel Maharero, who had led the fight against the Germans, died in exile in Botswana, his body was brought back to Namibia a few days later and he was given a grand burial on August 23 of that year. Although Maharero had been a Christian, as were many of the Herero who participated in the funeral, elements of pre-Christian Herero traditions were prominently incorporated into the festivities, with the use of the holy fire the major example. This funeral served as an important opportunity for the public reclamation of their roots for many Herero, and large numbers left the church following the funeral. For example, in

Windhoek more than one-third of the Herero Christians abandoned the mission church; in some places, the exodus was even worse. Some three decades later, as we will see later on, Herero leaders established their own national church. Even before that, in 1946, Nama-speaking congregations in southern Namibia broke off from the RMS and affiliated with the African Methodist Episcopal Church (AME), an African American sect.

Oruuano Independent Church of Namibia

Today, the Oruuano Independent Church, which seceded from the Rhenish Mission Church in 1955, is one of the most important churches in Namibia. The 1950s, which saw the establishment of the Oruuano Church, have been described as a period that saw a Great Revival, especially in northern Namibia, as already noted. The 1950s were a major moment for the churches in Namibia. Apart from the Great Revival and the formation of the Oruuano Church, all three of the major Lutheran churches held independent synods in that decade. At these synods the agenda was determined by local concerns and resident church leaders.

The Oruuano Independent Church sought to integrate the liturgical tradition of the Rhenish Church within a Herero cultural tradition. The word *Oruuano* means "community" in OtjiHerero. The desire of Christians all over the African continent for a Christianity that allowed them to honor important aspects of their cultural practices and beliefs that predated European missionary activity is hardly unique to the Herero, and scholars have long been fascinated with this phenomenon, variously termed syncretism, acculturation, or accommodation.

In the case of the Oruuano Church, many of the mainline churches in Namibia initially refused to recognize it as a Christian church, condemning it as heathen. Some European missionaries, however, saw the church as the inevitable result of the failure of the missions to speak out against the abuses and racism of the state. Chief Hosea Kutako, the Namibian leader popularly considered the "father of the nation," played an active role in the foundation of the Oruuano Church. The 1950s were a moment of great ferment in the religious as well as the political domain: At the same time as the Great Revival was underway, civil society groups were coming into being, demanding equality and justice for all Namibians.

APOSTOLIC AND FAITH CHURCHES

Pentecostal churches appear to be gaining ground rapidly, at the expense of the mainline churches. The first Pentecostal church to be established in Namibia was the Apostolic Faith Mission (AFM), which began proselytizing in 1942. Pentecostal churches emphasize the role of the Holy Spirit and the need for a person to be reborn (or, as it is more usually styled, "born again") in Christ by receiving Spirit or water baptism. Namibia's neighbor, South Africa, had a long history of Pentecostal churches for many years before this time, and thus it is no surprise that many of the earliest Pentecostal churches to emerge in Namibia had links with South Africa. Pentecostal preachers from as far away as Nigeria and the United States travel to Namibia to preach and hold prayer rallies; broadcasts by televangelists are hugely popular, drawing interdenominational audiences. There are a host of Pentecostal churches in Namibia today, including various congregations of Assemblies of God, the Church of the Nazarene, and the Full Gospel Church. Many churches may be classed as both Pentecostal and African independent.

ISLAM

There are no reliable sources on the number of Namibian Muslims, with estimates ranging from a few hundred to several thousand. The earliest Muslims in Namibia came from South Africa and were mostly likely of Indian and Cape Malay (South African) descent. Some believe that a majority of the Muslim population belong to recently converted Khoisan families, but Muslims can be found in all ethnic groups, and Islam is believed to be growing. There are about a dozen mosques in Namibia, half of them in the capital. Funded by Iran, the Quba Mosque Foundation and Islamic Center, located along one of the busiest streets in the capital, is a sprawling compound.

***

Although Islam is growing, the vast majority of Namibians remain Christian. To some, it is a fair question to ask how many of these are only nominally Christian since they continue to practice and believe in aspects of pre-Christian rituals. The percentage of Namibians who combine Christian worship or beliefs with older beliefs and practices is difficult to ascertain, but it is undoubtedly high. However, the question of separating nominal Christians from true Christians is a complicated one. In this regard, it is crucial to recall that in its more than 2,000 years of history, wherever it has flourished, Christianity has always taken root in preexisting soil, absorbing some prior practices, displacing others. It may be useful to think of the spread of Christianity from its Asian (or Middle Eastern) homeland to western Europe. Western Europeans celebrate the birth of Christ on a day that was already redolent of ritual significance in the period before Christ. When we think about Europe today, we think of a population that is predominantly Christian. Yet European Christian populations are considered Christian, without any qualifications, even though survey after survey shows only a minority of these Europeans attend church regularly or self-identify as Christian. Despite Europeans' exceedingly low church attendance rate (especially when compared with a country such as Namibia), few pose the question of how many European Christians are *truly* Christian and how many only nominally Christian. It is worth remembering, however, that religion is a living thing, and so it is, of course, impossible to draw lines to separate what is traditional and what is Christian religion. When individuals embrace a new religion, they bring with them aspects of their former belief systems. Namibians might be heard imploring the ancestors to help and, at the same time, invoking the Christian trinity.

Globally, evangelism has been on the rise since the 1980s, and new religious groups and movements have come to the fore all around the world. Namibia has not been excluded from this. Africa is the site of great dynamism with regard to the new Christian evangelism. The long-established churches are often accused by the newer ones of being too liberal in their theology. Some of the new churches criticize the seminaries in the country for being too focused on producing a professional class of religious leaders and less on fostering "real" spiritual life. In 1989 the Namibia Evangelical Fellowship was founded to address what it saw as an absence of deep faith among a population that was, nominally at least, overwhelmingly Christian.

In Namibia today many churches, including the mainline ones, have become acculturated, allowing members to express themselves in ways that make meaning locally. For example, dancing is incorporated into many church services, typically at the end of the religious service. The singing in church often features hand-clapping and swaying bodies, features that were widely frowned upon and not seen as appropriate to church service in the missionary period. All churches provide a variety of social services to members, from day care to AIDS counseling and care. The ELCRN has a Media Centre. It also owns a number of guesthouses, which provide a means of income to help sustain some of the activities it underwrites. The ELCIN owns a printing press and a museum. Churches play an important part in daily life in Namibia. Church members have even served in the government: In the elections that marked the end of South African rule, six ministers were elected to serve in the National Assembly. The six were also members of the South West Africa People's Organisation (SWAPO). With or without an official role in the government, centers of faith and their leaders continue to exert an influence over the public as well as private lives of Namibian citizens.

NOTES

1. See, for example, Meredith McKittrick, *To Dwell Secure: Generation, Christianity, and Colonialism in Ovamboland* (Portsmouth, NH: Heinemann, 2002).

McKittrick discusses the impact of ecological challenges, but she focuses on the generational differences in the responses of the Ovambo of northwestern Namibia to Christian evangelization.

2. We should note that the European wives of missionaries fare little better in the missionary records, their accomplishments rarely noted. Sometimes not even the wife's given name is noted!

3. Her name is also spelled Urieta. She was baptized as Johanna and later became Mrs. Gertze, giving birth to nine children.

4. See Tilman Dedering, "The Prophet's 'War against Whites': Shepherd Stuurman in Namibia and South Africa, 1904–7," *Journal of African History* 40, no. 1 (1999).

3

Literature and the Media

ORAL LITERATURES AND POETRY

Namibia has a rich and varied oral literature, but written literatures are a relatively new development. The oral traditions include poetry, storytelling, myths and legends, songs, and praise; some of this oral literature is now available in print. The various ethnic communities in Namibia each have their own traditions of oral storytelling. These folktales serve to educate, inform, and entertain. The tales of San, Nama, and Damara communities especially have received a fair amount attention from folklorists. Among the Ovambo in rural areas, unmarried young women may gather in the evening to sing songs known as *oudano*. At these performances, women share their concerns, problems, and successes, composing songs about their lives, often in a jocular way, even when dealing with weighty matters. These songs can also be somber, and such performances are an opportunity for creativity as well as a mechanism for relieving stress and receiving the support of one's peers.

Poetry

Poetry is a favorite among Namibians, and one can find poems in daily newspapers and even in the in-flight magazine of the national carrier, Air Namibia. According to Orford and Becker,[1] Oshivambo poetry typically either is historical in nature or offers a reflection on contemporary life. Memorable actions and events, positive as well as negative, are memorialized in this way.

Some performances of oral recitations have been recorded and reproduced in books.

The earliest published Namibian poems are to be found in the magazines put out by the various church groups. Naturally, many of these poems spoke of spiritual matters and Christian charity. By the early 1970s, however, many of the poems had a strongly nationalist tone. For example, "Psalm 23," a poem written in 1973 by Zephania Kameeta, then a recent graduate from seminary school, leaves no doubt about its political inclinations.

> The Lord is my shepherd;
> I have everything I need.
> He lets me see a country of justice and peace
> And directs my steps towards this land.
> He gives me new power.
> He guides me in the paths of victory,
> As he has promised.
> Even if a full scale violent confrontation breaks out
> I will not be afraid, Lord,
> For you are with me.
> Your shepherd's power and love protect me.
> You prepare me for my freedom,
> Where all my enemies can see it;
> You welcome me as an honoured guest
> And fill my cup with righteousness and peace.
> I know that your goodness and love
> Will be with me all my life; and your liberating love will be my home
> As long as I live.[2]

This poem, an adaptation of the Christian psalm of the same title, clearly does not subscribe to the injunction "render unto Caesar that which is Caesar's." Kameeta, now a prominent religious and political leader, was one of the key theorists of liberation theology in the 1970s and 1980s, and he continues to call for greater social justice in Namibia. Kameeta was the president of the Namibia National Convention (NNC), a group founded to promote Black Consciousness, a political movement that also had important cultural dimensions.[3] Namibian pastors played a leading role in advocating for their country's liberation, and church magazines often provided an outlet for them to get out their views. The poem reproduced in the preceding, for example, was published in the church magazine *Immanuel*.[4]

The year 1982 is a signal moment in the history of written Namibian poetry. A short anthology, *It Is No More a Cry: Namibian Poetry in Exile*, edited by the political scientist and activist Henning Melber, made written poetry available to a relatively wide audience. The title of the collection was taken from one of the poems; indeed, the titles of the poems in this collection speak directly to their dominant theme. The poems include "Good Old Days," "Before the White Man Came," "Namibian Contract Worker," "Namibia," "Evil of the World," "The Turnhalle Circus," "We Are Leaving You," "Tears of Africa," "The Voice of Namibia," "Freedom," "For Anti-Imperialists," "The Fighter's Courage," "Southern Africa," "Imperialism and Africa," "Freedom Fighter," and "People's Warrior." Every single one of the poems speaks to the desire for freedom or the injustices of colonial rule. Two new essays were included in a new edition of *It Is No More a Cry,* published in 2004.

One of the poems in this landmark collection, "Cry the Land between Two Deserts," recounts the suffering and struggles of the Namibian people to end colonial rule:

> Your children are scattered all over the world
> as they're fleeing the enemy's merciless sword
> but one day they'll come back
> with newborns on their backs.
> …
>
> Cry the land between two deserts
> cry the tenth of December!
> cry the Kassinga massacre!
> cry the Namibian masses![5]

Another poet dedicates a poem to the Cassinga (Kassinga) massacre:

> I heard a cry of a little baby,
> I heard a cry of a school going child,
> I heard a cry of a pregnant woman,
> A cry with pain and longing for freedom.
> …
>
> Their blood is shed—but not in vain!
> Their highest sacrifice—won't be in vain!
> Ensure the success of the struggle!
> Defend the revolution for the good of all![6]

The poems not only commemorate historical episodes in the liberation struggle but also serve as a call to arms and offer encouragement. In one poem, "Freedom Fighter," the author ties the nationalist struggle to end South African occupation to the earlier resistance against settlers; after detailing the hardships of armed combat and exile, the poet ends on a positive note.

Like our forefathers in those troubled years
You went away
Away to the bush
Carrying a gun in your hands
Travelling thousands of kms on foot
Heavily armed fighting the enemy
Minute after minute
Fighting for the freedom of the Motherland
…

A Luta Continua
A Victoria E Certa[7]

Some of these poems had circulated previously, albeit in very limited fashion, prior to 1982; all the poems were written by students at the United Nations Institute for Namibia (UNIN), based in Lusaka, Zambia. These students were Namibians in exile, and thus it should come as no surprise that the issues of liberation and apartheid were foremost in the minds of Namibian poets.

Mvula ya Nangolo's *From Exile,* a chapbook containing 13 essays, is considered the first book of poetry in English by a Namibian. Nangolo went on to become one of the most distinguished Namibian poets, with his works included in a number of international anthologies of poetry. Nangolo, as well as several of the contributors to the first published anthology of Namibian poetry, subsequently combined a literary career with prominent public service. For example, Albert Kawana was Permanent Secretary and then minister in the Ministry of Justice between 1990 and 2010, when he was appointed Attorney General. Nguno Wakolele, who passed away in 1997, served for several years as the permanent secretary to the Ministry for Information and Broadcasting.

After independence, young people continued to be active in the arts and to form groups to produce poetry in print or to perform their poetry. In 1993, the Young Writers' Club, a group of students at the Augustineum Secondary School, put out a collection of poems, *The Innermost Explosion.* The chapbook was published by a new initiative, New Namibia Books, a publishing house that had just come into existence, with the aim of fostering the production of works on Namibia and by Namibian authors. New Namibia, now a leading publisher in Namibia, has published a number of poetry collections. In 1998, it produced a slim volume entitled *New Namibian Poetry and Short Fiction,* collectively edited by a group known as the Kitso Poets.

Post-independence poetry continues to be politically engaged. In 2000, a group of young Namibian poets, collectively known as PAWN (Poets against

War, Violence and Nuclear Weapons) took part in an international celebration of poetry at the Franco-Namibian Cultural Centre, a venue that plays a key role in the cultural life of the capital. Many of the poems were subsequently published in a volume by Macmillan, *Poetically Speaking, Words Can Come Easy: An Anthology of Contemporary African Poetry*. The poems were listed under five categories: African renaissance, globalization, national identity, gender issues, and social responsibility. Siballi Kgobetsi, a contributor to and the compiler of the collection, dedicated the book to "those who pledge themselves to and defend the culture of peace and tolerance."[8]

Other notable Namibian poets include Abednego Lesheni Nghifikua, Dorian Haarhoff, Andre du Pisani, Kavevangua Kahengua, and Christi Warner, who is a founding member of PAWN, Kitso Poets, and Ama Poets. Ama Poets is a group of poets dedicated to making poetry accessible to a wider audience by focusing on its performativity, incorporating music, and making their performances interactive. Kitso Poets is also a collective that blurs the lines between oral literature, poetry, and music, consciously drawing on indigenous African traditions of performance. Warner has released one full-length album, another reminder perhaps of the impossibility of drawing hard-and-fast lines between genres such as music, poetry, and performance. Some of the young artists making music in Namibia today consider their work primarily as poetry.

A number of things are immediately striking about Namibian poetry. First, there is an intense sense of engagement with political and social concerns. Second, Namibian poets have often sought actively to address the gulf between the intellectual elite and the masses. For instance, although many of the poetry collections available for purchase have been spearheaded by students (at the Augustineum, the University of Namibia, and the UNIN), there is also a strong tradition of performing poetry in more popular locales. Venues in Katutura have often been the sites of poetry readings. Some poetry collectives, such as the Kitso Poets, incorporate elements of so-called traditional poetry into their performances, for example, by using indigenous musical instruments or singing, thus blurring the lines between poetry, storytelling, and singing in ways that reconnect with older traditions. Some of the poetry of Dorian Haarhoff, a South African–born Namibian poet, author of children's books, and teacher, can be located within the genre of praise poetry, which is typically seen as traditional. Examples of Haarhoff's work that can be considered within the praise genre include "Hendrik Witbooi" and "Umeani (Samuel) Maharero." Given the linguistic history of the country, it is not surprising to discover that some poets write in more than one language. The poet Luna Ramphaga, for example, has published poems in English and Afrikaans.

In an introduction to a recent collection of Namibian poetry, Volker Winterfeldt argues that contemporary Namibian poetry continues to be inflected by a sense of social consciousness.[9] The 2005 publication gathered the work of poets who had performed at the occasion of the republication of the first collection of Namibian poetry, *It Is No More a Cry* (1982, republished 2004). It must be noted, however, that Namibian poetry, like the country's other art forms, ranges from the politically engaged to the playful to the romantic.

OTHER WRITTEN LITERATURES

Written literatures date from mission days. Prior to the arrival of European missionaries, the literatures of the African communities in what is today Namibia were maintained orally; the literatures ranged over a diverse vista of styles and included songs, proverbs, tales, praise poetry, and riddles. The earliest written collections of these indigenous literatures are to be found in the volumes put together by Finnish, German, and other missionaries. With regard to the production of written literatures by black Namibians, two facts are critical to keep in mind. First, Namibian communities have a long and dynamic history of oral literatures; second, postprimary formal education became available to nonreligious black Namibians only in the mid-20th century. Before the 1950s the only postprimary school open to Namibian blacks was for the training of black catechists and pastors. By 1964, only 16 black Namibians had advanced as far as senior secondary school in the entire country.

Scholars of Namibian literature typically use an inclusive definition of literature, one that embraces the diaries and correspondence of historical figures as well as autobiographical accounts. The most famous in the first category is *The Diary of Hendrik Witbooi*, which was published in 1929. Witbooi was a *kaptein* (leader) of his Nama clan from the late 19th century until 1905 when he died as a result of battle wounds sustained fighting against German forces. Witbooi maintained an active correspondence with German missionaries and colonial officials as well as other African leaders. Witbooi, who was born in South Africa and educated by Rhenish missionaries, was fluent in and corresponded in Dutch. In the tumultuous late 19th century, he emerged as the most defiant resister of German imperial ambitions. In 1892 he sought to enter into alliance with the Herero, but two years later he signed a peace treaty with the Germans following brutal wars that had resulted in major casualties on both sides. In 1904, Witbooi's response to Maharero's letter calling on him to mount a joint campaign against the Germans appears to have been delayed as a result of treachery on the part of messenger. In the autobiographical category, John Ya Otto's *Battlefront Namibia* (1982) is the most widely cited example. Other autobiographers include Sam Nujoma, the first president of Namibia, and Ellen Namhila, who has written biographies also.

Joseph Diescho (born 1955), who currently lives in South Africa, where he is a distinguished professor of political science at the Nelson Mandela Metropolitan University, is the best-known Namibian author and the first Namibian-born writer to publish a novel in English. Diescho's *Born of the Sun* was published in 1988; Diescho published a second novel in English in 1993, *Troubled Waters*. Diescho has also produced two novels in his maternal language, RuKavango. The chief protagonist in Diescho's first novel is a mine worker who becomes politically engaged and is subsequently arrested and jailed, all elements that mirror the author's own experiences. Diescho holds two doctorates (from Fort Hare in South Africa and Columbia University in the United States) as well as a slew of other degrees and has also written several scholarly books on politics. Diescho taught briefly at City University of New York's Law School. Giselher Hoffman (born 1958) writes in German; he has written historical fiction dealing with conflicts between German settlers and indigenous populations. Other well-known contemporary Namibian writers include internationally recognized theater director Keamogetsi Joseph Molapong and Petrus Haakskeen, who write both plays and poetry. In 2009 Haakskeen published a chapbook, *Tales of Katutura,* his third volume of poetry.

Women too have been making a mark in literature, as well as other branches of the arts. In 1986, the Namibian feminist scholar Ndeutala Hishongwa self-published a short novel entitled *Marrying Apartheid,* considered the first novel by a black Namibian woman. Two years later Hishongwa was awarded a doctorate by La Trobe University in Canada for her dissertation "Comparative Study of Women's Education in Namibia." Hishongwa's novel explores the issues of domestic violence, women's labor migrancy, and the difficulties faced by young Namibian women who challenge the status quo. Novelists Neshani Andreas and Kaleni Hiyalwa have published works that have been well received. Andreas's 2001 novel, *The Purple Violet of Oshaantu,* recounts the story of a widow who refuses to mourn her deceased husband, with whom she had had an unhappy life, in the way expected of her. While he was alive, the husband was a womanizer and wife-beater; following his death the widow is forced out of her home by her husband's greedy relatives. While the portrayal of Shange's unhappy marriage offers a harsh portrait of male brutality, the novel is actually told from the perspective of Shange's friend, Ali, who has a very different kind of marriage with a wonderfully supportive husband. Hiyalwa's novel *In Meekulu's Children* deals with exile and return. The central character, Ketja, is a young girl who returns home one day to find both her parents dead, their home ransacked and her siblings gone. Ketja goes to live with her grandmother (or "meekulu" in the OshiKwanyama language of northern Namibia), whose fervent hope is for the return of her two other grandchildren. The feminist collective Sister Namibia has been at the forefront of providing a space for women's voices. In 1994 Sister Namibia published a collection of Namibian women's short stories and poetry. Two years later, Margie Orford and Nepeti Nicanor produced another collection of women's writing, *Coming On Strong*. The activist Elizabeth !Khaxas compiled a third collection of women's writing, *Between Yesterday and Tomorrow: Writings by Namibian Women*. Laurinda Oliver-Sampson and Tania Terblanche are the best-known Namibian women playwrights. There is a small but growing number of Namibian women filmmakers including veteran Bridget Pickering (Namibia and South Africa), Oshosheni Hiveluah, and Genevieve Tanya Detering, who tend to function in multiple roles, as writer, producer, and director.

LITERATURE IN OTHER LANGUAGES

Although this chapter has focused on literatures in English, Namibian writing, like the country itself, is multilingual. A few Namibian authors have published works in European languages such as Finnish and Swedish, the languages of the countries in which they spent their years of exile. Many more authors, however, have published in the languages of their home country. Hans Daniel Namuhuja was the first to write a novel in OshiNdonga. Namuhuja's *Omahodhi Gaavali* (*Parental Tears*) appeared in 1959, almost 20 years before Diescho published the first Namibian novel in English. Altogether, Namuhuja wrote a dozen novels—one of which was translated into Finnish—and translated Shakespeare's *Julius Caesar* into OshiNdonga. Abednego Lesheni Nghifikua, who writes poetry in Oshivambo, has also written a novel in that language. The polyglot politician Andrew Nick Matjila has published a drama as well as a number of poetry chapbooks in SiLozi, designed specifically for use by schoolchildren. Namibian authors (such as Giselher Hoffman, who was already mentioned) are also creating and publishing literature in German and Afrikaans.[10] Ironically, although the colonial period is essentially missing from contemporary German school textbooks, in an earlier era, the colonies featured prominently in literary and popular culture. In the late 19th and early 20th century, novels set in the colonies were very popular in Germany. Frieda von Bulow, a German woman born into an aristocratic family of modest means, was the best-known writer of such colonial fiction. A number of her books went into several editions in just a few short years. Although none of her novels were set in Namibia, she exemplifies the style of colonial fiction.

Von Bulow traveled in German East Africa but was barred from taking up residence there to run a farm she inherited when her brother died fighting against African rebels. The German government refused her permission because she was a single woman. Some contemporary Namibian authors continue to create works in German, which is one of the recognized national languages.

Radio, Television, and Print Media

As of 2010, Namibia had three television stations, Namibia Broadcasting Corporation (NBC), One Africa, and Trinity Broadcasting Namibia (TBN), an independent, family-owned, and privately operated affiliate of the evangelical Christian and U.S.-based TBN International. Television programming is around the clock, and many of the shows on television are from South Africa, the United States, and Latin America; viewers who subscribe to satellite networks are able to access a large number of international channels. In 2007, Sam Nujoma, the first president of Namibia, castigated the state television channel for showing a South African reality show, *Big Brother,* rather than, as the president said the channel should, documentaries about life in Namibia. Despite the former president's criticism, there are in fact homegrown shows on Namibian television. A number of NBC shows highlight Namibian culture, contemporary issues, and debates. *Tutaleni* is a television news magazine show, while *Tupopiyeni* is a talk show that highlights problems and solutions to social problems; *Know Namibia,* which broadcasts from different parts of the country, is another popular weekly show. News is broadcast in all the major languages of the country, including SeTswana, Damara/Nama, Afrikaans, and German. A sign language interpreter provides news daily during the evening broadcast.

Namibia has at least a dozen radio stations, three of which are national: NBC broadcasts all across the country, as do Kudu FM and the Christian Channel 7 (also Kanaal 7). Channel 7 broadcasts in Afrikaans and Oshivambo primarily, mixing Christian and other contemporary music, news, and talk. Kudu FM broadcasts in English, although it takes and airs calls in Afrikaans and German. Kudu FM's target audience is those under 50. In northern and central Namibia, listeners can also tune in to Angolan radio stations; those in the south of the country are able to listen to South African stations. The regional radio stations include Katutura Community Radio, Oshivambo Radio, Radio Omulunga, and Rukavango Service. The latter stations tend to play mostly Namibian-language music and are really the ones responsible for making the transition from airwaves dominated by foreign music to increasing popularity for local artists.

Namibia has five major daily newspapers. *New Era* is government owned. The German *Allgemeine Zeitung,* founded in 1916, is the oldest newspaper in the country, while the English-language *Namibian* has the largest circulation. The *Namibian* was founded by Gwen Lister, a South African–born Namibian who began her career at the *Windhoek Advertiser.* Started in 1985 as a paper dedicated to press freedom, the *Namibian* reported on the activities of the South West Africa People's Organisation (SWAPO) and the repression by the South African government; today, the paper maintains its independent stance, often finding itself in conflict with the ruling SWAPO government. In 2000 Lister was honored as a Press Freedom Hero by the International Press Institute. The Afrikaans-language *Die Republikein* and the *Windhoek Advertiser* are the other dailies. *Tempo* and the *Windhoek Observer* are also published weekly, as are the very colorful tabloids, the *Weekly Sun and Informanté. Insight Magazine* is a monthly news journal, and the *Namibian Economist,* another weekly, targets upper-income educated professionals. The *Namib Times,* based in Walvis Bay, is a biweekly regional paper. All of these publications also maintain Web sites. Namibians also have access to South African publications, widely available throughout the country; some vendors in Swakopmund and Windhoek carry newspapers from Germany.

Although Namibia has a relatively large number of newspapers given its population and a high literacy rate, bookshops are few and far between. Many bookstores stock mostly or only textbooks, so it is probably accurate to state that Namibia as a whole does not have a strongly developed culture of reading. Oral literatures remain very much alive and relevant in Namibia. Spoken-word performances, which are very modern but with roots in the past, can be heard on the television and radio. In the discussion of poetry earlier in this chapter, we noted the roots of written poetry in the liberation movement, as an arm of resistance and revolution. Oral poetry also continues to recall history, as well as reflect on the present. In an essay on Ovambo literature by women, the authors quote from a poem composed to welcome the young people born overseas to Namibian parents in exile who returned to the country at the end of the South African occupation. This poem, "Children of Namibia," was composed by the oral poet Mekulu Mukwahongo Ester Kamati.

> You returned
> Calves with no horns
> Left in the kraal
> Howling like hyenas
> Faces and mouths pointed northwards

Welcome friends
You returned gracefully

Children of Namibia
Like a joke, we see you
Like a dream we look at you
Your faces were not visible in this land
Your shadows were seen in death

Our cry as parents
Has resulted in jubilation
Though not all returned
We say thank God
For bringing along a nation.[11]

This poem was originally performed on television and subsequently reproduced in print, underscoring again the impossibility of making hard-and-fast distinctions between oral and written literatures.

NOTES

1. Margie Orford and Heike Becker, "Homes and Exiles: Ovambo Women's Literature," in *Contested Landscapes: Movement, Exile and Place,* ed. Barbara Bender and Margot Winer (Oxford: Berg, 2001).

2. Psalm 23. Used with permission from Zephania Kameeta.

3. Kameeta is currently the bishop of the ELCRN (Evangelical Lutheran Church in the Republic of Namibia), having been elected to the post by a resounding majority vote in August 2001. Known affectionately as "the people's bishop," Kameeta served from independence in 1990 until 2000 as the deputy speaker of the National Assembly.

4. The 1971 "Open Letter" to the South African prime minister from Bishop Auala and Pastor Paulus //Gowaseb also appeared in a church magazine. The letter called for an end to South Africa's occupation of Namibia, the authors noting their support of the World Court decision that declared the occupation illegal.

5. Gerson Uaripi Tjihenuna, "Cry the Land between Two Deserts," in Henning Melber, ed., *It Is No More a Cry: Namibian Poetry in Exile* (Basel: Basler Afrika Bibliographien, 2004), p. 39. Reprinted with the permission from Gerson Tjihenuna. It was on December 10 1959 that South African policemen killed more than a dozen peaceful demonstrators who were among those protesting the forced removals from the Old Location to Katutura. The Cassinga massacre took place on May 4, 1978, in Angola, leaving hundreds dead and hundreds more wounded.

6. Nguno Wakolele, "Kassinga," in Henning Melber, ed., *It Is No More a Cry: Namibian Poetry in Exile* (Basel: Basler Afrika Bibliographien, 2004), p. 55. A decisive event in Namibian modern history, Cassinga has been commemorated

many times in poetry and song by various artists, including well-known reggae star Ras Sheehama and the poet Mvula ya Nangolo.

7. Jimmy Seth Isaacks, "Freedom Fighters," in Henning Melber, ed., *It Is No More a Cry: Namibian Poetry in Exile* (Basel: Basler Afrika Bibliographien, 2004), p. 65.

8. Siballi E. Kgobetsi, *Poets Against War, Violence, and Nuclear Weapons (PAWN): An Anthology of Contemporary African Poetry* (Windhoek, Namibia: Gamsberg Macmillan, 2000).

9. Volker Winterfeldt, "Introduction," in *In Search of Questions: A Collection of New Namibian Poems,* ed. Keamogetsi Molapong, Christi Warner, and Volker Winterfeldt (Basle: Basler Afrika Bibliographien, 2005).

10. At independence, as noted, Afrikaans was the most widely spoken language. But because of its association with the South African apartheid regime, it was essentially demoted when English was made the official language. Debates continue about what role Afrikaans should play in Namibian cultural life. Supporters of Afrikaans frequently point out that it is the mother tongue of some nonwhite groups (for example, Basters and many Nama groups).

11. Mekulu Mukwahongo Ester Kamati, "Children of Namibia" in Margie Orford and Heike Becker, "Homes and Exiles: Ovambo Women's Literature," Barbara Bender and Margot Winer, eds., *Contested Landscapes: Movement, Exile and Place* (Oxford: Berg, 2001), 299. Translated by Kaleni Hiyalwa and Ndeshi Immanuel. Mekulu Mukwahongo Ester Kamati 1997, oral performance filmed for the series *Stories of Tenderness and Power,* OnLand Productions.

4

Arts and Architecture

WHAT IS ART? Should objects created for utilitarian purposes—such as pots and baskets—be considered art? Are woven textiles and homes (constructed or painted in a distinct style) art? Specialists in art disagree about how precisely to decide what is a work of art. In addition to the discussion about how to define art, we should note, too, the transformations in the ways African objects are displayed. In the colonial period, African objects were typically seen in museums, included in ethnographic exhibitions. Increasingly, African objects, including those not specifically made for exhibition, are presented in galleries, independently or alongside work from other parts of the world. The question of who or what determines art will continue to be heated. While some will claim a mass-produced urinal displayed in a gallery to be art, others may reject that but claim that label art for an anonymously produced hand-made basket.[1]

For our purposes we treat as art all expressions of cultural life, excluding the literary and the strictly spiritual. This includes paintings and sculpture but also basketry, woven cloth, carved masks, musical instruments, and tools for everyday life. Art thus has always been a part of life for Namibians; creativity in Africa has often worked along radically different lines from what obtains in the West. Nowadays, however, an ever-increasing number of African artists work in what we might describe as a Western model. By Western model, we refer here to the idea of a creator whose name is attached to his or her work and who, usually, exhibits his or her works in a gallery or some similar space. In the African past, art was an intimate part of daily life, and there was no tradition of art galleries. Art served a purpose, which could be utilitarian, spiritual, didactic, or diversionary. And some artists, though not all, often engaged in other functions, such as farming, cattle rearing, or serving as a healer or leader. Europeans brought new traditions of art production and consumption.

In Namibia today there are art galleries all over the country, and they display a diverse range of works. The most important is the National Art Gallery of Namibia in Windhoek; several other galleries are also located in the capital, including the John Muafangejo Art Centre. Bank Windhoek is a major sponsor of the arts in Namibia. The bank hosts a biennale, and its Bank Windhoek Omba Gallery is a major exhibition space for new as well as established artists. The government plays an active part in sponsoring the arts in Namibia, as do a number of foreign governments, notably that of France, which cosponsors (with the Namibian government) the Franco-Namibian Cultural Centre-FNCC). In 2008, the government awarded N$760,000 to artists in a variety of fields, including poetry, dance, theater, music, and crafts such as Himba metal jewelry making and weaving. The Ministry of Youth, National Service, Sport and Culture houses the Directorate of National Heritage and Culture Programmes, the portfolio of which is to promote the country's rich and diverse cultures. Officials speak about the need to preserve and affirm cultural traditions; at the same time, sometimes the urgency seems to be to revive and maintain traditions that no longer exist or are seen as threatened by extinction. Naturally, this tension is one that leads to debates and controversies about cultural identities.

THE MATERIAL ARTS

Painting

We tend to think of painting as an art form that is distinctly modern and recent. Yet some of the oldest paintings to be found anywhere in the world can be seen in Namibia. These are, of course, the famed rock paintings (and engravings) of southern Africa. The most famous site of rock art in Namibia is Twyfelfontein in northwestern Namibia. The rock art at Twyfelfontein depicts humans and a variety of animals, including rhinoceros, giraffes, and ostriches. Twyfelfontein has the most concentrated and largest collection of petroglyphs in Namibia, and Namibian rock art, which has been dated to 25,000 B.C.E., is considered by some the oldest in the world. In 2007 the paintings and engravings of Twyfelfontein were declared a United Nations World Heritage site. Rock art includes paintings and engravings, and stylistically, the works vary greatly, from the very naturalistic to the symbolic and impressionistic. The scenes in the rock art show animals as well as people engaged in a variety of activities, from hunting to fighting to dancing. Some images appear to be mythical or imagined creatures, and there is also abstract nonrepresentational art, some of which consist of geometric designs. More recently, some archaeologists and religious specialists have argued that some of the dancing scenes depict trances and thus say something about the spiritual world of the people who made them.

At one point, some European specialists speculated wildly about the creators of rock art. One foremost expert insisted that the rock art must have been made by Sumerian or Egyptian conquerors as Africans were not capable of producing such artistically stunning work. Experts now believe that the earliest Namibian rock art was created by the ancestors of today's San.[2] Before this connection was made, the San were dismissed most typically as primitive people who lived in a timeless space. Even modern-day images of the San tend to present them quite stereotypically as people who live a simple life in close harmony with nature, removed from the corruption and complexities of the modern world. In reality, the vast majority of San today work as day laborers on white-owned farms or are unemployed. Even in the pre-colonial past, the San were not isolated primitives living cut off from any contact with others. Famed scientist and eugenicist Francis Galton, who traveled to the area of modern-day Namibia in the 19th century, described

Prehistoric rock art, Twyfelfontein, Namibia. (Shutterstock)

San engaged in trade with Ovambo and other groups and also working in copper mining. In 1857, the missionary Carl Hugo Hahn, who figures prominently in the early history of Christianity in Namibia, wrote, "We met two Bushmen [San] today who were taking copper ore from Otjorukaku to Ondonga on their own account where they would sell it for corn, tobacco, and calabashes. This I never expected from Bushmen."[3] Colonial settlers and governments, who wanted land, erected laws and restrictions that subjugated many San communities; San access to land was also curtailed by other Africans. The history of San dispossession continues in contemporary Namibia as San populations find themselves forced to move off land they occupy to make way for national parks and other conservation programs designed by the national government. San children report a high incidence of bullying and teasing by their peers. While San individuals and communities continue to face great challenges, in the art world contemporary works by San artists have become highly valued. There is also a new appreciation of the ancient rock art.

Today, art galleries and museums all over the country display paintings, sculptures, and other works of art by Namibian artists of all ethnic backgrounds. Until the mid-1980s, however, art galleries in Namibia displayed, almost exclusively, the work of white artists who painted landscapes, portraits, and wildlife. With few exceptions, the only art to be seen publicly told of a country of enormous beauty, not of the politically charged situation in the country. Among the most celebrated Namibian painters are Adolph Jentsch, Axel Eriksson, and Carl Ossmann. These artists, almost all born in Germany, established a tradition of landscape and wildlife painting that continues to be important in Namibia today. Nico Roos (1940–2008), one of southern Africa's most distinguished artists, must be included in any discussion of Namibian modern art. Born on a farm in South Africa, Roos studied art at the University of Pretoria in South Africa. He is best known for his landscape paintings, especially those of Namibia, which, in later years, became quite abstract in style. Roos was awarded the Medal of Honour by the South African Academy of Arts and Sciences in 1998. Roos was heavily influenced by the German-born Jentsch, who was already a well-known and established artist when Roos was still a young pupil.

Printmaking

The work of the most-renowned Namibian artist of all time, John Ndevasia Muafangejo (1943–1988), could not be more different from that of the landscape and wildlife artists of European extraction. Instead of the colorful palettes of landscapes and wildlife, Muafangejo's work focuses on peoples and events, depicted in potent images in black and white. Born into an Ovambo community that straddled the Angolan-Namibian border, Muafangejo moved, with his family, to Namibia when he was 12 years old. Muafangejo received his early education in Namibia before continuing at the Lutheran Rorke's Drift Art and Craft Centre in Natal, South Africa. Muafangejo later made his home in Katutura, a place with which he continues to be associated because of the living monument to him there.[4]

Muafangejo is known primarily for his linocuts, and it is in part due to his stature that printmaking remains an important medium in Namibia. At the National Art Gallery in Windhoek, three entire rooms are devoted to Muafangejo's art. His images are didactic and archival, detailing events (for example, *Anglican Seminary Blown Up*) or practices (for example, the depiction of the Ovambo wedding in *A Kuanjama Wedding*). Indeed, the artist spoke about his work as being made in "a teaching style." His works recount life in colonial Namibia—for example, the work *South West Africa in 1976* has at its center a border labeled "artificial boundary" (separating Angola and Namibia)—but he also depicted scenes from the history and culture of his Ovambo people.

Muafangejo's linocuts often combine words and images, with text in English or OshiKwanyama, Muafangejo's maternal tongue. Since Muafangejo was an Ovambo belonging to the Kwanyama (or Kuanjama) subgroup, much of his art refers to the history and culture of the Kwanyama. A 1981 print, *Oniipa Rebuilding of Printing Press,* commemorates the rebuilding of the influential Lutheran church press, which offered a space to those critical of the South African government repression. The press was bombed in 1975; most people believed the bombing was carried out at the instigation of the South African government. In this work, Muafangejo shows Bishop Auala, a key figure in Namibia's struggle for independence, presiding over the Mass celebrating the new press, with a congregation of blacks (mostly) and whites. Bishop Auala was one of the two clerics who wrote the "Open Letter" to the South African government protesting the harsh conditions of the occupation and calling for Namibian independence. The churches in Namibia played a central role in the struggle to end the South African occupation. Another of Muafangejo's linocuts is entitled *Hope and Optimism: In Spite of the Present Difficulties.* In it we see white and black, male and female, gathered together, holding hands.

One of the most poignant images produced by Muafangejo deals with the death of his mother. His mother died in their home, on the Angolan side of the border, in 1979. Just four years previously the South African government had passed a law making it illegal to cross the border between Angola and Namibia without government permission. The text in this cut, made in 1980, the year following his mother's death, tells of Muafangejo's inability to attend his mother's funeral: "I was sorry also that John could not get to Angola to attend his mother's funeral service. The war stops me to go to one I love." The Namibian war of liberation was fought mainly in the north and in Angola, with rebels based in that neighboring country and government forces making strikes there. Muafangejo (1943–1988) remains the most celebrated Namibian artist ever, and one of the best-known African artists of the 20th century. Muafangejo rose to international prominence at a very young age; unfortunately, the life of this prolific artist was cut short by a heart attack. His prints are in museums and private collections throughout southern Africa, Europe, and the United States, including the Schomburg Center for Black Culture in the city of New York. Many young and rising Namibian artists make prints in the tradition of Muafangejo. Among the best-known contemporary Namibian artists is Joseph Madisia (b. 1954). As well as making lithographs, Madisia works with watercolors and metal. His prints are not made using linoleum and thus are not linocuts; instead, Madisia uses cardboard and paperboard to make his prints.

Sculptural Forms and Installations

One of the most exciting Namibian artists must be Hercules Viljoen, who makes enormous interactive sculptures and installations using wood and sticks but also plastic and mass-produced found objects. For a work entitled *From /Ae//Gams to Salazie: A Project for Sharing,* Viljoen constructed a giant replica of a kudu horn, made mostly of wood, with real kudu horns and telephone handsets attached as well as steel and text. To the 15 telephones and kudu horns Viljoen attached messages about waiting for rain in the different languages spoken in Namibia and Reunion. (Salazie, referenced in the title of Viljoen's sculpture, is a town and department on the French Indian Ocean island of Reunion.) Viljoen's work, which includes photography and drawings, has been exhibited all over southern Africa as well as in Europe. The equally prominent painter Francois de Necker often creates works that, while constructed on a flat canvas, are three-dimensional and may include wood, metal, and plastics. Necker is best known, however, for his abstract landscape paintings. In half a century of artistic production, sculptor Dörte Berner has held numerous exhibitions throughout southern Africa, Europe, and North America; her works may be seen in public spaces all over Namibia. Some of her works include *Tired Woman, Lonely Old Woman, House Arrest, Diver, Miners,* and *Porcupine.* The Polish-born Berner works in stone and marble, usually creating human forms, even when they have abstract titles such as *Sorrow.* Berner has been a central figure in promoting the study and production of art, especially in the workshop setting that is so popular in Namibia.

Pottery

The creation of many art forms proceeds along gendered lines. Pottery, for example, is typically, though not always, done by women in Namibia, as is generally true over much of the continent. Pottery is an ancient art form, going back to the dawn of human existence, a skill critical for daily life: One needs vases and bowls to hold water and food.[5] Some potters use a wheel, whereas others mold and shape the clay by hand. There is a large variety of pottery shapes and styles, which vary according to the region, maker, and use. Some pots are for the preparation and storage of foods and beverages (water, milk and saps, and fermented drinks); sometimes, however, pots hold items for beautification (i.e., makeup).[6] Patterns of ornamentation vary greatly among communities and over time and, of course, depending on the intended use as well as the creator.

Basketry and Weaving

Using a variety of raw materials, basketry is usually, but not exclusively, done by women. Typically the baskets are made using leaves from a sturdy plant such as the Makalani palm tree, reeds, or grasses. After the leaves are harvested, they must be prepared and dyed prior to use. Basketmaking is a laborious process because first the leaves or bark to be used must be collected and then prepared for weaving; the various colors to be used must also be prepared. Dyes are made from a variety of sources, including fruits, leaves, and other parts of the tree. In the case of some trees, the inside root must be pounded to make a powder, which is then made into a paste before it can be used to soak the fibers for the basket. Baskets are used for fishing and for straining beer in many parts of Namibia; baskets are also used to store dry goods but also for milk. Mats for sleeping and sitting, and fishing nets for fishing, are also woven using palm fronds and grasses. Today, baskets and mats are also made from plastic, a wonderful way to recycle plastic that otherwise might simply be discarded.

In Namibia today, most people wear ready-made clothes. The secondhand clothing market is huge all over Africa, with vast quantities of used clothing being shipped to Africa from the countries of the global north. In the not-so-distant past, most people in Namibia wore locally produced clothing, made out of a variety of materials. Clothing was made out of skins as well as bark and cotton. Although skins and woven cloth are not commonly worn everyday, weaving continues to flourish in contemporary Namibia, supported in good measure by a relatively robust international demand. Weaving is done with a variety of different fibers, including raffia and karakul wool. As well as textiles, weavers make carpets and wall hangings. Wool from the karakul sheep is the most common fiber for these products; linen, cotton, Kalahari silk, sisal, bamboo, merino wool, and other fibers are also used. The most common styles depict animals, the dramatic landscape, and geometric patterns. Custom-made designs may also be ordered. Ibenstein Weavers, a company founded in 1952 by Marianne Krafft, a German immigrant, is the best-known company producing Namibian woven carpets. The company employs Namibian men and women artists to make handwoven carpets and wall hangings; it exports almost all of its products. Ibenstein wall hangings depicting scenes from the Bible can be seen in several churches in Germany and Scandinavia.

Carving

While women usually make pottery, it is typically men who work with wood and iron, fashioning canoes from tree trunks, making musical instruments, and working with iron to make knives and other tools. Carvers make headrests for sleep, combs, walking sticks, masks, and a large variety of decorative, everyday, and ritual items. Wood is carved into such useful tools as spoons, bowls, mortars and pestles, walking sticks, and fire sticks; puppets are also made out of wood. Caprivians and the Kavango especially are noted as skilled wood-carvers; wood-carvers often set up shop along the country's major highways to sell their wares. The San carve wood as well as bone. Ivory from elephants and hippopotamuses is also used to carve decorative objects; utensils as well as jewelry are carved out of bone.

The carving of masks is a very important aspect in this field of art. Masks typically represent spiritual forces, such as ancestors and divinities, male and female. When worn by an initiate, the mask becomes an embodiment of the force it represents. Some masks are used for initiation ceremonies, and some may be used only for chiefly installation. As representations of forces connecting this world and other worlds, masks are thus imbued with power and must be treated with respect. Masks are associated with individual or communal rites of passage, such as initiation, funerary rites, and the harvest season. Carved figurines may be made for healing purposes at the recommendation of a spirit medium. Carved figures and masks often are made of mixed media, with feathers, mirrors, and beads, which reference the power of the spirits they represent. Carved objects are a significant part of the goods produced for sale to tourists in Namibia, and while there are occasionally large carvings, such as of animals or furniture, most are small pieces, such as carved animals, pens, bowls, and decorative spoons.

Beading and Other Arts

Beadwork is widely associated with southern Africa in the popular imagination, with the Ndebele of Zimbabwe probably the best-known producers of beadwork in the region. In Namibia, the San are considered the best beadwork artists. San jewelry made out of beads and ostrich-egg shells can be found for sale throughout Namibia, in little gift shops, at the Hosea Kutako International Airport in Windhoek, and at roadside stalls along the country's highways. Cattle are an important aspect of life for many of Namibia's peoples, so it is no surprise that there are well-developed traditions of leatherwork in the country. Body art and ornamentation are other forms of art found widely in Africa, including parts of Namibia. Headdresses, jewelry, and other forms of body adornment are often made using a variety of materials and methods; for example, a headdress may be carved out of wood and include leather, beads, ostrich-egg shell, and copper as embellishments. The intricate hairstyles worn by Himba women are a favorite subject for photographers; the hairstyles of Himba men and women reflect their life stage.

Arts Training

The post-independence government continues to assert that culture is essential to nation building, and it sponsors the arts in a variety of ways. Workshops are a popular avenue to encourage and produce art in Namibia. A significant development in the art scene in Namibia was the inauguration of the John Muafangejo Art Centre (JMAC) in Katutura in 1994. The JMAC was a joint effort by the Ministry of Education and Culture and local artists. When it first opened its doors, the JMAC offered printmaking classes to economically disadvantaged youth; over the years, the JMAC has expanded its repertoire of classes to include painting and other visual art forms. Today, students from neighboring countries also enroll at the center, and a number of established foreign artists have led workshops there. The center has an art gallery, and its annual student exhibition attracts regional and even international attention.

In 1994, the same year the JMAC opened, the Visual Arts Department at the University of Namibia held the first Tulipamwe International Artists' Workshop. This two-week residential workshop, which has become an annual event, brings together international and local artists. Although the European population in Namibia is a minority, it continues to exert an impact on Namibian life disproportionate to its numbers, and many of the gallery owners and sponsors of arts training in Namibia are of European descent. European and African approaches to art have been, until relatively recently, quite distinct. As Hercules Viljoen, practicing artist and the head of the Visual Arts Department at the University of Namibia, puts it, "Large sections of the Namibian population are indifferent to visual art—especially gallery art, which is simply not part of their cultural awareness."[7] The Visual Arts Department is part of the School of the Arts, which also has drama and music departments.

While new centers for the study of various art techniques (for example, weaving and pottery making) continue to emerge, older forms of learning and teaching—based essentially on apprenticeship—do continue to exist. Many new centers focus on reviving or preserving old forms. Frequently, centers for art education offer training in old, new, and emerging art forms, all under one roof. Dozens of centers for the promotion and production of arts and crafts exist all over Namibia including the Caprivi Art Centre, the Khorixas Community Craft Centre, the Tsumeb Arts and Crafts Centre, the Rossing Foundation Craft Project (Windhoek), Chabura, and the Opuwo Art Promotions (the latter two in the Kunene region).

The Future of the Arts in Namibia

Muafangejo was the first black Namibian artist to garner regional, and then international, attention. Since independence black and white Namibian artists have been able to work in a freer environment and to interact with artists and people from other parts of the country, the region, and the world. The National Art Gallery in Namibia exhibits and encourages artists working in all kinds of media; both the permanent and temporary collections display functional (such as pottery and baskets) as well as nonfunctional art (paintings, for example), including the works of well-known artists alongside anonymous pieces.

Tourism and international demand have been a motor for the encouragement of certain art forms in Namibia. For example, artists can be seen selling their creations, such as carved animals, bowls, and utensils, along Namibia's major roads. International interest in African arts has created a market for Namibian arts. In a number of instances, astute entrepreneurs with capital have been able to marshal local talent and gather artists together in a single locale, providing them with the resources to produce, and thus maintain, old artistic creative traditions, or to modify them to satisfy contemporary markets. A good deal of the art that is produced by Namibian artists—such as woven wall hangings and carpets, jewelry, and baskets—enters the international marketplace in this fashion. So there is an interesting irony here: In the first instance, European colonialism introduced mass-produced material goods that competed with and threatened local manufacture, but now it is the international interest in African crafts that is spurring on and reviving

Namibian arts. For those able to find employment in the collectives and studios set up by fellow Namibians, the income is very welcome. But some people worry about how foreign interests are shaping manufacturing habits and styles; some dismiss much of the contemporary production of material arts in Namibia as simply "airport art." It is important to keep in mind that Namibian artists have long been producing for a paying market. The fame of the Kavango wood-carvers is hardly recent. The various peoples of Namibia have been producing utilitarian and purely aesthetic pieces for themselves as well as for sale to their neighbors for a very long time. The arts, like all aspects of culture, are dynamic and ever-changing. The arts in all their guises, including so-called traditional dances, music, and drama, have never been static and were certainly not so in the period before the Europeans' arrival. Cultural habits and patterns change in response to internal as well as external forces. Namibia has long been open to a variety of external sources. Some of the external factors that impinge on culture in more recent times include migrant labor, forced migrations and the creation of Bantustans, the modern school calendar, and improved communications.

ARCHITECTURE

Vernacular Architecture

Although Namibia is rapidly urbanizing, more than 50 percent of the population continues to live in rural areas. Even those who spend the majority of their time in the city maintain ties to a rural home community. Building styles vary all over Namibia—in materials used for construction, in size, and in shape. Traditional homes come in a variety of shapes, but the type of dwelling most often associated with rural life is the *rondavel*. A rondavel is a round hut typically with a conical thatched roof; ordinarily, several rondavels are built inside a *kraal* within which members of an extended family make their home. *Kraal* refers to any enclosed space for humans or animals, so a cattle enclosure, a small compound (or homestead) with two dwellings, or a vast compound with many dwellings may all be properly described as a kraal. The distinguishing feature of the kraal is that it is surrounded by a fence, which is usually constructed of twigs and tree branches. These fortified enclosures probably served as a protective barrier in the old days against animal as well as human intruders. Cattle kraals also, of course, ensured that the cattle did not wander off. The rondavel is typically constructed of mud (adobe), but building materials vary almost as much as styles in construction. In the countryside one also finds rectangular homes, built with mud or cement, and with a flat tin roof. Wealthier residents are able to build multiroomed homes of brick and mortar. In addition to mud, brick, and stone, other materials used in the construction of modest dwellings and commercial structures include logs, sticks, cow dung, and grass. The skeleton of a small home may be made of deadwood and sticks, with a mixture of clay and cow dung filling in the frame. The structure may be topped with a roof of grass, woven reeds, zinc, or some other material. In Ovambo communities, spherical granaries dot the landscape. These grain-storage baskets, which are very large and placed on stilts, have been described as womb-like.

Colonial Architecture

Namibia is noted for its large number of well-preserved colonial buildings, constructed in stone. In Windhoek, the capital, visitors encounter a city with many German colonial-era buildings alongside some very new modernist buildings. The buildings as well as the street names are a window into the country's past. Important offices in town are located along Independence Avenue, formerly Bismarckstrasse. Surely Windhoek must be the only major world city with streets named after both Fidel Castro and German colonial officials! Streets in Namibia honor German and Namibian heroes; Bismarck remains a popular street name throughout Namibia, although Sam Nujoma probably holds first place now. The oldest building in Windhoek is the Alte Feste, or the Old Fort, which was built in 1890. Formerly, the fort was the headquarters of the *Schutztruppe,* the colonial army. Today, it serves as the State Museum, housing a diverse collection of artifacts spanning the colonial, resistance, and contemporary periods. Other important monuments to Namibia's German past in Windhoek are the Lutheran Christuskirche (1910) and the Tintenpalast (Ink Palace), where Namibia's parliament meets, which was formerly the headquarters of the German colonial administration. The train station (1912) and Gathemann Haus are other important examples of colonial architecture.

The architecture in some parts of Namibia seems as if it was lifted up and transplanted from Germany—and indeed sometimes it was. In most cases, some or all the materials were brought from overseas and then used to construct familiar buildings in Namibia. Sometimes a watchtower or stained glass windows would be brought from Germany. In the case of the Rhenish Mission Church in Walvis Bay, the entire edifice was constructed in Germany in 1879, then dismantled and transported to Walvis Bay, and reconstructed there in 1881. Other towns along the coast have examples of German architecture. Although the German colonial period ended in 1915, German is still heard on the streets and in the cafés and homes of Swakopmund. Posters in German announce events; bookstores sell works in German. The ties with Germany remain strong; Swakopmunders of German descent actively maintain their heritage, and today a significant number of German tourists

Colonial-era buildings, Swakopmund, Namibia. (Julian Love/JAI/Corbis)

and migrants visit or live in the town. In 2001, following bitter debates, the town council approved a decision to change the names of four streets in the historic city center. Kaiser Wilhelm Street was renamed Sam Nujoma Avenue.[8] One of the most famous structures in Swakopmund is the lighthouse, completed in 1903. The Public Library and Swakopmund Arts Association are housed in the Woermann Haus (1903), which was completed in 1905 as the headquarters of the Damara and Namaqua Trading Company. The Hohenzollernhaus (1905) was the residence of visiting German aristocrats; now, it is an apartment building. The former railway station (1901) is today a resort, the Swakopmund Hotel and Entertainment Centre. The Kaiserliches Bezirksgericht (magistrate's court), built in 1901, is now the summer residence of the president of the republic. The German Evangelical Lutheran Church (1911) is another example of late 19th- and early 20th-century German architecture.

In Luderitz, about 280 miles (450 kilometers) down the coast from Swakopmund, the Deutsche-Afrika-Bank (1907), the Lutheran church, the train station, and the Magistrate's Residence (1908) are other examples of German architecture. Still further along the coast lies the ghost town of Kolmanskop. Kolmanskop used to be a boomtown, with many examples of fine German architecture in the mansions constructed by gold barons in the early 20th century; these stately homes are almost entirely covered in sand now. Other towns with notable German architecture are the southern towns of Keetmanshoop (with its famed Rhenish Mission Church, which is now the Keetmanshoop Museum, and the Kaiserliches Postamt or Imperial Post Office) and Bethanie, the site of Schmelen's house (Schmelenhaus) and its own Rhenish Mission Church.

Schmelenhaus, the modest home built by Johann Heinrich Schmelen in 1814 in Bethanie in southern Namibia, is the oldest building in Namibia. In the 19th century, some of the earliest colonial settlers from the Cape built even simpler homesteads made of mud with thatched roofs. Very wealthy settlers, on the other hand, sometimes had colossal baroque homes erected for themselves. Three notable examples are the Schwerinsburg, Heinitzburg (1908), and Duwisib (1909) castles. All three were designed by the architect Willi Sander; the first two belong to a trio of castles in the capital city, while the third, Duwisib, is 150 miles from Windhoek, just outside the small town of Maltahohe. Baron Hansheinrich von Wolf commissioned the Duwisib castle for his American heiress wife Jayta, née Humphreys; however, after her husband died in World War I, Jayta never returned to Namibia. The Duwisib is now a museum operated by the government; the Heinintzburg, also built by a lovestruck man for his beloved, has been transformed into a luxury hotel, and the Schwerinsburg is a private residence.

One of the houses in the ghost town of Kolmanskop Namibia. (Riana444 | Dreamstime.com)

Contemporary Architecture

An ever-growing number of Namibians are moving into urban areas seeking to make a living. Often, there are as few opportunities in the towns as in the rural communities Namibians left behind. With few resources, these migrants are forced to construct their dwelling places by recycling found items. Some scholars describe this as "scavenger architecture," the results of which often demonstrate remarkable creativity. Such homes are constructed of a variety of materials: corrugated iron, cardboard boxes, wooden boards, wood, and all manner of found objects. In a book on photography, there is a striking image of a remarkable home constructed of soda cans in Kavango. The soda cans have not been flattened but retain their cylindrical shape; hundreds (thousands?) of Coke, Fanta, and Lion lager cans have been used to fashion the wall of the rotund home, the roof of which is thatched.[9]

Housing in Namibia bears distinct reminders of the country's colonial past quite visibly. In 1948, the government issued a report on "Housing for Non-Europeans in Urban Areas." The South African government, which ruled Namibia, began to implement apartheid policies in Namibia, just as it was doing in South Africa. The ideas in the report drew on earlier European colonial ideas about the need to segregate Europeans in African cities from "the natives" in order to protect the former from disease and also to enforce modern standards of hygiene and sanitation. The fundamental principle of apartheid was, of course, segregation and the maintenance of a black population as a source of cheap labor for the white minority. In addition to the physical layout of communities, the designs of homes, as well as the terminology used to describe spaces, all referenced apartheid principles. Before independence, the town (or city) was for Europeans, and blacks were considered strangers in town; blacks had to live in townships or locations. Independence ended all that officially, and individuals are free to live where they wish. Yet, even 20 years after independence, the terms *township* and *location* are still reserved for describing the urban spaces in which blacks dominate; whites live in *towns*. This distinction is not based on any difference in the comparative size of these urban sites: Some townships are larger than their adjacent towns. Indeed, in a country whose total population is much smaller than that of major cities in other countries, all towns are relatively small. Windhoek, the capital and by far the largest city, has a population well under half a million. Probably more than half of Windhoek's population resides in Katutura, and that is also the fastest-growing sector of the capital city.

Katutura

One of the most arresting examples of contemporary architecture in Namibia surely must be the two-story zinc residence in Katutura, a warren of single rooms occupied by more than two dozen tenants. Katutura was founded in 1959, a result of the government's apartheid policies and the forced resettlement of blacks in this new location. When the government established the settlement by forcibly bringing Africans to live there, different ethnic groups were assigned to different locations. The different neighborhoods have names such as Nama Location, Damara Location, or Nama Seven, reflecting the history of their founding. Most of the homes in Katutura are made of corrugated iron or zinc and are small relative to the homes in the neighboring wealthy suburb of Klein Windhoek. The flat roofs are typically of corrugated iron. Of course, this means homes may be exceptionally hot during the day and cold at night, especially in the winter months. Billboards advertising beers, soft drinks, and a host of other communities abound, as many of the homes and other constructions use billboards as building materials.

Life in Katutura is inescapably communal; many live in single rooms in shared homes. Also, in many instances homes do not have fences separating them from one another, and so the sense that the open spaces between homes belong to this or that individual or family is often necessarily fluid. That many people have to fetch water from communal pumps also heightens the sense that privacy is often quite a limited commodity. The relative absence of privacy has both its positive and negative aspects. On the one hand, it means that quiet solitude is a chimera and that keeping one's affairs private is almost impossible; on the other hand, it means that help is always nearby—at least theoretically—in the case of any emergency, big or small.

Some homes do have fences, constructed sometimes with interesting material such as discarded auto parts, tires, or wooden and wire fencing. Perhaps the most striking thing about Katutura is how tidy those who have private yards keep them. Found objects such as bottles, tires, and other detritus from abandoned cars may be used to mark boundaries, with carefully tended flowers in pots and beds. Homes that look extremely modest from the outside may be surprisingly well stocked inside with modern gadgets such as television, washing machine, stove, stereo, and other household appliances. A home constructed almost entirely of tin may house an entire family and have several bedrooms and modern appliances but no indoor toilet. Electricity and indoor plumbing especially are luxuries not available to all of Katutura's residents.

If the word *township* conjures up images of a chaotic and dirty ghetto, a visit to Katutura will quickly dispel such notions. Potted plants and small gardens are common; colorful flowers sprout from the most unlikely spots. Another surprise may be that the homes in Katutura are not all modest, or all constructed from found objects, zinc, and tin. With an estimated population of some 200,000 people, Katutura is actually a sprawling city of its own, with distinct neighborhoods and a broad range in terms of architectural styles and the size of homes. There are rows and rows of matchbox homes of brick, cement, and mortar. Many churches are also constructed of such permanent materials. Katutura is home to a visible minority of well-off residents, who live in large homes and drive expensive cars.

At first, a new migrant from the countryside may have to squat with a friend or family member, perhaps as one of several living in a single room. With more resources a Katutura resident is able to rent her own room for herself and any children. Those who are lucky and industrious will build a home, constructed most likely of zinc and aluminum. A zinc and aluminum house is quicker and cheaper to put up than a more permanent brick or stone structure; it also makes very good sense to have such a house while one waits to receive a permit from the government to build a permanent brick home. A permit may take a long time to secure, and renting a room, or building an aluminum home, allows one time to save up money for the more permanent structure.

Even though there are some primarily commercial districts, Katutura's neighborhoods are all effectively mixed in terms of use, with residences and commercial enterprises sometimes sharing space. The high percentage of drinking establishments in Katutura can be a challenge, even if the *shebeen* in question is not in such close proximity to residences. In the Greenwell Matongo neighborhood in Katutura, for example, there are numerous shebeens along one street. For women workers who have to leave for work early in the morning, at more or less the same time as some visitors to the shebeens are leaving to go home after a night of drinking, the relative proximity of drinking establishments to their homes, and the density of these, is a source of abiding dissatisfaction. Pan-Africanist sentiments are echoed in the signs on commercial buildings in Katutura: There is a minimart named Kissangani on Julius Nyerere Street, not far from Mandela Bar, and the central market is Soweto. It is worth noting that at independence, the first president of Namibia, Sam Nujoma, made his home in Katutura. Proprietors of bars, shops, and other enterprises do not limit themselves to the African continent in their naming practices; there are businesses with names such as Manhattan, Times Square, and Tokyo.

Contemporary Architecture Elsewhere

Much of Namibia's contemporary architecture is designed and built by individuals for their own private use; however, Namibia does have many professionally trained architects who design private homes as well as commercial buildings on commission. There are a number of associations for architects, such as the Namibia Institute of Architects (NIA), and Namibian architects usually receive training at home or in South Africa. Among the best-known architects are Kerry McNamara and Jaco Wasserfall. Another Namibian architect gaining international acclaim is Nina Maritz, who is known for incorporating elements from the natural environment in which she works as well as the practices of the local populations. Maritz designed the Habitat Research and Development Centre in Windhoek. The center works to encourage and provide sustainable housing and construction in Namibia. Maritz used recycled oil drum lids to make doors, screens, and signage for this striking work. Maritz also designed the Visitor Centre for the Twyfelfontein Rock Art Museum and again made use of discarded oil drums, in this case for the roofing and washbasins in the public bathroom. Before the new construction, visitors to the site would often climb over the ancient rock art and pour soft drinks over the rock in order to wet the surface and make the petroglyphs easier to photograph. In designing the center, Maritz sought to minimize damage by visitors. Maritz's architecture, in which found objects figure so prominently, is reminiscent of township constructions. Along with fellow Namibian architect Paul Munting, Maritz designed the Football for Hope Centre in Katutura, which was officially opened on September 25, 2010, by Namibian Prime Minister Nahas Angula and the secretary general of the Fédération Internationale de Football Association (FIFA, or International Federation for Association Football).

Adequate housing continues to be a major problem for local authorities throughout Namibia as more and more people move into urban areas. Shacks constructed of tin and aluminum are unlikely to disappear any time soon, especially in squatter settlements. Such housing can be erected relatively quickly by the ever-growing number of rural–urban migrants as an immediate solution to their need for housing. Usually this is seen as a temporary solution, to be utilized until one finds a job. But with the high rates of unemployment and underemployment, most of those who find themselves in the city struggle continually to make ends meet, and what was conceived as a temporary solution too often becomes permanent housing.

Some urban activists point out that the slums and the temporary shacks that the urban poor erect must be seen as a natural stage in the growth of urban environments in countries of the global south. Certainly, it is true that in Namibian history there are examples of former slums that have been transformed into relatively attractive neighborhoods with more permanent constructions and access to municipal services. In the period after World War II specifically, large numbers of immigrants moved from war-torn Europe to Namibia, and many were forced to live in temporary housing before they were able to move into better dwellings. One no longer extant neighborhood in Windhoek, Steenskamp, had prefabricated homes and apartment buildings; most of the residents were Dutch immigrants. For too many Namibians today, however, there are few signs that they will be able, in any foreseeable future, to exchange these structures that were intended originally to be transitory for the more comfortable homes they desire.

NOTES

1. In 1917, French artist Marcel Duchamp purchased a urinal, placed it on its side, and displayed it as art alongside other works. Many consider this the beginning of the Dada movement in art.

2. Rock art was not made exclusively by San (ancestors); Nama and Bantu-speaking peoples also made petroglyphs, and some scholars focus on the differences in the rock art created by different populations and/or in different geographic locations.

3. Quoted in Robert J. Gordon and Stuart Sholto-Douglas, *The Bushman Myth: The Making of an Underclass* (Boulder, CO: Westview Press, 2000), p. 26. Francis Galton's observation appears also on the same page in this book.

4. I refer here to the cultural center dedicated to him, a major center for art training.

5. Using basically the same essential material, men are more likely to make figurative than utilitarian objects. It is interesting to note how language sometimes serves to draw gender or racial distinctions that obscure commonalities: Figurines made by men are typically described as "terra-cotta"; buildings constructed of identical material are referred to as "mud" in the African context and "adobe" elsewhere.

6. Gourds and other storage containers are made not only of pottery but also of skins and even grasses and reeds, which are then treated to ensure impenetrability.

7. Hercules Viljoen, "Is Namibian Art (Still) Provincial + Regional + Untouched?" in *Transitions: Botswana, Namibia, Mozambique, Zambia, Zimbabwe, 1960–2004*, ed. Barbara Murray and John Picton (London: The Africa Centre, 2005).

8. As late as the mid-1990s there were reports in the media that some shops were selling Nazi memorabilia, while such evidence tells us little it may offer some indication of unresolved racial tensions. However, it must also be noted that there have been many important shows of unity at significant times since independence, such as, for example, following the murder of a young woman by her spouse in 1999.

9. Editions Revue Noire, *Namibia* (Paris: Editions Revue Noire, 1994). See image no. 32.

5

Cuisine and Dress

Namibia does not have a single national cuisine. The diversity of the country's cuisine reflects the diversity of the ethnic communities within the state. Nevertheless, there are some foods that are relished the length and breadth of the country; at the top of this list must be meat: Namibians are avid meat eaters. A host of domesticated and game animals are consumed. Wild game (such as kudu and springbok) can be found on the dining table in all parts of Namibia and among all ethnic and social groups. Game is so popular that restaurants frequently offer a variety of steaks and sausages made out of game, including kudu, springbok, crocodile, and ostrich. Beef and lamb are also popular. Indeed, many Namibians happily proclaim Namibian beef the second best in the world, after Argentinean beef; much of the beef produced on ranches is exported to South Africa. Namibians hold their lamb and goat meat to be second to none. Biltong, a cured meat snack, is popular throughout southern Africa. Biltong may be made out of virtually any kind of meat, from ostrich to kudu to zebra to farm-grown beef.

One popular way to consume meat is the *braai*. *Braai* is both a verb and a noun. To braai is to barbecue, and, as with sausages and biltong, virtually any meat may be braaied. The braai is any social gathering where family and friends or colleagues gather to eat outside, in a park, at the beach, or in someone's backyard. At a braai, in addition to the meats, other dishes are

Various meats at a barbeque in Namibia, including zebra, impala, warthog, and ostrich. (Unique2109 | Dreamstime.com)

served, such as potato salad, *mahangu* (millet or sorghum meal), and *potjiekos* (a stew cooked slowly in a three-legged pot over an outdoor fire). Although meat is extremely popular, it is not necessarily on the menu daily because it is expensive, and hunting is not an option for most. Meat is always served at important occasions, such as weddings and funerals, no matter the economic situation of the family. Certain foods are considered an essential component at particular events; for example, at a Herero wedding one can expect to drink *tombo* (home-brewed sorghum or millet beer), *omaere* (sour milk), and *oshikandela* (a type of yogurt drink) and to eat *vetkoek* (fried dough with a sweet or savory filling) and a great deal of meat.

Another item that is eaten by almost all Namibians is mahangu (millet or sorghum meal) porridge.[1] Mahangu can also be made using maize (corn) meal. Mahangu is served with a variety of meat or vegetable sauces. There are a variety of spinach-like leafy green vegetables eaten in Namibia, and these are often served with mahangu. Millet and sorghum, both of which tend to be drought resistant, are indigenous to Africa, but most experts believe that corn was introduced to Africa from the Americas. The popularity of corn (known locally as maize) in Africa is phenomenal, especially in southern Africa. Corn and millet are widely available in Namibia and are used in a great variety of ways, including to make thick fermented drinks, whose alcoholic content rises with age. Whole corn is also roasted or boiled. Legumes are popular in Namibia, as in other parts of Africa; pulses of different types, including beans and peanuts, are widely consumed, as snacks and also at meals. Local varieties of leaves in the spinach family are used to make different dishes, including sauces to accompany the mahangu.

Widely touted as a Namibian national dish, *smiley* (goat head) is not a delicacy of which everyone partakes. One dish almost all southern African peoples share is the mealie made of maize (sorghum or millet) and curdled milk, often served as a breakfast food. When the grain is prepared in this way it is not as stiff as the mahangu served with meat and vegetables; the latter is typically served at lunch or dinner. The cuisines of peoples such as the Herero, the Ovambo, the peoples of Caprivi, and the San have much in common with those of their compatriots in neighboring countries (namely Angola, Zambia, and Botswana). German and northern European food has penetrated deep into daily life in much of the country, not just in towns. Namibian cuisine has also been influenced by Afrikaans cookery. For its part, Afrikaans cookery is a cuisine built on Dutch foundations and heavily inflected by the foodways of the various populations of South Africa, including African, Malay, and Indian. Northern European food traditions were brought by missionaries from Finland, Germany, Sweden, and other places, as well as by the large numbers of Afrikaners who settled in Namibia during the long South African occupation (1915–1990). In towns, restaurants often serve German foods such as schnitzels, apple strudel, and a large variety of sausages. At home, many urban families eat rice or pasta on a weekly basis.

Apart from meat (whether domesticated or wild) and dairy, a great deal of what is eaten in Namibia is imported. Even grains are imported from South Africa, although a substantial amount is grown domestically in the north. This high level of importation is, of course, linked to the difficult terrain: Namibia has very little land that is suitable for cultivation. A great deal of the fruits and vegetables available for purchase are imported from South Africa. However, Namibia is fortunate in that often what plant foods do grow are extremely versatile. The leaves of the baobab tree, for example, make a delicious and nutritious relish when cooked; the pulp from the fruit is used to make a satisfying, creamy drink, and the seeds, eaten raw or cooked, supply good quantities of protein and omega oils. Loaded with antioxidants, the baobab is considered a superfood whose fruit supplies many times more vitamin C than the equivalent amount of orange and more calcium than spinach. Dried baobab-pulp powder is sold in health food stores throughout the United States, marketed as a healthy addition to smoothies and cereals.[2]

Nara melons. (Alexander Mitrofanov | Dreamstime.com)

Plant food species rarely found elsewhere include the Nara melon, the Tsamma melon, and the Gemsbok cucumber. The Gemsbok cucumber is usually round or oblong with a prickly outer layer; it can be fried but is typically eaten roasted. The flesh of the Tsamma melon is usually cooked and pounded to make a porridge-type dish; the seeds, which are high in protein and oil, are usually roasted and eaten as a snack food. Roasted or dried seeds are sometimes ground or made into a paste, to be used in the preparation of other dishes. When the Tsamma melon is sweet, it may be eaten raw. In the past especially, the San, who sometimes must endure long periods without access to water, depended on these wild melons and cucumbers because they have a high water content. The whole of the Nara melon can be utilized— the peel is used for animal feed, and the flesh and seeds are consumed by humans. The seeds are extremely nutritious, and some Khoisan communities are reported to have been able to subsist for significant periods of time on the seeds alone. When dehydrated, the seeds can keep a very long time. The seeds are more than 50 percent oil and about 30 percent protein, making them remarkably providential in times of food scarcity. The oil from the seeds makes an excellent moisturizer for the skin, and today, the seeds are exported or used locally to make cosmetics. *Marula* oil, extracted from the seed of the fruit, is a staple of Ovambo cuisine. One traditional Ovambo dish consists of spinach seasoned with marula oil. Many Namibians cook their food outdoors on an open fire. This is true for rural dwellers as well as a significant percentage of urban residents who subsist on meager wages and do not have modern kitchens. Ironically, many who live in town and have modern kitchens look forward to returning to the village to sample food cooked over an open flame, with the distinctive taste imparted by the smoke.

Restaurants

While there is a great diversity in Namibian cuisine, visitors to Namibia will encounter much the same cuisine in commercial establishments throughout the country. The cuisine in restaurants that cater to the Namibian middle classes and most foreign tourists is based in significant measure on what is described around the globe as "international cuisine," with heavy influences from the country's German heritage. In all the major urban centers in Namibia, one is sure to find at least one or two pastry shops and cafés where apple strudel, Black Forest gâteau, and heavy black breads are on the menu. Hearty savory pancakes with meat or seafood and cheese are popular at any time of day. There are German beer halls and German-style restaurants throughout the country, and it must be noted that international staples such as pizza and beefsteaks, hamburgers and fries, scampi, and spaghetti are readily available. Sometimes, even when the menu is full of easily recognizable items—sandwiches, wraps, and barbecue—the ingredients may be less familiar. For example, the menu may offer a kudu salami pita bread sandwich, biltong and avocado salad, or fillets of crocodile, ostrich, or oryx. Other items unfamiliar to most Americans include snails, frogs' legs, smiley, and *mopane* worms. On the coast and in Windhoek, seafood is readily available. Lovers of snails will find they are readily available in many areas. In Windhoek and Swakopmund, German-style cafés are numerous, serving the sorts of cakes and cookies one can find in such establishments in Germany or Austria. Hot meals are available at major supermarkets; since these cater to working-class Namibians, the foods on offer are often of a greater variety than is generally found in most restaurants, and items such as mahangu and sour greens or beans and tripe are likely to be available. Restaurants that serve foreign cuisines (for example, Japanese, West African, and French) can be found in larger towns, especially Windhoek.

South African chains dominate the food and retail sectors in Namibia. For example, Nando, a South African fast food chain, can be found in major towns in Namibia. Nando has restaurants in more than 30 countries, including the United States, the United Kingdom, and Pakistan. Although founded in South Africa, the chain is most famous for its *chicken peri peri,* which the company describes as "Portuguese-Mozambican." Peri peri is an African hot pepper used in the preparation of the Nando chicken; peri peri chicken is a well-known chicken dish throughout southern Africa.

In 2008, a Namibian woman entrepreneur, Kayenda Nangolo, opened what she hoped would become the first homegrown franchise in Namibia, the Nanken restaurant, which opened in Windhoek in November of that year. Although the restaurant offered a range of fast foods such as hamburgers and fries, its promotional efforts focused on its "Owambo chicken." With about 90 percent of new restaurants closing in their first year and given the dominance of the fast food chicken market by two South African chains (Nando and Hungry Lion), it is not surprising that this venture folded. Another Namibian woman, Twapewa Mudjanima, runs a restaurant-cum-cultural center in Katutura serving Ovambo food, catering to locals as well as tourists; the restaurant caters and also delivers to offices and hotels. In addition to the restaurant, the Xwama Cultural Village houses a craft workshop and a store that sells locally produced crafts as well as cosmetics. The city of Windhoek promotes the diverse cuisines of Namibia via its annual /Ae//Gams, a cultural festival. This is a great time to see and taste the great range of Namibian cuisines.

Snacks and Delicacies

Biltong is probably the most widely available snack in Namibia. This is often referred to as "jerky," much to the annoyance of those southern Africans who are familiar with the American variant. (South Africans also eat biltong.) Biltong can be made out of essentially any meat: There is biltong made of beef, kudu, ostrich, and other game in shops and in gas stations throughout Namibia. Unlike jerky, which is cooked, biltong is air-dried. *Kapana* is another popular meat snack: It is barbecued meat that is served with a dry dipping sauce and is usually eaten on-site. Meat pies, sausage rolls, and such savory or baked snacks are also available generally at gas stations throughout the country, and in bakeries. Other flour-based treats include a variety of roasted and pan-cooked breads, such as the ash bread made by the Nama; Herero bread is available from supermarkets, but is best when homemade and baked outdoors.

Major supermarkets, *cuca* shops (small shops that sell snacks, toiletries, and drinks including beer), and gas stations sell a variety of hot and packaged snacks, including biltong, meat pies, sausage rolls, and dried fruit such as Nara leather. To make the Nara snack, the melon pulp is removed, boiled, and made into a puree, which is then dried for several days. Once it is completely dry, it is cut into strips and sucked or licked like the fruit leather one finds in health food stores in the United States. Street vendors are a common sight in even the smallest towns, selling noncomestibles as well as a host of snack foods. More adventurous foreigners may try the delicious and nutritious fried mopane worms, available from street vendors, in shebeens, and at local markets.

Both the eggs and the flesh of the ostrich, which is a low-fat dark meat, are eaten, the latter in a great variety of forms, made into salami, as biltong, or as steak. Ostrich eggs are enormous; one ostrich egg is easily the equivalent of two to three dozen chicken eggs. There are wild ostrich as well as farm-raised ostrich. The ostrich shell is so strong that it may be used as a receptacle to hold water; artists also use it to make jewelry and artwork. During the rainy season, huge mushrooms grow in the termite hills that dot the country. These mushrooms are very rare as they grow so infrequently and are difficult to find because other animals often get to them first. These are considered a great delicacy and are said to be more delicious—as well as rarer—than French and Italian truffles; there is also another variety of seasonal and highly prized mushrooms, the Kalahari truffles. These mushrooms are very versatile and can be eaten raw or cooked, in a variety of ways.

Drinks

Cattle rearing is widely practiced, and so milk is an important part of the Namibian diet. The Herero, who in the past were mostly cattle herders,

A 1955 image showing Khoisan man drinking water from his ostrich egg containers. (Getty Images)

consume fresh milk as well as curdled milk and yogurt drinks. The European communities all use milk and milk products too, manufacturing yogurt and cheese; indeed, dairy drinks are popular throughout Namibia. Many different types of dairy drinks are prepared at home or commercially and are available throughout the country. Ginger beer, in its homemade and commercial varieties, is popular. The Nama prepare a beverage using maize, *maxau,* which may be served before meals as a sort of nonalcoholic aperitif. Beer is another favorite throughout Namibia, and there are varieties of beer, from German-style lagers to home brews. Home-brewed beers using millet, corn, and sorghum can be very low in alcohol; such beers are usually thick and are more rightly considered a food. The longer these drinks are left to ferment, the more potent they become; if they are drunk soon after being made, they are extremely mild and suitable even for children. The marula fruit, already mentioned, is used commercially to make a popular liqueur available throughout southern Africa. Juice can be extracted from the versatile marula fruit. Berries, fruits, and nuts are also used to make beers and stronger liquors. *Kashipembe,* the name used to describe any number of extremely intoxicating home-brewed brandies made using different fruits, has come under great public scrutiny, with many decrying the combustible mix of its elevated alcoholic content, its great affordability, and Namibia's staggering levels of unemployment.

Namibian commercial beer is reputed for its high quality. Windhoek Lager is produced locally but proudly advertises that every year it sends samples to Munich's Beer Institute to make sure that its beers meet the standards set in 16th-century Bavaria. Castle is another Namibian beer; the most popular beer, however, is Tafel Lager, which is produced by Namibia Breweries. There are other bottled drinks, including soda and waters flavored with local fruits. Regional wine is available, almost all of it from South Africa, as is a liqueur made from the marula fruit. A small amount of wine is produced in Namibia, mostly in the Omaruru River valley area, but domestic vintners are not yet producing enough for broad distribution. It is interesting to note that, although wine production is on an extremely small scale in Namibia, viniculture has a relatively long pedigree historically. The first Namibian grape wine is believed to have been produced in 1904 by French Catholic missionaries who had imported seedlings from the region of Alsace-Lorraine. As well as beers, teas, and coffees, restaurants and cafés may offer a variety of shandies (soda or bitters and beer) and the malted nonalcoholic beverage Horlicks.

DRESS

Everyday Dress

In urban areas, most Namibians wear what is commonly referred to as Western dress. Women wear dresses, pants, and skirts (which are rarely

Tabelo Timse Mamtlatso Sealola holds dry Marula fruits during a Marula festival. Marula is a natural fruit that is used to produce many products such as the Marula traditional beer and juice, Marula jam, and Marula oil. (AFP/Getty Images)

worn above the knee) with tops, which, occasionally, may be rather low-cut. Although ceremonial or national dress is more usually worn on special occasions, it is not too unusual to see the occasional Herero women in a traditional outfit going about her daily life or engaging in street-side vending. Among men, the business suit is the exception rather than the rule in offices. Uniforms, however, are common for both men and women, and one frequently will see employees in banks, beauty salons, cafes, supermarkets, and commercial offices dressed in the particular uniform of their place of work. Although some young people have adopted the contemporary international style of droopy pants and women's tops that expose the belly button, it is rare to see Namibians in towns wearing extremely skimpy clothing such as very short shorts. However, in nightclubs, at dance parties, and in the rural areas, one will often see people wearing revealing clothing. For example, in the northwest of the country, Himba men often wear leather thongs, and young children may be seen going about their business naked throughout the country. However, Western dress is extremely common in rural as well as urban areas. In nightclubs and bars, and in Namibian popular music videos, women wear the kind of clothing familiar to anyone who watches American music videos.

The best-known traditional dress in Namibia is that worn by Herero women. Herero women can be seen throughout the country, dressed in their traditional attire, the lineage of which can be traced to the costume of 19th-century European missionary women. To the layers of skirts, the Herero women add a headdress designed to recall the horns of cattle, which play such a central role in Herero culture and life. Instead of wearing layers of petticoats, which add to the weight of the outfit, today women sometimes use a sponge or stiff netting under the dress to achieve the same effect. The headdress, considered a sine qua non with regard to Herero women's national dress, is made using two pieces of cloth. The Herero women's outfit is completed with a shawl. Shawls are in fact a common component of the national dress of many Namibian communities; Nama, Damara, Baster, and Coloured women all typically include a shawl when they dress traditionally. Herero, Nama, and Damara women frequently wear an apron over their long dress. While the headdress is nonnegotiable in constituting Herero women's national dress, the apron is optional. Bonnets (or other head coverings for women) and hats (for men) are a common feature of the traditional dress of a large number of communities, including Herero, Ovambo, Basters, Coloureds, Damara, and Nama. Nama women's national dress is a gown made of patchwork; for

Handmade leather bags, Namibia. (Courtesy of Anene Ejikeme)

Herero woman in traditional dress. (Urosr/Shutterstock)

Ovambo women this is a pink dress, below the knee or longer, with a border around the hem. Of course, there are many variations on this theme.

The Himba are an even more popular sight for photographers than Herero women. Himba women often go topless, and they wear skirts fashioned out of leather. Himba men also wear animal skins. The women use red ochre on their skin, giving it a red hue, thus their designation as "red women." Oils and herbs are mixed into the ochre to create a highly effective moisturizing skin balm. The hairstyles worn by the Himba indicate their stage of life. Adult women often wear their hair in very intricate braids with leather woven in. It is possible to determine the life stage of a Himba individual—male or female, including children—from his or her particular hairstyle.

Ceremonial Dress

Dress not only serves as a covering but also conveys symbolic meaning. For example, during the initiation ceremony of Herero girls into woman-hood, the transition into adulthood is marked when the initiate puts on a special headdress made of leather. This leather headdress has three horns, to represent cattle, and may be decorated with beads. Increasingly, the leather

Himba woman arranging her hair prior to having her picture taken. (Courtesy of Anene Ejikeme)

headdress is no longer used and instead the initiate puts on the horned cloth headtie that forms part of Herero women's national costume.

Not surprisingly, dress for special occasions can be quite elaborate. For example, at funerals or royal functions individuals may dress in skins or have whiskers and horsetails attached to their clothing. Herbalists and healers sometimes wear ceremonial dress or outfit their ordinary attire (for example, a T-shirt and shorts) with horns, horsetails, and other accoutrements. Dance troupes typically wear special costumes; groups that perform dances associated with a particular ethnic community may wear dress that is culturally appropriate. It is common to see people wearing the national costume of their own or another ethnic community to weddings and church. Interestingly, West African dress (especially from Senegal and Nigeria) is sometimes seen on such occasions. Namibians typically dress up for church; casual clothing at a Sunday service is unusual. For weddings, funerals, and ceremonial events such as Maharero Day, Namibians dress up. The dress worn on such occasions is typically made by a tailor. As well as custom-made clothes for their clients, many tailors also display and sell ready-made clothes; clients bring their own fabrics to the tailor or they may select from the tailor's stock. Having clothes custom-made is more expensive than buying imported clothes. The Herero dress for women, for example, requires a great deal of fabric, which is expensive to buy and which also attracts a much higher fee to have made relative to other, less time-consuming, styles.

The sartorial habits of Namibians reflect both the history and heritage of the country as well as individual preferences. It is important when talking about the dress of Namibian ethnic groups not to fall into the pattern of talking about the traditional as some unchanging, timeless entity. Herero fashion history is a wonderful reminder of this: Contemporary Herero national dress is so clearly a riff on European missionary clothing that it makes it impossible (or should make it impossible) to speak or think about timeless native costumes.

NOTES

1. Some, for example in Caprivi, refer to mahangu as nshima.

2. Another Namibian native plant that has become celebrated internationally in health-conscious circles is *hoodia*. Besides its appetite-suppressing qualities, hoodia is believed to be an effective medicinal treatment against a variety of diseases, including high blood pressure and diabetes. For years, a controversy involving the multinationals Pfizer and Unilever, U.K.-based Phytopharm, and San communities in southern Africa raged over attempts to patent the chemical component in hoodia that suppresses the appetite.

6

Gender Roles, Marriage, and Family

AFRICAN WOMEN ARE widely seen as overwhelmingly oppressed, victims of an African cultural tradition that is deeply patriarchal. Indeed, many people in contemporary Namibia, like their counterparts elsewhere in Africa, eagerly call upon tradition to challenge any attempts to institute equality for women or groups such as homosexuals. However, one effect of this is that it presents a picture of African cultures as static and fixed, impervious to change through the centuries. The reality, of course, is quite different. For instance, some historians of the Ovambo insist that prior to the 19th century, women enjoyed relatively high status, being valued in their families (which were matrilineal) and serving as healers and even occasionally as clan chiefs. Among the Ovambo, with their strong tradition of social hierarchy and chieftaincy, there is a record of some women rulers and lineage heads. Royals, including women, enjoy high status and privilege in Ovambo society.

Most scholars agree that the majority of Namibians trace their descent primarily matrilineally, even though in the contemporary period and, indeed since the coming of European Christian missionaries, the patrilineal principle has been rapidly gaining in importance. The Kavango, the second-largest ethnic group, trace descent matrilineally, while the Herero trace descent bilaterally. Among the Herero, each individual belongs to an *eanda* (i.e., the matrilineal descent group) as well as an *oruzo* (the patrilineal descent group).

Matrilineality alone, however, cannot be taken as proof of high social status for women. In pre-colonial Namibia, women's participation in politics varied from society to society, and there is disagreement as to whether women in pre-colonial Namibia had recognized avenues for making their collective will known. H. Becker argues that even prior to colonial rule, class, not gender, was the central factor in terms of social identity in Namibia. According to Becker (2007), colonial authorities ignored this, choosing instead to recognize only those male leaders who were willing to cooperate with them. For instance, the Native Reserve Trust Fund Proclamation 9 of 1924 allowed only male "natives" to represent the "native reserves." In every instance, the prerogatives and claims of male elites were enforced. Practices that had formerly been fluid and often diverse were increasingly fixed and enshrined as "customary law" and "tradition."[1]

In the more recent past, tradition did not prevent women from actively participating in the liberation struggle. Namibian women did everything from acting as spies to giving moral and material support to also fighting in battle. However, as has been the case with other armed resistance struggles in Africa (for example, in Zimbabwe and Eritrea), even if a few women rose to very high rank in the armed resistance, after the war, questions of gender equity were shunted to the sidelines. Having taken part in a liberation struggle does not by itself guarantee gender equality in peacetime. Nevertheless, the participation of women in the resistance struggle did have an enormous impact on those women who participated, in terms of the acquisition of skills and knowledge. A study of women exiles, conducted after independence, found that these women were five times more likely to have graduated from secondary school than their counterparts, male or female, who had remained in Namibia. The Ovambo regions in the north were the most actively involved in the liberation struggle; in consequence, Ovambo women also had a higher level of participation in the struggle than women in the other areas. Some commentators have suggested that this has made Ovambo women more willing than many other Namibian women to take active roles in community meetings and organizations.

Women often organize through their churches for a variety of activities, from self-help to community-focused events. In Windhoek and other towns, women's groups work to provide skills training and child care, as well as to agitate for the provision of better services, such as housing and sanitation. Namibia has seen a remarkable explosion in the education sector since independence, with the numbers of literate Namibians at a very admirable level. Women too have been beneficiaries of these positive developments. In 2000 the government passed the Traditional Authorities Act, requiring that traditional authorities achieve gender balance. The Constitution of Namibia, one of the most egalitarian in the world, provides for equal rights to men and women. However, as is often the case in many other places, reality and the law are frequently out of sync.

WOMEN'S ECONOMIC STRUGGLES

While a significant portion of Namibia's total population is economically disadvantaged, as elsewhere, women and children are affected disproportionately by poverty. About 40 percent of all households (rural and urban) in Namibia are headed by women. The number of children born out of wedlock has also increased tremendously since independence. According to the United Nations, almost 40 percent of 19-year-old Namibian young women are mothers. This is an astonishing figure, especially given that according to the same 2005 United Nations Population Fund (UNFPA) study, the average age when girls have their first sexual experience is 19 (and 18 for boys). This would seem to suggest a very low level of contraceptive use, if almost half of all girls become pregnant the first year (time?) they engage in sexual activity.[2] Some suggest that young women choose to get pregnant for a variety of reasons, including to manipulate the father (and perhaps collect child support) and to gain the respect of others by ascending to the status of an adult in public opinion. In reality, however, it is more likely that the majority of single mothers do not receive any regular support from the fathers of their children. A large percentage of girls drop out of school once they become pregnant, some due to the fear that they will become targets of teasing and public humiliation. Life as a single mother is extremely challenging. The fact is that there are many reasons that children are born out of wedlock and that women are marrying later. The impact of migrant labor over the generations cannot be overlooked. The exorbitant cost of a wedding is another factor: A wedding

Table 6.1: Distribution of out-of-wedlock births, percent married, and average number of reproductive partners (women only), N = 341

Women born between	# Women	% Births out of wedlock	% Married	Average # reproductive partners	
				Ever married	Never married
1916–34	35	55%	80%	1,7	*
1935–44	44	81%	59%	2,4	3,5
1945–54	47	90%	29%	1,9	3,0
1955–64	57	91%	38%	2,5	2,9
1965–74	68	93%	(22%)	**	**
1975–84	90	97%	(5%)	**	**

*Not enough cases
**Still in childbearing age
Source: *We All Have Our Own Father!* Reproduction from "Marriage and Gender in Rural North-West Namibia," in *Unraveling Taboos: Gender and Sexuality in Namibia,* eds., Suzanne LaFont and Dianne Hubbard (Windhoek, Namibia: Legal Assistance Centre, 2007), p. 206.

requires a significant outlay of cash to purchase meat, foods, and drinks and to provide entertainment. One reason so many couples choose to cohabit, but certainly not the only one, is the expense associated with nuptials.

On the economic front, Namibians are overwhelmingly dependent on agriculture and animal husbandry. The majority of Namibians live in rural areas, and their lives are governed less by stipulations in the Constitution and more by practices and rituals that have become hallowed as tradition. Access to land is a critical issue for women; women's access to land is usually through fathers or husbands.[3] With many men engaged in migrant labor that takes them to South African and other urban areas, women are often the ones left de facto in charge of farms in the rural areas. Yet women's hold on land remains tenuous, as dictated by customary laws, which were inscribed under colonial rule. In terms of government policies regulating the farm sector, women are often excluded or simply invisible. Land has long been a major source of conflict and tension in Namibia, a former settler colony. Under German and South African colonial rule, government policies benefited white farmers, and black farmers faced discrimination and marginalization. Under South African rule, black farmers wishing to form cooperatives, which the government saw as challenges to white farmers, faced enormous barriers. The Communal Land Reform Act 5 of 2002 gave widows protection from any threat of eviction if their spouse died. This law is not always implemented.

With many fathers engaged in migrant labor, away herding cattle, or simply absent from the picture, and with so many children born out of wedlock, Namibian women face enormous burdens. Often, women must look after their children alone, all the while eking out a difficult rural subsistence or engaging in extremely low-paying jobs. Women in towns have more choices than those in rural areas with regard to the range of employment options. Women migrate to towns for similar reasons as male migrants—to find work—and the economic autonomy that is associated with wage labor gives them a measure of independence. However, it would be wrong to imagine that life in town is idyllic. The unemployment rate is high, wages are low, housing is substandard and overcrowded, and migrant women may find themselves forced to stay with abusive partners for financial reasons. Independence has brought neither racial nor gender parity. Some see the numerous women's rights groups in the country as a positive sign, embracing the elevation of the Office of Women's Affairs to a ministry as an indication that the government is heading in the right direction. Many government critics, however, are not mollified by this ministerial appointment.

WOMEN'S POLITICAL ACTIVISM

Women's groups in Namibia fight to end gender discrimination. One prominent organization in the campaign to improve the lot of women is the

Women's Leadership Centre. It organizes meetings and workshops, issues educational bulletins, and speaks out against practices harmful to women and women's exclusion from political power. In 2005, for example, the group issued a statement against "Harmful Cultural Practices and Beliefs for Women." The statement condemned harmful cultural practices such as child marriage and the levirate, which allow women no choice in determining their destiny. Some of the discriminatory laws against women that are in effect are remnants of laws inherited from the apartheid regime of South Africa.

The feminist collective Sister Namibia, which was founded in 1989, has long encouraged political parties to advance so-called zebra candidate lists, which is to say lists in which there is an equal number of male and female candidates. In 1989, the South West Africa People's Organisation (SWAPO) sought to guarantee that women had a voice in the political process, and the party mandated that lists of candidates supplied for the elections must include women. This stipulation applied only to local elections. Since independence, there have always been women councilors at the local level, as well as some women at the ministerial level. However, the percentage of women in these latter positions, which are appointive offices, remains abysmally low. At the regional level, where no affirmative rules are in place, the percentage of women in elected office is the lowest. On the economic front, a few women occupy very prominent positions; for example, the executive director of the state-owned Namdeb Mining Corporation is a woman.[4] Most women, however, are self-employed, operating modest roadside shops selling food or other commodities.

Sister Namibia has been extremely active in keeping women's issues at the forefront of national awareness, if not always national debate. The group publishes a magazine, hosts a radio show on Base FM (formerly Katutura Community Radio), hosts workshops, publishes pamphlets, and even produced one of the best-known collections of Namibian women's writing. To mark its 20th anniversary in 2009, Sister Namibia hosted a celebration that featured a performance of the well-known play *Vagina Monologues* by U.S. playwright Eve Ensler. In 2009 Sister Namibia launched a special one-year, four-issue magazine aimed at girls between 14 and 20. The magazine, *Real!* was produced largely by a group of young women selected to participate in the project, and these young people did everything from writing the stories to working in production.

In the 2009 campaign season all the political parties made ending gender discrimination and violence against women a key campaign promise. In the December 2009 elections, however, women actually lost ground: Women won only 22 percent of seats in the National Assembly, a drop from the 30 percent prior to the elections. Following SWAPO's victory at the polls, the SWAPO Party Women's Council (SPWC) began to call for the government to change the constitution to guarantee greater female representation in government. The SPWC pointed out that the goal of the African Union "Protocol on the Rights of Women in Africa" is the achievement of gender equity in politics by 2015. Namibia is a signatory to the protocol.

The Namibian constitution, similarly to its South African counterpart, is extremely progressive. Article 10 of the constitution bans all discrimination on the basis of sex. Subsequent amendments have been promulgated to ensure women's equal treatment before the law. For example, in 1996 the Married Persons Equality Bill was passed. The period leading up to the passage of the law saw a great deal of emotional debate. Many self-professed traditionalists and "God-fearing" Christians expressed dismay at what they considered the wrong direction the country was going; others cheered the proposal, which they thought long overdue. In 2003, two further laws targeted at protecting women were passed: the Maintenance Act, which sought to guarantee that women were not left without any financial support from the fathers of their children, and the Combating of Domestic Violence Act. Today, the laws assure women of equality, but the lived reality for most women falls far short of this ideal. In October 2009, the Women's Leadership Centre in Windhoek organized a forum to which it invited leading politicians and women from various walks of life to discuss the issue of women's place in Namibian society and the fact that women still did not enjoy equality.

MARRIAGE AND FAMILY

Although a small number of young people in towns perform only a simple civil ceremony, marriages for most Namibians involve extended kin. If problems arise later in the marriage, the couple may turn to family members for counsel. The involvement of family members of both the groom and the bride begins before the actual wedding ceremonies with the ritual of the "asking of the hand" (which can last from a day to several weeks) and extends beyond the wedding, which itself can be a very elaborate and expensive affair. In the asking of the hand (also known as "opening the door"), members of the groom's family visit the wife's family to formally request the marriage. At this stage, of course, the prospective spouses have already agreed to the marriage and may even have been living together for some time, but this does not mean that the woman's relations cannot delay the wedding by making numerous or difficult requests of their prospective in-laws. The asking of the hand can be long and exhausting, with the girl's kin eagerly demonstrating their reluctance to "give away" their daughter; the family of the prospective groom must show their patience and goodwill. The whole process is highly ritualized.

There are three types of marriage: church, civil, and customary marriage, and individuals usually combine these in various ways, whether sequentially or concurrently. Marriages are held usually on the weekend and last for two days or longer, involving considerable expense. Typically, the traditional marriage begins on a Friday and is not over until Sunday; many couples combine the traditional and church ceremonies into a single weekend of festivities and rituals, with ideas about what constitute relevant elements of tradition and church varying. Other couples marry in court, delaying the traditional and church weddings (both or either) until they have saved up enough money. Some couples have only one type of marriage; many cohabiting couples have no marriage ceremony at all.[5] Couples who have a civil marriage are free to determine whether they want to commingle their assets or to keep them separate; if a couple does not state whether they wish their marriage to be out of community of property or not, then, in the instance of a divorce, property matters are decided automatically based on residence.[6] The civil marriage of those who live north of the "Red Line" is automatically out of community of property, while for those south of the line the marriage is in community of property. This peculiarity of the Namibian legal system goes back to colonial era laws which divided the country into two distinct zones, one (in the north) where Africans supposedly were allowed to live more or less according to their cultural traditions and the south, which came under much more direct colonial government control.

There is a great deal of feasting, dancing, and singing at traditional wedding ceremonies. Music, song, and dance play important roles at wedding festivities among all ethnic groups. At Coloured weddings there is even dancing in the church as well as at the reception. In most communities women ululate at different moments during the ceremonies to express their delight. Among the Ovambo, Damara/Nama, and Herero, festivities take place at the homesteads of both the groom and the bride. For a lavish wedding, huge tents are set up outdoors to entertain the invited guests, and vast amounts of food are served. As well as the family members and invited guests who sit under the tents, other well-wishers who drop by are also offered drinks and food. Goats, fowl, and perhaps a cow or more are slaughtered to prepare the food for the guests.

Among the Ovambo and other Namibian communities, the wife is supposed to show reluctance to leave her own family and single status to become married and join her husband. The families of the bride and groom engage in lighthearted competitive singing to see which group can out-sing the other. During the Ovambo traditional wedding ceremonies, when the groom's family arrives at the home of the bride, the groom's party has to dance and sing to the satisfaction of the bride's family before they are invited in. Naturally, this is a moment of great festivity and merrymaking. Once welcomed inside the homestead, the groom's party presents the wife's family with the gifts they have brought. Members of the bride's family may engage in a ritual in which they carefully examine each item, commenting on its beauty, quality, and value. Among the Ovambo, although members of the same matriline should not marry, the ideal marriage is a union within one's subgroup but out of the clan. Cross-cousin marriage (i.e., to the daughter or son of a paternal aunt) remains popular, but not all Ovambo groups allow this, because some Ovambos classify such cousins as siblings. The Herero also prefer cross-cousin marriage.[7] At the conclusion of the Herero wedding, the new bride may remain in seclusion for a period of three days (or longer, if the family can afford it); during this time she does no household chores and is fed and cared for by her husband's family. While some see this ritual as confining, others see it as a welcome opportunity to rest and be pampered. Nowadays, when many have salaried jobs that make it impractical or impossible to do this ritual is often not observed at all. Among the Damara/Nama, the husband's people present a gift of cattle (*aba gomas*) to the wife or female guardian of the bride. This gift is sometimes described as *lobola*, many reserving the term *lobola* only for the gifting of cattle or money, although in the past, and now, the gifts could be items such as hoes and cloth. Among some communities in the past, the prospective groom had to perform services for his future mother-in-law; nowadays, this practice has been replaced by the gift of money. There is a wide misconception that the exchange of gifts (especially in the form of cattle or money) is an indication that women were seen as commodities and thus a man purchases a wife. This was certainly not the case in the past because societies distinguished between wives and slaves; nevertheless, the system is clearly one that is open to manipulation by elders. Today, some couples choose to exchange only symbolic, rather than expensive, gifts.

If the traditional marriage is a stand-alone affair, then it may be preceded or followed by a church wedding, after which there is a reception, usually in a hall. At the reception hall, there is further music and dancing; there are also numerous speeches and a master of ceremonies to keep the event proceeding according to plan. The newlyweds sit at a "high table" with a few honored guests and family members. There might be a band or simply a deejay; a cultural dance troupe might perform to entertain the guests. The grandeur of the reception is determined, not surprisingly, by the family's economic situation. Some weddings are extremely opulent, with feasting for days, hired limousines to ferry the bride and groom, and imported flowers at the reception. Such weddings are, of course, in the extreme minority. With the increasing influence of Pentecostal churches, it is no surprise that some weddings do not include any alcohol, which is shunned by many Pentecostals.

Marriage is considered an essential rite of passage into adulthood, for both men and women. For Ovambo women, in the past, the *ohango* ritual was performed to mark the transition into maturity and signal a girl's readiness for marriage. A girl who had not performed the ohango ritual could not marry and was deemed not yet ready for parenthood. Ideally, the ohango was performed about the time a girl reached puberty, but families could choose or prefer to delay for any number of reasons, including financial. Getting pregnant before one had performed the ohango was a crime of enormous proportions; indeed, some contemporaries claim that in the old days the punishment for both the girl and the man involved was to be burned alive for their transgression. Nowadays, the ohango ritual marks the transition into married life, and the term *ohango* is typically translated as "traditional marriage." One effect of this linguistic choice is that the changes that the ritual has undergone over time are obscured, and ohango is seen as fixed and ahistorical. The evolution of the ohango ritual points to an important facet of all cultural practices—their dynamism—one that is often overlooked in discussions of African communities and their cultural practices.

If they are able, a couple may decide to establish their own individual compound. In the old days, patrilocal residence was widely practiced, with wives moving into the household of their husband's family. This was not universally the case; sometimes husbands and wives set up a separate residence, or the wife lived with her own family, or (as with the Damara in former times) the couple established residence matrilocally. In a matrilineal community, the husband and his family may be happy to have the wife (especially if she has children) live with her own family as it reduces the burden on their own resources. A wife typically has her own dwelling and lives with her children; she is, in the words of Felicia Ekejiuba, in charge of her "hearthhold."[8] At adolescence boys and girls may move out and live in a communal setting with their same-sex peers. In matrilineal societies, a wife retains membership in her own lineage, as do her children, and the children are supposed to inherit from their maternal uncle; however, while they are living, fathers may bestow property on their children. Nowadays, matrilineal principles are often not observed, especially in families that live as a nuclear unit in the capital or other urban settings.

Women often find that they are prevented from inheriting property from parents and spouses, making them especially vulnerable in the event of the death of loved ones.[9] Many women's groups focus particular attention on the plight of widows. Some widows are provided land and other property; however, there have been instances where the widow is forced to move out of her home and is left landless. Some point to the levirate (or "widow inheritance") as a system designed to offer protection to widows. The Ovambo, Herero, and SiLozi-speaking groups in the Caprivi Strip practice the levirate and the sororate ("widower inheritance"), but the practice is far from universal and it is difficult to know the percentage of widows involved.

Matters related to marriage, divorce, and inheritance are governed by two distinct sets of legal codes, civil and customary. The result is that the two systems often clash. There is only one civil law, but there are different customary systems, depending on the ethnic community. For instance, inheritance is affected by whether the community is patrilineal or matrilineal. Namibia has one of the lowest incidents of civil divorce, no doubt due in large part to the fact that couples are not allowed to divorce simply because of irreconcilable differences. For a civil divorce to be granted, one party must be at fault. Not surprisingly, this has produced a number of high-profile divorces in which the parties exchanged unflattering accusations, eagerly recounted in the tabloid media. The High Court in Windhoek is the only court in all of Namibia that may dissolve a civil marriage. Under the customary system, spouses may dissolve their marriage in consultation with their family (who also played an important role in the marriage) or by application to chiefly authorities. Reasons for divorce typically have to do with neglect of the children, antisocial behavior, adultery, or the husband's marriage of a second wife without the first wife's consent.

Under civil regulations, the costs of child care are supposed to be shared by both parents in cases of divorce. This is according to the Maintenance Act of 2003. The act made the civil authorities responsible for locating parents and determining their assets. According to many mothers, who are typically the custodial parents, some fathers meet their obligations only in part or not at all. In July 2004, women in Swakopmund organized a demonstration to voice their discontent over the court's handling of maintenance payments. Children born outside legally sanctioned marriages have, by law, the same rights as children born of a civil marriage in the event of a separation. Since a significant number of Namibian couples, especially in urban areas, do not perform any sort of marriage, a notable number of children are born out of wedlock, so the Child Status Bill is a significant landmark.

DOMESTIC VIOLENCE

The Combating of Domestic Violence Act, a landmark, was passed in 2003. Apart from provisions in the constitution guaranteeing equality before the law, the government has created specific offices to handle women's issues and matters to do with gender. There is a Ministry of Gender Equality and Child Welfare; there are also offices in other departments that deal with women and gender, such as the Woman and Child Protection Unit in the

Police Department. However, no matter how good a piece of legislation, if it is not implemented, or cannot be implemented, it has no practical value. With regard to public life, it is easy to assess the impact of laws that address gender equality. Many women's groups are particularly interested in seeking ways to address, as well as improve, the quality of women's private lives. Domestic violence is one aspect of women's private lives about which politicians, women's groups, church leaders, and civil society groups express great concern.

Activists and women politicians point to the incidence of rape in Namibia and insist there is a crisis that requires urgent action. For the two years 2006 and 2007, there were almost 1,000 reports of rape each year. Many complain that despite legislation protecting women, the government has not done enough to address the problem of domestic violence. One male letter writer to the *Namibian* hoped to see "a day when NO government will think it acceptable to send rapists to prison for 10 years, while someone caught stealing some goats or smoking cannabis can be locked up for 20 years or more."[10] In 1998, Namibians all over the country were shocked by the heinous murder of a young Swakopmunder, Monika Florin, by her husband. Hundreds of women marched, in a multiethnic show of solidarity, through the streets of Swakopmund to honor the murdered woman and demand greater protection for women from domestic violence. A reporter for the *Namibian* newspaper described the march as a "an unprecedented show of sisterhood at the coast."[11]

While the almost-total absence of men from the Swakopmund demonstration may be startling, around the world the fight to end gender discrimination tends to be exclusively or overwhelmingly female. Yet there are in Namibia some exclusively male feminist groups such as the National Organisation for Men against Sexism. Namibia has a branch of the White Ribbon Campaign, an international organization that claims to be the largest antisexist male group in the world.

Domestic violence is a concern among all groups of women, including the San, who have a reputation for greater gender equity than other communities. Richard Lee's *The !Kung San,* L. Marshall's *The !Kung of Nyae Nyae,* and Majorie Shostak's 1981 classic *Nisa: The Life and Words of a !Kung Woman* are the best-known works on the San. These authors essentially concur with anthropologist Eleanor Leacock's argument that women in gathering and hunting societies have greater equality than women in agricultural, pastoral, and industrial societies.[12] There is serious debate about how gathering and hunting societies have been studied and the conclusions that have been drawn about them. Whatever San women's social position in the past, in modern Namibia, although the San are extremely marginalized, their lives, like those of other communities, are largely shaped by the social and economic realities of today as well as policies being put into place by local and national governments.

Despite SWAPO and President Sam Nujoma's much-touted insistence on the need for gender equality, women activists in Namibia continue to decry the situation of women and to agitate for further changes to bring about real transformation. In 2008 the Women's Actions for Development (WAD), the University of Namibia, and the Namibia Prison Service published a report, "Understanding the Perpetrators of Violent Crimes against Women and Girls in Namibia." The study found that "cultural factors, alcohol consumption, low levels of education, lack of employment, socio-economic marginalization, broken family systems, and poor socialisation" were factors in domestic violence.[13] They found that most respondents were unaware of the new rape act contained in the constitution that made it a criminal offence to have sex with a wife or partner against her will. Individual women and women's groups continue to fight for greater gender equality.

SEXUAL ORIENTATION

Homosexuality was declared illegal by the Combating of Immoral Practices Act 21 of 1980. On the question of homosexuality, as with abortion and prostitution, neotraditionalists and church leaders find themselves in agreement. On more than one occasion, Sam Nujoma, leader of SWAPO and first president of Namibia, publicly declared homosexuality "un-African." Politicians and church leaders who decry homosexuality as un-African apparently do not acknowledge the irony in their selective insistence on African authenticity. In 2000 the Minister of Home Affairs, Jerry Ekandjo, declared that "we never had moffies [a derogatory term for homosexuals] in mind when SWAPO drafted the Namibian Constitution ten years ago."[14]

Despite the extreme homophobic vitriol emanating from the political leadership in Namibia, some brave activists have challenged such hate-mongering. These include Elizabeth !Khaxas and Liz Frank, who have headed the Namibian feminist group Sister Namibia, and Ian Swartz, head of the Rainbow Project (TRP). In 2001 hundreds of Namibians took part in a demonstration in support of homosexuals following more incendiary remarks by President Nujoma. The president had given a speech at the University of Namibia in which he declared, "The Republic of Namibia does not allow homosexuality, lesbianism here. Police are ordered to arrest you, and deport you and imprison you too."[15] In that same year, foreign-born Elizabeth Frank, a well-known lesbian activist, was granted permanent residence in Namibia. In 1998 Frank had taken her battle to secure residence on the basis of her same-sex relationship with a Namibian national all the way to the High Court.

The donkey cart is a typical mode of transport for many among Namibia's rural Damara people. (Dr. Fatima Mueller-Friedman)

The High Court decided in Frank's favor, but that decision was overturned by the Supreme Court on appeal from the Immigration Selection Board. In 2001, Frank's application for residence was approved on the basis of her two decades of anti-apartheid and education activism.

!Khaxas, a Damara woman who is openly lesbian and a well-known Namibian feminist, insists that "many women in same-sex relationships among the Damara live their lives more openly than women of other ethnic groups in Namibia" because "Damara culture still has remnants of traditional values such as egalitarianism and peace."[16] In the past, the Damara were gatherer-hunters and pastoralists, living in small bands of a few dozen people or so; residence was matrilocal, with men, who were the hunters and caretakers of the cattle, staying in homes built and owned by the women only occasionally, and it is believed that polygyny was not practiced. Today, in postcolonial Namibia with its exceedingly high unemployment rate, most Damara work on farms owned by others or are unemployed.

HIV AND AIDS

AIDS and HIV have hit southern Africa particularly hard, and the rates of HIV and AIDS in Namibia are among the highest in the world. Often, non-governmental organizations based in the global north seek to combat AIDS by implementing policies aimed at educating the populace, especially in the rural areas. In an illuminating study, Ida Susser and Richard Lee demonstrate that in fact what ordinary people knew often outstripped statements issued by the local political and religious authorities. In interviews with rural women in Ovambo communities in northern Namibia, Susser found that both women and men knew about AIDS, feared it, and sought out biomedical treatment when they got sick. At the same time, local church authorities were insisting that people didn't really believe AIDS was a disease. In extensive interviews in rural communities in 1996, the researchers found that people "knew about AIDS" and "were not dying in ignorance."[17] They contrasted this reality with continuing attempts to eradicate or reduce AIDS in such places by focusing on the need to educate. The authors also did not find secrecy surrounding AIDS, as is widely reported in the Western media. In recent years local news media have published accounts about prominent Namibians afflicted with AIDS, so although having AIDS is not yet entirely stigma-free, enormous progress has been made in this regard.

Susser and Lee found that while ordinary people were aware of AIDS and sought access to condoms, including female condoms, as a means to protect themselves, often church authorities were reluctant to distribute or encourage the use of condoms as they argued condom use was counter to Christian moral ethics. The biggest hindrance to effectively addressing the challenge posed by HIV/AIDS is probably the government's insistence on blaming HIV/AIDS on homosexuality and claiming that homosexuality is un-African and has been introduced into Africa by foreigners.

With regard to knowledge about AIDS and HIV, researchers also found that even the extremely marginalized San, often squatting in public areas, know about AIDS and how it is transmitted. And, interestingly, unlike the Ovambo women interviewed by Susser and Lee, San women were willing to use condoms if they could get access to them. While the Ovambo women who were interviewed preferred the female condom because it was less dependent on the man's participation, San women indicated no reluctance to ask their male partners to use a male condom. However, there is also alarming data with regard to knowledge about HIV/AIDS treatment. Robert Lorway (2007), who has spent a lot of time researching same-sex practices in Windhoek, found that men who sleep with men often have the mistaken idea that heterosexual sex is risky while homosexual sex is less dangerous.

In light of the AIDS pandemic, which continues to exact a severe toll, sexual relations outside of marriage are receiving especial attention. Activists, journalists, and community leaders all express alarm at the apparent rise of the "sugar daddy" and "sugar mummy" phenomenon. Some HIV/AIDS activists point to polygyny as a practice that contributes to the spread of the virus. However, it remains to be seen whether targeting polygyny is a tactic that can be effective in the fight against HIV/AIDS. For some African neotraditionalists, polygyny is an integral part of their cultural tradition and thus nonnegotiable.

Many African men—and their critics—point to polygyny as license (or reason) for Namibian men to have multiple sexual partners. However, this claim rarely receives serious scrutiny. Polygyny, found widely throughout Africa, does not justify promiscuity. One aspect of polygyny that is rarely discussed is that, typically, in the past sexual intercourse was not supposed to take place outside of marriage, whether the marriage was monogamous or polygynous. Yet, today, supporters and critics of polygyny point glibly to the practice as one that encourages promiscuity. The real issue is that men pick and choose from tradition as it suits their purposes.

Numerous organizations have sprung up to address various aspects of the AIDS epidemic. Some are small and local, with a limited focus, such as trying to alleviate the plight of AIDS orphans or AIDS sufferers in their immediate community; other organizations are national in scope. !Khaxas, who has worked with Sister Namibia, founded the Women's Leadership Centre, whose mission statement calls for it to focus its energies on ways to address HIV and AIDS that engage sufficiently with the cultural practices and values of the communities themselves. The Women's Leadership Centre organizes writing workshops and promotes women's writing, arguing that women can use writing as a form of resistance and self-determination. In 2007, !Khaxas, Frank, and A. Rimmer edited a pamphlet entitled "We Women and Girls of Namibia Claim Our Right to Survive HIV and AIDS by Challenging Poverty, Oppression, Cultural Practices and Violence."[18]

It is interesting to note that researchers have found that some men now believe that the criminal justice system is biased in favor of women, charging that the pendulum has swung too far and that there is too much focus on women's rights and women's issues. Comments attesting to this position can be found also in the print media and online discussion groups. Some men claim that the laws regulating marriage and divorce discriminate against men. In 2004, Namibian Women's Day was celebrated for the first time ever (December 10).[19] Male critics complained that there was no equivalent, Namibian Men's Day.

It will be interesting to see how a country such as Namibia, which has been independent for only two decades and has come out of decades of a harrowing racist apartheid rule, navigates the future, especially with regard to issues of gender and gender equity. On the one hand, the government has passed legislation outlawing discrimination on the basis of sex, giving Namibians a constitution that is recognized as one of the most advanced in the world. Yet the realities of Namibian women's lives continue to be shaped by long years of social, political, and economic injustice.

Notes

1. Martin Chanock has written about the manufacture of customary law under European colonial rule. See Chanock, "Making Customary Law: Men, Women and the Courts in Colonial Rhodesia," in *African Women and the Law: Historical Perspectives,* ed. Margaret J. Hay and Marcia Wright (Boston: African Studies Center, Boston University, 1982). For the invisibility of women in the ethnography and archives of colonial South West Africa, see Patricia Hayes, "'Cocky' Hahn and the 'Black Venus': The Making of a Native Commissioner in South West Africa, 1915–1946," in *Gendered Colonialisms in African History,* ed. Nancy Rose Hunt, Tessie P. Liu and Jean Quataert (London: Blackwell, 1997).

2. These UNFPA figures are taken from Panduleni Hailonga-van Dijk, "Adolescent Sexuality: Negotiating between Tradition and Modernity," in *Unravelling Taboos: Gender and Sexuality in Namibia,* ed. Suzanne Lafont and Dianne Hubbard (Windhoek, Namibia: Legal Assistance Center, 2007), pp. 131 and 133.

3. Some scholars reject the notion that in the past Namibian women could access land only through a male relative, maintaining that women had access to communal land on their own account.

4. Namdeb is jointly owned by the Republic of Namibia and diamond giant De Beers.

5. While it is possible to have only a traditional marriage or only a civil marriage, most church authorities insist that a couple married in church marriage must also sign a civil union.

6. Couples may sign a prenuptial agreement, which essentially provides them an opt-out from the community of property. This is rare, practiced by a small minority of the economic elite.

7. Consanguinity functions differently in matrilineal and patrilineal systems. In the United States, for example, the children of a brother and a sister are first cousins, thus close kin and intermarriage in such a case is taboo. In a matrilineal system, the children of a sister and a brother belong to entirely different kin groups.

8. Felicia I. Ekejiuba, "Down to Fundamentals: Women-Centred Hearthholds in Rural West Africa," in *Readings in Gender in Africa,* ed. Andrea Cornwall (Boulder, CO: Westview Press, 1995).

9. This is, of course, a topic novelist Neshani Andreas tackles in her first novel, *The Purple Violet of Oshaantu* (Oxford: Heinemann, 2001).

10. Letters to the Editor, Hugh Ellis, Windhoek, "Gender Issues and Mungunda," *The Namibian,* March 4, 2007.

11. Elizabeth !Khaxas and Saskia Wieringa, "Same-Sex Sexuality among Damara Women," in Lafont and Hubbard, *Unravelling Taboos,* p. 312.

12. Eleanor Burke Leacock, *Myths of Male Dominance* (New York: Monthly Review Press), 1981.

13. "Understanding the Perpetrators of Violent Crimes against Women and Girls in Namibia; Implications for Prevention and Treatment," Windhoek, Namibia, 2008. Available from the Konrad Adenauer Foundation, Windhoek.

14. Max Hamata, "Namibian Minister Elaborates on Anti-gay Stance," *The Namibian,* November 3, 2000.

15. These statements were widely reported in *The Namibian* and some international media at the time. See the coverage in *The Namibian* of March 20, 2001; also Nangula Shejavali, "Political Parties Ponder Homosexuality," *The Namibian,* November 2, 2009.

16. Elizabeth !Khaxas and Saskia Wieringa, "Same-Sex Sexuality Among Damara Women," in Lafont and Hubbard, *Unravelling Taboos,* pp. 296 and 312.

17. Ida Susser and Richard Lee, "Confounding Conventional Wisdom: The Ju'/hoansi and HIV/AIDS," in *Updating the San: Image and Reality of an African People in the 21st Century,* ed. R. Hitchcock. Osaka, Japan: National Museum of Ethnology, 2007.

18. The booklet was published by the Women's Leadership Centre, based in Windhoek.

19. Namibian Women's Day has not become a major national holiday.

7

Social Customs and Lifestyle

GENERALLY SPEAKING, NAMIBIANS are incredibly hospitable, and individuals readily go out of their way to help strangers or persons in difficulty. Polite behavior is highly valued, and those in the service industry treat customers with courtesy. Respect for elders is a universal trait shared by all Namibian communities, even as many complain that things are no longer as they used to be in the old days with regard to relations between the youth and their elders. Even in the workplace younger colleagues are likely to address older colleagues with honorifics such as *meme* or *madam* and not the elder colleague's first name.

Family and community are important in the life of most individuals, and festivities often involve family and extended kin, for example, at major moments such as marriage, birth, and death. Weddings and funerals bring together family and friends from different age and income brackets. Other social gatherings, however, may be much more restricted in terms of age or socioeconomic background, or both. Urban nightlife is one place where segregation on the basis of age and socioeconomic status is common, with some bars, clubs, lounges, and shebeens catering to a younger clientele and others to more mature patrons. Of course, some establishments attract a broad spectrum.

Daily life varies greatly depending on ethnic identity, religious affiliation, geographic location, and class. There is a great discrepancy between the lives of the vast majority and those of the small affluent minority. Slightly more than

Children playing billiards, Soweto Market, Katutura. (Courtesy of Anene Ejikeme)

half of all Namibians live in rural areas; in rural communities families farm and maintain livestock as well as small animals, such as chickens. Fetching water is a part of daily life in Namibia for a great many, even, for example, schoolchildren at boarding schools. For those who depend on water to grow crops or for their animals, fetching water may become a central focus of daily life. Rural communities cultivate maize, sorghum, beans, pumpkins, millet, peanuts, and yams. Fruits such as the *marula* and Nara melon are gathered. Many plants have multiple uses; an excellent example is the palm tree, which provides fluid, food, and resources for building homes and making mats and baskets.

Cattle are important for most Namibians, especially the Ovambo, Himba, and Herero. Cattle are signs of wealth and status. Cattle provide food (in the form of milk especially, and meat occasionally) and clothing, as well as serving as a form of currency. Often, various rituals surround the treatment of cattle. For example, the slaughter of cattle is typically done following certain rules that have become hallowed as tradition. Those who have a tradition of cattle rearing tend to have rituals associated with cattle. For example, the Herero headdress is designed to recall the horns of cattle, and among the Himba, some families continue the practice of the father handing his eldest son the ear from a special cow at his naming ceremony. Cattle herding is done by men and boys, while women grow crops and tend to the care of the home. In cattle-rearing communities, young boys are typically in charge of the cattle, while girls assist with chores closer to home. The boys must not only find adequate water and pasturage for the herds but also protect their animals from predators. Girls and women fetch water and cook and cultivate food, for their family use as well as for sale. Farming, raising cattle, and housekeeping all are time-consuming, especially if there are no modern gadgets to assist in the work. The plants must be adequately irrigated, and cooking food typically includes winnowing grain and pounding it into a flour before it can be cooked.[1]

For the urban poor, life means a high probability of unemployment. A large segment of those in urban areas must earn a living in the informal sector; thus, hawking is a common activity, one that does not necessarily require significant capital. Those with relatively little capital may be able to start a business for themselves, such as head dressing, tailoring, or selling cooked food from a kiosk. A very small percentage of Namibians maintain a pastoral way of life, moving with their animals according to the seasons and environmental conditions. Although the San make up a very small percentage of the total population of Namibia, literature on life in Namibia often focuses disproportionately on this community. Moreover, this literature often speaks of the San and their traditional practices as if the majority of San today live as gatherer-hunters. The ability of contemporary San to follow a gatherer-hunter lifestyle is extremely curtailed as many of the lands over which the San moved in the past have been declared national parks, or they are claimed by other ethnic communities. Some San enter into client-patron relations with Hereros and others or engage in contract labor. Contract and migrant labor remain important throughout Namibia: Landless black Namibians work for white farm owners, who produce the bulk of the food grown in Namibia.[2]

CEREMONIES

All societies perform certain rites and rituals to mark important rites of passage in the life of an individual. These include weddings and naming ceremonies. The need to register the birth of children is shaping naming practices: When a naming ceremony is held, the newborn most likely has at least one name already (the name on the birth certificate); it is becoming rarer to find a newborn who is not given a name immediately at birth, and indeed naming ceremonies are becoming less common. Indigenous Namibian names usually refer either to a significant event or to a physical location associated with the birth of a child. For example, among the Ovambo one may meet someone named Natangwe, which means "Praise God," perhaps a reference to a change for the better in the circumstances of the family or simply a declaration of faith. In the early colonial period, Namibians who wished to have their children christened were not allowed to use African names but had to choose a "Christian" (i.e., European) name such as Paulus or Frieda. Even today, many Namibians have at least two names, an indigenous one and a European one, and individuals sometimes choose to use different names depending on the setting; for example, an indigenous name may be used only by family members, while at school or work and with friends and colleagues the baptismal name is used. Today, some parents choose to baptize their children in church with indigenous names, but European names continue to be common. Initiation rites recognizing the transition from youth to adulthood may be performed, but not all Namibian communities engage in these rites for young persons, and even among those who do so nominally, not all members of the community do so. Historical accounts indicate that male circumcision was more widespread in the past, being widely practiced in Ovambo kingdoms of old, for example; at the present time, circumcision is most often associated with the Herero and Himba. However, because of recent medical indications that circumcision can be a powerful tool in the fight against HIV/AIDS, there are attempts to introduce (or reintroduce) circumcision all over the country.

Funerals and marriages are important occasions at which family members, often dispersed throughout the country and even overseas, gather. Among the Herero, who combine bilateral descent with patrilocal residence, it is at such moments that the members of an *eanda* (matrilineal group) typically attend to the functions of their group, which focus on issues of property and inheritance. Deaths are announced on the radio, a way to circulate the news widely and quickly. Most funerals start with a church service, ending with the burial; other ceremonies depend on the deceased's stature and ethnic group. Namibians are buried in their homesteads, in family burial plots, or in cemeteries owned and maintained by municipal or clerical authorities. As in many places around the world, local authorities in a number of towns in Namibia are concerned because cemeteries are either full to capacity or rapidly about to become so; the Windhoek municipal authorities are promoting cremations as an alternative that is also more affordable, but so far their efforts have not been very successful. The costs of burial include not only the plot but also the coffin itself, each of which typically costs more than the average worker's monthly salary. Whether the body is cremated or buried, costs associated with funerals include providing refreshments for mourners.

FESTIVALS AND HOLIDAYS

As well as ceremonies to mark key moments in the life of an individual, communities also hold celebrations to mark significant occasions on the community's calendar. In agricultural communities, for example, festivals are often associated with harvesting or planting. Such festivals involve the entire community, and family members who live elsewhere may travel to their hometowns for such annual festivities. Festivals also commemorate great moments in history, for example, victory in war or abundant rainfall. Festivals include music and dancing. Some dances may be associated exclusively with certain festivals and thus are performed and seen only occasionally. Dancers wear special costumes, which may include rattles and other acoustic elements, and are accompanied by musicians, who also may be wearing clothes designed for the occasion. The performers may wear painted body art.

Installations or funerals of chiefs and other important persons are major community events.[3] Funerals are important because death is an important moment of transition, significant for the deceased as well as the living, and disputes by family—or even community—members over the deceased's status may delay a funeral, sometimes for a significant length of time. In late 2010, for example, two brothers, including one who was the Deputy Minister of Fisheries and Marine Resources, took their fight over where their deceased uncle, a chief, should be buried all the way to the High Court in Windhoek. This community-wide dispute was related to disagreements about succession; the site of a person's grave, the nature of the funeral, and the role each participant plays are all important opportunities to make statements about who the deceased was in life, and they lay the groundwork for claims that may be made by his or her descendants about their own lives.[4]

One of the most colorful annual events in Namibia is the Maharero Day festivities in Okahandja, held on the Sunday closest to August 23, the date that in 1923 marked the start of the three-day funeral at which the remains of Chief Samuel Maharero were reburied in Okahandja alongside the graves of other Namibian national heroes. Although Maharero died in exile in Botswana, he was brought back with great pomp and circumstance to Namibia and given a grand burial. In addition to Chief Maharero, Maharero Day memorializes several other heroes who fought for independence.

Maharero Day is a spectacular day of commemoration, with processions of colorfully dressed women and men, the colors worn by each group indicating the branch of the Herero community to which they belong (Red Flag Herero, White Flag Herero, and Green Flag Herero). The women wear the Herero national dress, which is a floor-length gown worn over layers of petticoats that give the skirt its iconic full character, completed by a double-pointed headdress and shawl. Regiments of men on horseback in military uniform march in procession. Some regiments march on foot, as do the women. Troops of Boy Scouts, Girl Guides, and other organizations, all in their formal uniforms, take part in the parades. The procession makes stops at the burial sites of Maharero, his father, and his grandfather as well as the Nama leader Jonker Afrikaner and the Rhenish Mission Church. Performances reenacting events of the past, the recitation of poems recalling fallen heroes, cultural dances, and speeches are all part of the festivities. Some of the speeches function as history lessons, while others are best described as motivational and self-help in nature, exhorting the community to undertake projects to better the lives of individuals and the group. Over the years, such speeches have addressed everything from the rape of young girls to the need to uphold the practice of respect for elders.

Maharero is not the only one honored with a day of remembrance; there are other days to celebrate other leaders who fought against colonialism. For example, the life of the Nama chief Hendrik Witbooi, whose face appears on Namibian paper currency and who died in October 1905 fighting against German troops, is celebrated in October. The biggest Heroes' Day celebration is the national day of remembrance held every August 26th, which thus always falls on or very near Maharero day. Heroes' Day is a day of commemorative events around the country to remember those who fought against colonialism. Heroes' Day has multiple roots. It was originally the day when Hereros visited the graves of their chiefs to remember them and the devastation of 1904–1908. August 26, 1966, is also considered the official start of the armed struggle against South African rule. The largest Heroes' Day celebration of all is in the capital at Heroes' Acre, an imposing complex that was completed and dedicated in 2002. An almost 100-foot marble obelisk, in front of which stands a bronze statue of the Unknown Soldier, built by a North Korean company, dominates the Heroes' Acre complex. The Heroes' Acre monument remains controversial, with opponents charging that the statue glorifies only the role of the South West Africa People's Organisation (SWAPO) in the liberation struggle, ignoring other voices who also fought for freedom from colonial occupation. Critics charge that Heroes' Day has become hijacked by the ruling SWAPO party, taken as an opportunity to praise its members and allies, an effort to consolidate its hegemony, Others complain that young people—many of them born-frees, who have no first-hand experience with South African occupation—do not feel adequate reverence for the sacrifices made by those who fought for independence.

Christmas

Christmas is a major annual holiday in this overwhelmingly Christian country. With families typically scattered all around the country, many make a huge effort to return to their natal home for the holidays. Many Namibians who live overseas return home for the holidays. Friends and relatives who perhaps have not seen one another since the previous year, or longer, reunite.

As well as organized parties, there are also a great deal of unannounced visits to the homes of friends and relatives.

Some Namibians prefer to travel to the coast where temperatures are cooler for the Christmas and New Year holiday season, which occurs at the height of the Namibian summer. The resort towns of Swakopmund, Walvis Bay, and Henties Bay see their populations explode for the two-week holiday period between Christmas and the New Year, much to the chagrin of many residents, who complain about the traffic jams, noise, and long lines at supermarkets and shops. Rundu in the northeast seems keen to attract some of its own seasonal holidaymakers: In December 2010 many out-of-towners welcomed the New Year at a music concert and party extravaganza at Rundu Beach, organized by the town council.

With so many residents traveling home for the holidays to be with their extended families or escaping to cooler climes, the country's major arteries experience tremendous traffic jams during this period. Most people travel by road, in private cars, shared taxis, or buses, so the roads leading out of Windhoek, where more than 10 percent of the country's total population lives, become especially congested. Given the demographic makeup of the country, it should come as no surprise that the roads leading to northern Namibia are particularly clogged; northern towns such as Oshakati, Rundu, Grootfontein, and Tsumeb become centers of much hustle and bustle during the holiday season as people stop en route to their final destinations to make last-minute purchases or return to town for an occasional urban interlude.

Because of the volume of travel during the Christmas holidays, traffic checkpoints are set up by the police along all the major highways, and drivers must stop to have their licenses and their car safety stickers checked. It is illegal at any time of the year not to wear a seatbelt or not to have one's license and inspection stickers; during the Christmas holidays, fines are sometimes increased, more checkpoints are set up, and more police are put to work. Public service announcements on the radio remind drivers of the need to be extra cautious.

It is customary for salaried workers to receive a bonus with their pay in December, a Christmas bonus; even casual workers often get a bonus at this time from employers or clients, so those workers who do not receive a bonus can, understandably, be bitter. Although some do exchange gifts at Christmas, this practice is not commonplace everywhere, and children are more likely than adults to receive gifts. Families of German descent maintain a tradition of a German-style Christmas, complete with presents as well as special Christmas cookies, St. Nicholas (Santa Claus), and carol singing. For all Namibians, buying foods, decorating the home, and cooking are the major activities leading up to the big day. Small retail stores in provincial towns enjoy brisk sales at this time, provisioning travelers who stock up on food and supplies en route to their rural homesteads. Naturally, braai-ing (barbecuing) is a big part of the festivities for many people, and most people usually purchase a variety of meats, with whole goats being popular. Much of the partying is usually done outdoors, with festivities beginning on Christmas Eve and continuing through to the next day.

Although Windhoek is abandoned by many of its residents for the holidays, those who must remain, or those who choose to, at least get to enjoy whatever decorations and lights might festoon the downtown. Most businesses are closed, and even the government newspaper ceases publication. However, there is still fun to be had as those who remain behind throw house parties that last into the early hours of the morning. Festivities continue on the day after Christmas, Family Day. This is a public holiday, and many go to church to mark the day; visits to and from friends and family continue. New Year's Day is a public holiday. On New Year's Eve, family and friends celebrate with braais, dancing, drinking, and lots of eating.

Other public holidays include Labor Day (May 1) and Human Rights Day (December 10), both internationally recognized; Africa Day (May 25), and Cassinga Day[5] (May 4) are holidays that are celebrated continentally and nationally respectively. At least officially, the most important national holiday is, of course, Independence Day, March 21. Independence Day is marked by speeches, marches, parades, and musical and dance performances organized by the state. Businesses, private individuals, and centers of culture such as galleries and museums also organize exhibitions, special events, and parties to coincide with Independence Day celebrations.

Regional Festivals

Each of the 13 regions of Namibia hosts an annual festival that highlights aspects of its community, cultures, or history. For example, Tsumeb hosts an annual Copper Festival, the main aim of which is to stimulate the local economy and advertise the copper industry. From modest beginnings, the festival has grown to become an important community festival promoting local music and cultures as well as showcasing some foreign talent. The festival kicks off with a procession of floats down Tsumeb's main street. There are all kinds of other attractions, from the crowning of a Mr. and Mrs. Copper to bicycle races for all age groups.

The three-day annual /Aa//Gams Festival of Arts and Culture, which is held in Windhoek in September, is international in scope, bringing acts from all over the continent as well as local talent. It is a major event, with dance and musical groups from Namibia and overseas, Namibian foods, and arts of all kinds. /AA//Gams, which means "hot springs," is the Nama name for

Windhoek. Events take place in venues throughout the city, from Katutura to City Centre. This festival was started in 2000, 10 years after independence, as a means to promote Namibian artists and culture. There are other, older festivals in Windhoek, such as the annual Ocktoberfest in October, and the Windhoek Karnivale (better known as WIKA) earlier in the year, in late March or early April, another tradition originated by German immigrants. The highlight of this carnival is a masked ball at night. Swakopmund holds its own Oktoberfest as well as an annual carnival of its own, Küste Karnival, better known as Küska (usually in June). WIKA and Kuska continue to be affairs that have greatest participation by German Namibians, but schoolchildren of all ethnicities look forward to the candies tossed out to onlookers by the revelers who take part in the parades. Carnivals in Namibia, as elsewhere, give individuals an opportunity to leave behind the mundane parameters of their daily life and to dress up and engage in behavior that is quite literally out of the ordinary. Parties, drinking, food stalls, and children's activities are all part of the merriment.

Apart from the community, regional, and national festivals, there are others, such as the biennale sponsored by the Bank of Namibia and a number of film festivals, music award shows, or competitions sponsored by different organizations.

AMUSEMENTS AND SPORTS

Adolescents in town often complain of boredom and the absence of places of amusement, but those who live in Windhoek have possibilities available to them that those in rural communities do not have, such as shopping malls and movie theaters. Those too young to go to nightclubs and bars—and who have accommodating parents—hold houseparties (Houseparties are not, of course, the exclusive preserve of youth.) Having a boyfriend or girlfriend is normal, although many girls and women report that men do not invest significant energy in their amorous relationships as they are more career and job oriented. Many young men concur that they feel great pressure to get their work life in order before they can focus on a serious relationship.[6] There are relatively few movie theaters in Namibia as a whole, and even those who live in town are more likely to watch films on video. Hollywood films are popular, as are South African films and films from Nigeria's Nollywood, now the world's third-largest movie producer. In Windhoek, there is a multiplex at Maruea Mall. Films are also screened regularly at the Franco-Namibian Cultural Center, and other sites such as the National Theatre and the Goethe Centre.

In the larger towns such as Oshakati, Rundu, Oshikango, Swakopmund, and Walvis Bay, visitors and residents have a selection—albeit limited in comparison with the capital—of nightlife to choose from, including night-clubs, shebeens, bars, and restaurants. Some bars, lounges, and clubs cater to a very exclusive clientele or acquire a reputation for attracting only certain kinds of individuals or couples. Cafés tend to be the domain of German and Afrikaner Namibians, as black Namibians patronize these establishments a great deal less. The suburb of Katutura is the most vibrant part of Wind-hoek at night, and in the evenings, white residents and tourists, rare sights in Katutura during the day, can be seen partying inside some of Katutura's popular nightclubs. Of course, there are clubs, lounges, and bars in other parts of town as well. In Swakopmund, located just beside the desert, every year young people ring in the New Year on the dunes, drinking and mer-rymaking all through the night. Although Swakopmund has several cultural and arts venues, such as the impressive Krystal Galerie with its huge collec-tion of crystals and gemstones, Windhoek is the heart of the country in terms of entertainment and leisure-time opportunities.

Sports are popular in Namibia. Sprinter Frankie Fredericks is the most fa-mous Namibian athlete. In 1991, just one year after independence and with Namibia's newly minted certification to participate in international sport-ing events, Fredericks won a silver medal at the World Championships in Athletics held in Tokyo, Japan. In 1992 and 1996 he won two silver medals (in the 100 meters and 200 meters) at both the Barcelona and the Atlanta Olympics. His 1992 win made him the first Namibian ever to win an Olym-pic medal. Fredericks continued to win medals until his retirement in 2004. Fredericks remains a revered figure in Namibia today, and the image of Fred-ericks taking a victory lap with the Namibian flag held high above his head in 1992 remains cherished. In 2008, Fredericks was elected president of the International Olympic Committee (IOC) Athletics Commission.

Soccer (generally known as football in Namibia) is the number-one spec-tator sport, and, as in much of the rest of the world, many young people also play the game; in Namibia there are various leagues and teams. Sam Nujoma Soccer Stadium in Katutura, which has a capacity of about 10,000, is the venue for major matches. Other sporting as well as cultural events and musical performances are also held at the stadium. Girls' soccer is gaining in popularity in Namibia. In 2008, the Namibian Football Association, in part-nership with UNICEF, created a program called Galz & Goals to encourage young girls to get involved in soccer; a number of other groups promote girls' soccer. The idea is to use soccer to encourage physical activity and a healthy lifestyle and also to empower young girls by teaching them life skills. Young Namibian girls have local role models in women's soccer who have been doing well in regional and Africa-wide competitions. The best-known women's teams are the Okahandja Beauties and the Rehoboth Queens.

Mature women often have little leisure time, as much of their time is taken up caring for family members. So a story that appeared in the *Namibian* on January 8, 2008, about mothers and married women in Okahandja who gathered every afternoon to play soccer and netball informally was particularly interesting. The women interviewed indicated that they chose to take part because they saw it as a way to relieve stress and get exercise at the same time.

Boxing is another popular spectator sport, and Namibia has produced a number of well-known titleholders. The most famous Namibian boxer is Olympian Harry "Terminator" Simon, who has fought all over the world. Simon won the World Boxing Organization (WBO) light middleweight title in 1998. In 2002, he was stripped of his title when he was unable to fight a title defense due to a pending manslaughter case in Namibia. (At the conclusion of the appeal in 2007, Simon was found guilty and served a two-year sentence; after he was released in 2009, he returned to the ring in 2010.) In 2009, lightweight Paulus "The Hitman" Moses defeated Yusuke Kobori of Japan in Yohohama, Japan, to take the World Boxing Association (WBA) title. In May 2010 Moses lost his title to the Venezuelan Miguel Acosta in front of an international crowd in Windhoek, his hometown. The defeat must have been especially hard as it was Moses's first loss in his career; in his next major bout, in December 2010 against Argentine Sergio Omar Priotti at the Windhoek Country Club Resort and Casino, the site of the loss of his title, Moses delivered victory to the hometown crowd. In March 2011, in a match scheduled to coincide with independence day celebrations, Moses again cheered the hometown audience with a win over Argentine Miguel Lombardo.

Rugby is tremendously popular, and the national team is, fittingly, named after the *Welwitschia* plant, the country's national plant. In 2010 the Welwitschias won the International Rugby (IRB) Cup for the first time ever. Rugby, cricket, netball, field hockey, golf, table tennis, lawn tennis, horse riding, cycling, and gymnastics all have their devotees. Some might be surprised that sports such as rugby and hockey are already making noticeable progress toward becoming more integrated. Golf, on the other hand, continues to be overwhelmingly the preserve of whites, although blacks, of course, do play. This is due in great part to the fact that golf is a very expensive sport and until relatively recently clubs were exclusively for whites. Cycling is hugely popular, and there are cycling clubs and tours; each year the Rotary Club of Windhoek organizes a Cycle Classic, its largest fund-raiser. Camping is another popular pastime, and families often go camping for long weekends. Campers may choose between public campsites or private farms. Water sports, a variety of sports that take advantage of Namibia's sand dunes (such as quad biking and sandboarding), and more esoteric activities such as paragliding are available.

Sandboarders just outside Swakopmund. (AP/Wide World Photos)

All of the major churches have youth organizations, typically organized by sex. Boys and young men may join youth bands, which are typically for boys only. All-girl groups pursue a myriad of other activities. Boys Scouts and Girl Guides both have branches all over Namibia. For Catholics, there is a Youth Brigade for boys and the Blue Circle for girls; the name of the latter comes from the uniform worn by members, and these organizations are similar in structure and aims to the Scouts. Activities for young people are designed to attract them to the church or to provide assistance to working mothers. For example, some churches have kindergartens and after-school programs where schoolchildren may take lessons in karate, play games such as table tennis and card games, study ballet, and read or do homework.

For school-age young children in Windhoek and the larger towns such as Rundu and Swakopmund, there are clubs that organize sporting and other after-school recreational activities. Girls may play soccer or do ballet and judo. Naturally, these activities require fees, and most people cannot afford them. Children (and adults) who live in urban areas especially have access to individuals offering private lessons in everything from art and crafts to judo and ballet. There are also organizations and businesses that offer a menu of activities, such as team sports or lessons in music or art. The Sport Klub Windhoek (SKW), which fields its own teams in soccer and a number other sports, also offers the public opportunities to take part in go-karting, archery, soccer, tennis, volleyball, and fistball. The club's youth soccer academy is highly regarded.

Fee-paying sports are, of course, not the only options available to young Namibians. Interschool sports are commonplace, from the elementary to the tertiary level. Young Namibians engage also in spontaneous play, unsupervised by adult organizers. No matter what part of the country, in urban and rural areas, young children can be seen playing with homemade toys. A sport such as soccer requires little in the way of equipment, and it is thus easy to understand its universal appeal. Television is also a pastime enjoyed by many, if they have access to a television. Foreign shows are the mainstay of Namibian television. Like their counterparts around the world, Namibian young people consume contemporary American music eagerly. Radio is much more widespread than television, and radio shows are broadcast in all the major languages of Namibia.[7]

SCHOOLS, TEACHERS, AND LEARNERS

For those of school age, time at school, and getting to and from school, occupies a significant portion of their day. Years of unequal and racist education have left deep marks on the country's educational profile, even today. In 1990 the SWAPO government inherited an educational system that was designed to be iniquitous; the task that confronted the new government was enormous, and, whatever one's opinions about SWAPO and its ideology, it must be acknowledged that the government achieved a remarkable feat in a short space of time in terms of literacy rates, evidence of a strong commitment to education. Between 1990 and 1995 the government spent between 20 and 30 percent of its total annual budget on education every year. In the next five years, although the figures declined, the percentage of government expenditures spent on education (as on health) remained remarkably high.[8]

Namibia encourages early childhood education, but the availability of these facilities is extremely limited. Early childhood education is usually provided by private individuals, development agencies, and churches. In some small rural communities the school and church continue to be one and the same building. This should not be a surprise given the history of formal education in Namibia, as well as the high percentage of Namibians who are Christian. Education from grades 1 to 3 is available in their mother tongue for most children, with the notable exception of some San communities. From grade 4 on, students transition to English as the language of instruction.

Grade-level education is divided into four categories: lower primary, upper primary, junior secondary, and senior secondary. Passage from one grade to the next is automatic for most grades, but before one may proceed from grade 7 (upper primary) to grade 8 (junior secondary) in a public school, one must pass a state-regulated examination. To move up to grade 11, the first year of senior secondary school, a student must take and pass another statewide examination. In grade 12 students take an external final examination.

Education is mandatory for the first 10 years (i.e., from grade 1 to grade 10) and, officially at least, those who are unable to pay attend free. In reality, parents and guardians are sometimes called on to make contributions for specific supplies, sports, activities, or school-sponsored projects. There are other costs associated with education that may present a bar to attendance for some, for example, the cost of purchasing suitable clothing (which is usually a uniform).[9] Indeed, a study sponsored by UNICEF in 2009 found that well over 50 percent of young people believed the single best way to effect a decrease in the dropout rate among students was "to make education more affordable."[10] Children who are teased at school (for example, about their clothing) may play truant or drop out. Unplanned pregnancy is another reason often cited for student absenteeism.

Girls attend school at the same, or a greater, rate than boys at the elementary level. There is some debate about whether there is a discernible difference in attendance between boys and girls at the secondary level; there are indications that beginning in 2007 there have been more girls than boys at the secondary level, even though, at the secondary level and beyond, girls face unique challenges, including pregnancy. While the government has legislated that girls who have children should return to school, in practice this does not always happen. Sometimes the girl herself feels embarrassed or ashamed; in other instances the school denies the girl reentrance. Despite the unique burden girls and women who become pregnant may face, currently there are more women than men at the tertiary level in Namibia, according to the latest figures from the World Bank.[11] Men continue to dominate in certain fields that traditionally have been considered male areas, such as engineering.

Grades 11 and 12 are not found in all schools, so a student who wishes to continue usually goes away to a boarding school. There are concerns about inadequate supervision of boarders, especially on the weekend, and some girls report feeling vulnerable at boarding school. Girls who choose to be sexually active do not have ready, safe, and affordable birth control methods. Clinics are distant or nonexistent. When there is a clinic, the staff may refuse to provide birth control to school-age girls and young women.

Hostel Schools and Mobile Schools

Boarding schools are common in Namibia, and not just for the offspring of the elite; indeed, while a few are prestigious and have well-appointed facilities, the vast majority of schools are extremely modest. A significant portion of the school-age population comes from homes that are in isolated locations, making the provision of schools for all difficult. The solution in Namibia has been to provide "hostel schools," as they are termed locally. These are boarding schools in which children as young as seven and eight live in dormitories where they are supervised by matrons, who also, typically, are themselves effectively boarders, as they live away from their own families. Most boarding school teachers are housed in teachers' hostels or apartments on school premises. Depending on school policy and the distance between the school and the student's home, a student may go home every weekend, once a month, or a few times a term. Namibia also has some mobile schools that cater to pastoralist communities. The Namibian school year begins in January and ends in December.

Education remains a top priority for Namibia, and the quality of education and ways to improve it are popular topics of discussion. Despite the extreme level of unemployment, even among those with tertiary education, education is highly valued by Namibians, and it is not unusual to find a school-age young person living with relatives, rather than his or her own parents, in order to attend a nearby or better school. Nonetheless, only a minority of Namibians complete all grades of the primary and secondary levels; students often drop out as they progress through the ranks. As already indicated, the reasons for dropping out are many, and discussions are always underway in Namibia's educational and policy circles about how to bring down the dropout rate.[12] While the government has achieved a great deal, much remains to be done. Independent Namibia inherited a highly unequal system based on racial and ethnic segregation. Namibia achieved an astounding level of success quickly, bringing the country's literacy rate from 65 percent in 1991 to 81 percent in 2001. However, although there are many more schools and greater opportunities for the black majority to pursue education, huge disparities remain in wealth and opportunities. It is still the case today in Namibia that the best private schools have little in common with the most modest rural school offering just a few grade levels. The aim of providing education for all in Namibia's 13 major languages may be laudable, but it places severe burdens on the educational system. Critics charge the government with spending too much and not having enough to show for it, arguing that while the level of adult literacy may be high, the level of achievement for school leavers is inadequate.

Namibia continues to devote a significant amount of its fiscal resources to education. Yet concerns remain as to how long this can continue. In 2008 the long global financial crisis created deep anxieties about the vulnerability of the educational system in times of financial crisis. Another crisis that continues to have ongoing and severe consequences for the educational sector is the AIDS/ HIV pandemic. Like other southern African countries, Namibia has been particularly hard hit by this tragedy. According to the United Nations, about

15 percent of all Namibians between the ages of 15 and 49 are HIV-positive, and close to 7,000 die every year from complications related to AIDS.[13] This impacts schooling directly in a number of ways. In the first instance, many teachers have perished, and are still perishing, as a result of this health crisis. The remaining teachers cannot do both their own jobs and those of their deceased colleagues adequately. Also, when a parent or both parents die, the child becomes an orphan, and getting to school becomes difficult, if not entirely impossible, for that orphaned child. The incidence of orphans in Namibia as a direct result of HIV/AIDS is a major public concern.

Another noteworthy development in the educational sector is the emerging interest in the study of the Chinese language. In the last decade of the 20th century, China increased its presence in Africa in spectacular fashion: In 2000 Chinese direct investment in Africa was well under half a billion dollars; at the close of 2010, Chinese direct investment in Africa was about $10 billion for the year, and China overtook the United States and the European Union to become Africa's most important trading partner.[14] The University of Namibia has established a Centre for Chinese Studies. There are numerous Chinese private and state companies working in Namibia, and with the increasing Chinese presence in Namibia, many Namibians are eager to learn Chinese in order to get jobs working for Chinese companies. However, relations between ordinary Namibians and Chinese entrepreneurs can be fairly characterized as tense. Chinese employers and managers are often accused of implementing harsh working conditions and not paying the minimum wage, as well as withholding wages unilaterally. Other Chinese entrepreneurs, especially in the construction sector, are accused of importing workers from China, thus denying Namibians employment opportunities. The Chinese government provides a number of scholarships for Namibians to study in China; these scholarships have been the source of much controversy in Namibia, as critics charged that the offspring of top government officials seem to enjoy a near monopoly in acquiring these grants.

NOTES

1. In his autobiography, Sam Nujoma, first president of Namibia, recalls helping both of his parents with all the household chores, including cooking and looking after his younger siblings. Nujoma was the eldest of 11 children. It is not uncommon to find that the eldest or the only child assists with tasks without attention to whether the child is a boy or girl.

2. Under South African occupation, those wishing to become migrant laborers signed up with the SWANLA (South West African Native Labour Agency). Each applicant would be given a test of physical fitness, then classified and sent to a central workers' camp from where workers were shipped out to their individual assignments.

A worker did not have the right to reject a posting: You went wherever you were sent. In late 1971 to early 1972 roughly one-quarter of all Namibian contract workers took part in a strike that lasted several weeks.

3. The landscape of monarchical institutions in Namibia is a complicated one, exacerbated by conflicts propelled by the apartheid regime and occupation. Some chiefs and monarchs opposed the South African government; others worked with the government or were seen as stooges. Today, some rulers and houses are seen as illegitimate creations of the apartheid regime. In some communities, the monarchical system was forced underground during the occupation and was revived after independence. For example, when the Kwanyama king died in 1917, no other ruler ascended the throne until 1996. Not all monarchs are men; among the Ovambo there are, and were in the past, queens who ruled independently. The Modjadji dynasty in the Limpopo region has been ruled by women for many generations.

4. Traditional rulers in Namibia receive a modest monthly stipend. There are councils of traditional authority as well as a national Supreme Council of Traditional Authority.

5. On May 4, 1978, the South African Defence Force (SADF) attacked Cassinga, a South West Africa People's Organisation (SWAPO) encampment inside Angola, killing over 600 children, women, and men. For a long time controversy reigned over the terminology to use to describe this event and whether to call it a massacre. The SADF insisted that the attack was aimed at rebel forces with which it was at war. SWAPO, on the other hand, insisted that Cassinga was a refugee camp consisting largely of children, women, and the elderly. They rejected the South African authorities' claims that the camp was full of terrorists. It was only at the Truth and Reconciliation Commission, with the end of white minority rule in South Africa, that the South African government admitted that the attack on Cassinga had probably been carried out with the full knowledge that the majority of residents at Cassinga were not terrorists at all but ordinary citizens. For those who wanted an end to South African rule, Cassinga became a symbol of the callousness with which white South Africa treated black Namibians. On the 10th anniversary of Cassinga, Namibian students staged major demonstrations involving hundreds, perhaps thousands, of people.

6. Given the unbelievably high unemployment rate, it is no surprise that men, aware of societal expectations, may choose to expend more energy on trying to establish a career than on their romantic relationships. Yet the reality is also that Namibia has an incredibly high rate of unmarried pregnancy. Women complain bitterly that while men don't take their relationships seriously, fatherhood makes them proud, even when there is no marriage and the man has no intent or ability to support his child.

7. For more on the media, see chapter 3.

8. According to a recent news report, the percentage of the budget devoted to education continues to remain higher than 20 percent. See Antoinette Kakujaha, "Major Strides Have Been Made in Education," *Southern Times* (Windhoek), March 21, 2010, p. 19.

9. Schoolchildren in both private and public schools typically wear a uniform, but students report that it is not uncommon to attend school wearing something other than the uniform.

10. Theunis Keulder, "Catching the Voice of the Born-Free Generation of Namibia through Mobile Phones," Namibia Institute for Democracy (NID), December 2009, http://www.nid.org.na/pdf/publications/UNICEF%20final%20report.pdf. The research was conducted by the Namibia Institute for Democracy (NID) and contacted young people, who are traditionally very difficult to engage in such market surveys, on their cellphones.

11. For the latest and earlier World Bank data on "Ratio of Female to Male Enrollments in Tertiary Education around the World," please contact the World Bank statistics department.

12. In 1998, the government established the Namibia College of Open Learning (NAMCOL) to extend educational opportunities to adults and others who, for whatever reasons, had not been able to complete their education or were unable to enroll in the formal school system. Over the years NAMCOL has expanded its offerings to include certificates in managerial skills, early childhood care, computer literacy, and a host of other skills. There are dozens of NAMCOL centers all over the country, but students may also complete their coursework entirely online.

13. These estimates are from the United Nations for 2009, available at the UNAIDS Web site, http://www.unaids.org:80/en/Regionscountries/Countries/Namibia/.

14. The $10 billion figure is an estimate. As of the time of this writing the figures for 2010 are not available. China's direct investment in Africa in 2009 was $9.3 billion. China–Africa trade stood at over $120 billion dollars in 2010, more than a 10-fold increase from the beginning of the decade.

8

Music, Dance, and Performance

NAMIBIANS ENJOY A wide variety of music and dance forms. Dance and music are integral parts of events such as weddings, festivals, and funerals; indeed, it is hard to imagine a major event not accompanied by music, and usually dance as well. At independence celebrations, dance and music groups from all over the country are invited to perform and entertain the crowds that gather to mark the occasion. A large number of international musical headliners, including the Jamaican Ziggy Marley, as well as Namibian performers helped to mark the country's independence, attained in March 1990. Whenever an event of major significance on the social calendar takes place—for example, the inauguration of a community project—the speeches are often followed by performances by dance troupes, and usually music too. Major events sponsored by the South West Africa People's Organisation (SWAPO), the ruling party, are invariably accompanied by cultural dances.

MUSIC

Music accompanies all the key transitions in life. Music also accompanies more mundane activities, such as daily work and impromptu social gatherings. Songs may commemorate events or people, effectively functioning as historical texts. Musicians sometimes use their music to comment on contemporary issues (including AIDS, absentee fathers, drug use, and politics) as well as to recall injustice or demand justice. The group Ongoronomundu

Concert Group (OCG), which performs mostly in Herero, released a CD in 2004 entitled *Ondjembo ya Hamakari* (The battle of Ohamakari) in which it joined the call for reparations from the German government for the genocide against the Herero people under German colonial rule.

As well as at celebrations, music can be heard at venues all over the country, from bars and restaurants to nightclubs and concert halls, including Barth Hall in Omaruru and the Bank Windhoek NPS Kulturaula in Swakopmund as well as numerous locations in Windhoek. The Namibia National Symphony Orchestra performs western and Namibian musical forms. The College of the Arts (COTA) hosts an annual music festival in which its students perform. In 2006, the program included indigenous Namibian music for the first time, alongside European staples.

The SWAPO government, which assumed power in 1990, arrived with a progressive agenda, especially with regard to education and culture. Under German and South African colonial rule, African cultural practices had often been suppressed or relegated to secondary status. Schools did not generally teach African arts or music. A key objective of SWAPO was to raise the level of education in the country. We have already seen that the rate of literacy was dramatically increased in just under 10 years. In 1992, the government passed a law requiring that schools include Namibian musical traditions as well as music from around the world on the curriculum. Namibian artists are encouraged to register with the Namibian Society of Composers and Authors of Music. In 2005 there were just under 700 registered local artists; two years later, that number rose to 1,200. The government provides financial assistance, albeit quite limited, to the arts.

Even prior to independence, music in Namibian languages was heard on the radio, broadcast by both state-sponsored stations and nationalist stations set up in exile, each side aware that the use of local languages could be a powerful tool in the ideological war.[1] Foreign music from the United States, South Africa, and other African countries is very popular, but since the late 1990s there has been a phenomenal growth in homegrown talent and the popularity of local musicians. Today, there is more than one company that focuses on the production of Namibian traditional music. Omalaeti, a company founded in 2004, is assertively nationalistic in its ambitions, proclaiming its raison d'etre to be the promotion of the musical traditions of every Namibian ethnic group. Beginning in 2003, the Namibia Broadcasting Corporation (NBC) has hosted a much-anticipated annual music awards extravaganza. In 2009, out of 250 entries, 87 contestants were selected to compete. A number of companies also host their own annual musical competitions. The growth in the number of competitions for singers and groups has seen an explosion in the number of professional musicians in Namibia. While local talent is extremely popular, making a living from music alone remains an elusive goal for the vast majority of Namibian musicians.

Minette Mans, a specialist on Namibian musical forms, has researched differences in singing styles in the different regions of Namibia. According to Mans, in the northeastern portions of the country, women sing in a tone that is "clear, sharp and thinly pitched," whereas in the northwest, women sing in an entirely different register, one that Mans describes as "deep in the throat."[2] Mans identifies three general tendencies in Namibian music, corresponding to the country's broad geographic divisions. The first music type is located in the north, involving the use of drums, call-and-response singing, and dancing that focuses on the hips, feet, pelvis, and shoulders. The second category is the music of southern Namibia, which shares much with music across the border and is derived from Afrikaner, German, Nama, and Rehoboth Baster traditions; the prevailing characteristics here are choral singing and keyboard instruments. The third musical category is found in the central highlands of Namibia, where the capital is located. Here, Mans finds that the dominant theme is international and multiple influences. Of course, this is an idealized typology, and one can enjoy all genres of music throughout the country, especially thanks to the radio and touring musical groups.

Musical instruments such as the guitar, cello, and piano are part of the musical landscape of Namibia, but so are instruments that are unfamiliar to Western audiences such as the thumb piano, mouth bows, and a host of other bowed instruments, each known by different names, depending on the ethnic community. While drums are certainly part of the musical landscape of Namibia, it must be said that drums are not as evident in Namibia as they are quite typically in many places elsewhere in Africa. Interestingly, the term *ngoma,* which is found in Bantu languages, is used in Khoisan languages in Namibia, but the meaning here is different. Whereas in Bantu languages, ngoma refers to the drum, in Khoisan languages it is used for bowed instruments. Experts point to this as underlining the centrality and greater antiquity of musical bows in Namibian musical expression.

Like the country itself, Namibia's musical landscape is multilingual. Many musicians sing in more than one language, sometimes on a single track; there have even been instances of songs sung in one language, then subsequently translated into another. One of the best-known musicians in Namibia is the so-called granddad of Namibian music, Jackson Kaujeua, better known as JK, who had been in the music industry for four decades when he passed away in 2010. A Herero by birth, JK grew up in a Nama community, was multilingual, and sang in a variety of Namibian languages. He is widely regarded as the liberation artist par excellence, having composed a large number of anticolonial songs during the liberation struggle. Other well-known artists include reggae star Ras Sheehama, Kenyan-born Faizel Bashir (also known as Faizel MC), Sunny Boy, Swart Baster, rising rhythm and blues (R&B) star Tequilla, and the group Gal Level, whose songs often combine several languages including Afrikaans and English and mix the modern and traditional in their dancing and often-revealing outfits. Among the most popular female solo performers on the scene today are Lady May, who has had a string of recent hits, and Monika "Diamond" Shafooli, both of whom make videos featuring skimpy clothing and suggestive dancing. Veteran reggae artist and Rastafarian Ras Sheehama, who spent much of his life prior to independence in exile in Angola, Zambia, and Nigeria, returned to the country in the second half of 1988, just before independence, along with tens of thousands of other exiles. One of Ras Sheehama's earliest hits was the song "Cassinga," which commemorates a major event in the struggle to end white apartheid rule. Ras Sheehama has performed all over the world, has several albums to his credit, and remains one of the most respected Namibian artists. A two-girl group Vanity (Candy, also Matilda Simasiku, and Sisty, also Victoria Naunyango) burst on the Namibian music scene in 2008. A group that is currently making its name on the music scene is the Remember Concert Group, one of whose lead vocalists is a teenage girl. A recent hit, "Ozombara," memorializes the Ovambenderu chief Munjuku II Nguvauva and the Herero chief Kuaima Riruako. The music of some now-defunct bands, such as Ugly Creatures, Poppets, Baronages, and Purple Haze, remains popular, especially among more mature audiences.

The best-known contemporary Namibian musicians are The Dogg and Gazza, popular musicians who play *kwaito,* a brand of music that first emerged in the townships of South Africa in the early 1990s. Kwaito has often been compared to house music. It is a style that was and remains heavily influenced by different genres, including hip-hop, R&B, and reggae. Kwaito artists speak of the genre as encompassing more than music, insisting that kwaito includes one's style and attitude toward life. Like house music, kwaito performers use a backdrop of studio-mixed music rather than live music. Debates rage about whether kwaito at its start was apolitical or political; there is, however, general agreement that kwaito emerged following the election of Nelson Mandela as president in the first democratic elections in South Africa, marking the end of white minority rule.

Today, some kwaito artists are decidedly purely commercial, promoting sexism and "bling bling," while others speak about urgent social issues such as unemployment and lack of services for those living in townships. Young people in towns tend to favor kwaito, rap, and reggae. Kudu FM, which specifically targets the age-group from 14 to 49, plays these musical forms.

Other musical forms include *kwasa kwasa* (a kind of rumba), *kwiku, ndombolo, oviritje, Damara panchi,* and *shambo.*

One cannot speak of the musical landscape without mentioning gospel and other church music. With a population that is more than 90 percent Christian, Christian music, including church, choral, and gospel music is obviously widespread. Church music is performed in a host of languages, depending on the congregation. Young people often take part in youth choirs organized by churches or other groups and individuals, such as the Macasto Coastal Youth Group, based in Swakopmund. Macasto was founded by Eve Venter, who also serves as the group's conductor. The group, which is composed of high school students, has performed in several foreign countries, and its polyglot repertoire includes Namibian music as well as music from African and other countries. Soloist Erich Mahua, scion of a family with a long and distinguished musical heritage, got his start singing at his school and in church choirs and has been collaborating with a group of other musicians in a project that aims to "rediscover and rekindle traditional music forms from different parts of the Namibia."[3] The Sidadi Band, which grew out of this collaboration, sings in various Namibian languages.

Classical Western music is also popular, as are jazz, country, and rock. All these forms have regular homegrown groups that perform; South African, Congolese, and Zimbabwean performers, as well as performers from other parts of the world, also make visits to Namibia. In 2012, the choir Cantare Audire will celebrate its 40th anniversary. Even though it was established before independence, the group, founded by choirmaster Ernst van Biljon, was multiracial and multicultural from the very outset; its repertoire consists mostly of Western classics. In 1984 the group won first prize in the mixed choirs category in the prestigious International Eisteddfod in Llangollen, Wales. Van Biljon, who is also a composer, conducts the Namibia National Youth Choir as well as the Namibia Children's Choir.

DANCE

Typically, dance is part of a larger complex of artistic expressions, involving dance, music, and poetry, as well as theater, thus making it often impossible to isolate dance from its associated artistic expressions. Indeed, in Namibian languages, a single word usually denotes dance as well as music. Like music, dance in Namibia is an important part of many rites of passage, such as marriage, entrance into adulthood, or other initiations. Dance may be an integral part of healing ceremonies in some communities, and in this context dance is not primarily or just entertainment but also medicine. Some dances are performed in public and may even invite—or require—audience participation; other dances may be secret, to be viewed only by initiates. Ritual and closed dances may involve esoteric symbols, with or without music. Forms of dance performance well known in the West, such as ballet and modern dance, are also part of the Namibian cultural landscape.

In earlier times, Africans were often presented as perpetually engaged in frantic "barbaric" dancing. In this worldview, African dancing was the antithesis of Western forms, which were considered rational and ordered. Christian missionaries often attacked African forms of dance, sometimes because they were associated with and performed during religious rituals, but at other times for being, to European sensibilities, debauched or vulgar. Europeans introduced new forms of dance to Namibians, who often adapted them and made them their own. The Rehoboth Baster dance, the *langarm*, is clearly an offspring of European dance styles, as is the music that accompanies it. One of the best-known indigenous dance forms in Namibia is the *namastap* of the Nama and Damara, performed at celebrations and other gatherings. This is an energetic dance, done in a circle, involving the stamping of feet and hopping in rhythmic fashion. Today, African dance is admired in many quarters, even though it is rarely accorded the same sort of status as the ballet. Nevertheless, we know less about indigenous African traditions of dance than of music because, even today, dance remains more challenging to fix in writing than music. While Labanotation was developed in the early 20th century as a system to record dance movements and is highly praised by its users, it remains relatively little known and even less used.

Dance in Namibia has always had a social function, and contemporary groups continue this tradition by using dance to address issues such as AIDS, homelessness, youth truancy, drug use, xenophobia, and the need for unity in diversity in the country. An example of this is Omaleshe, a dance group that uses music and dance to bring joy to orphaned and blind youth in northern Namibia and also offer them practical life skills. Omaleshe was founded by Doris Mukensturm, a South African Zulu by birth. One of the more prominent dance groups in the country is the OYO Dance Group, which is affiliated with the Ombetja Yehinga Organisation (OYO), directed by French-born scholar and artist Philippe Talavera. The focus of the organization is to encourage open discussion about sexuality, sexual health, HIV, and AIDS, especially among young people. In 2008 OYO unveiled a dance at the National Theatre of Namibia titled *The Namibian Odysseus*. In this adaptation, Penelope is a married woman whose husband, Odysseus, is a migrant worker. As already noted, sometimes the line between dance and music is difficult, or impossible, to determine. A striking example of this is the group Ghetto Fabulous. Ghetto Fabulous began as strictly a dance group, performing at the invitation of well-known Namibian musical groups at concerts; now, the members of Ghetto Fabulous are branching out to become musicians in their own right, and the group is currently working on its first album. Between 2009 and early 2010 the group released several songs, including the popular music video "Kwaito Party."

THEATER AND OTHER PERFORMING ARTS

Local and national groups give theatrical performances that address social issues such as HIV/AIDS, the plight of orphans, domestic violence, and a range of other concerns. Performance has always been an integral part of Namibian life, whether in the historical reenactments on Maharero Day or in masked performances at chiefly installations in the past. In health and healing rituals among a variety of Namibian peoples, performances may play a part. Performance can also serve the purposes of commemoration and education. The annual Herero Flag Days (Maharero or Red Flag Herero in August, Green Flag in June, and White Flag in October), which take place over several days, are characterized by ritual performances commemorating various moments in the long struggle for independence. There are songs, visits to the ancestral graves of the heroes, and processions of women spectacularly attired in national dress and men in striking military uniforms.

Experts argue, however, about what, properly speaking, constitutes drama. Some insist that drama must have a dramatist, a cast, a script (even if unwritten), and an audience to be so labeled; others insist that certain religious rituals, including spirit mediumship, masquerades, and other rituals, are all as much drama as a play performed in a theater. Are the performances at the annual Herero Heroes' Day drama? If not drama, what are they? Is there a distinction between ritual and drama, or are the two synonymous (especially in their origins)? Is the assumption by the performers of a role other than as themselves what distinguishes drama from other types of performances? What are the basic requirements in order to classify a performance as drama? Is it props, costumes, professional actors, characters, script, plot, or other elements? In chapter 4 we noted that many specialists believe that some of the ancient rock paintings and engravings depict shamans performing trance dances. If that is indeed the case, we may point to rock art as providing evidence of the oldest recorded dramas (as well, of course, as the oldest known dances) in Namibia. Of course, not everyone accepts the images in the petroglyphs as ritual performances, much less as drama.

The best-known contemporary playwright in Namibia is South African–born Frederick Philander, who moved to Namibia in 1980. Philander is considered "the father of community theater" and was honored for his work by the Namibian National Theatre Awards in 2007. Philander created the first black theater group in the capital, the Windhoek Theatre Association. At the time the only other theater group in the city was under the umbrella of the all-white South West African Performing Arts Council. Later, Philander created another group, the Committed Artists of Namibia (CAN); the latter and the Windhoek Theatre Association are both still in existence. Philander uses both professional and amateur actors. Like many other Namibian artists, in the pre-independence days Philander focused his critiques on the political situation, and post-independence he has turned his attention to the socioeconomic situation. A number of Namibian theater groups, including Philander's, tour regionally and internationally. For example, in 2008 Committed Artists of Namibia traveled to Belgium where they staged a one-week run of a play in Afrikaans. OYO has performed in South Africa and Europe.

The Windhoek State Theatre was launched in 1960. It maintained a whites-only policy until just before independence in 1989, when it officially abandoned that policy and changed its name to the National Theatre of Namibia. The National Theatre of Namibia, which seats almost 500, mounts its own productions and also hosts foreign productions. Other spaces where performances can be seen in the capital include the National Gallery, the Warehouse, Bricks, the Drama Department at the University of Namibia, and the Boiler House Theatre in the Katutura Community Arts Centre (KCAC). The KCAC was originally a hostel for contract workers under the hated apartheid contract-work system instituted during the South African occupation. Built as a hostel in 1962 for 3,000 migrant contract workers, the hostel soon became, like similar places in South Africa, extremely overcrowded. Over the years, the hostel compound was often the site of bitter and violent opposition to the policies of the apartheid government. So it is fitting that in post-independence Namibia it should serve as a venue that promotes progressive and politically engaged artistic endeavors. Thirteen years after independence the former workers' hostel compound was transformed into the KCAC; over the years hundreds of youth and adults have received training there, and the center also houses a gallery where art exhibitions, poetry readings, dance performances, and plays may be seen. The gallery is named after John Muafangejo (1943–1987), Namibia's best-known artist, whose work reflected his compatriots' nationalist struggles. It is worth noting that during the long liberation struggle, SWAPO actively promoted the arts, just as it established educational institutions to cater to the large numbers of youth who fled into exile to join the liberation movement. Theater, which can be very mobile, was a feature of SWAPO's art program. Community theater, poetry, and music, all art forms that travel well and easily, played important roles in the nationalist struggle to overthrow white minority rule and apartheid.

Plays and theatrical performances are popular in Namibia, and there are theatrical troupes throughout the country. In 2001 and 2002, Macmillan Namibia published two volumes, *New Namibian Plays I* and *II,* which are used in secondary schools all over the country. The youth play a significant role in the arts in Namibia; students participate in theatrical productions in school as well as in semiprofessional troupes. Students often take on the role of showcasing the cultural traditions of the country, mounting traditional dances for fellow students and other audiences. This is true for students at all levels, from the elementary to the tertiary level. Schools hold cultural festivals; each of the country's tertiary-level institutions holds an annual cultural festival. Festivals are also organized by arts centers and others, for example, the Franco-Namibian Cultural Centre. The KCAC holds an annual art and cultural festival. On the eve of Independence Day in 2010, students gave several free performances at the National Theatre of original works created by two Namibian choreographers, affiliated with Namibia's premier arts school, COTA.

COTA offers instruction in dance, as well as classical music, contemporary music, theater, and the arts. Established in 1971 (albeit under a different name), COTA is the largest arts educational institution in the country, with 17 centers throughout the country. The college consists of several campuses all over the country, including one in Katutura, the KCAC. In 2003, the Arts Performance Centre, better known as the APC, was founded in Tsumeb to provide for the education of youth. A varied art curriculum is available, including music, dancing, theater, and painting; there is also instruction in hygiene, world politics, and religion. The University of Namibia provides training in music, dance, drama, and visual arts.

FILM

While it certainly cannot compete on this front with its better-established and economic powerhouse neighbor, South Africa, Namibia has a burgeoning film industry. Namibian filmmakers include Bridget Pickering (who is of South African and Namibian parentage and has done work in both countries and worked as a producer on *Hotel Rwanda*), short-film veteran Cecil Moller, German-born Tim Hubschle, newcomer Joel Haikali, and Perivi Katjavivi, who launched his own production company, Old Location Films, in 2009. Moller has made numerous feature-length documentaries as well as shorts and currently heads the Namibia Film Commission (NFC). Namibian directors often deal with social issues, such as AIDS, early pregnancy, and cross-cultural marriages. The 2006 film *Tate Penda* by Errol Geingob is about a young Ovambo woman, her Damara boyfriend and her father's attempts to break up the relationship because he is eager to marry her off to a well-to-do Ovambo man. Philippe Talavera, the director of OYO, has also made a number of films, including one that tackles the issue of rape. In 2010, the young actor-director Haikali premiered his first feature-length film, *My Father's Son,* at the National Theatre in Windhoek. The 82-minute film, in English, Afrikaans, and Oshivambo, was also selected for screening at the 2011 FESPACO Festival, Africa's most prestigious film festival, held every two years in Ouagadougou, Mali. (FESPACO is the French acronym for "Festival panafrican du cinéma et de la télévision de Ouagadougou," or the Panafrican Film and Television Festival of Ouagadougou.) The arts organization Africavenir, which cosponsored the screening of Haikali's *My Father's Son,* was founded in 1990 in Douala by the indefatigable Cameroonian historian and man of letters Professor Kum'a Ndumbe III. Africavenir opened a branch in Namibia in 2007 and runs a year-round African film series in Windhoek where films by filmmakers from all over the continent are screened. In 2009 Africavenir, in collaboration with the Franco-Namibian Cultural Center, launched the Namibia Movie Collection, a depository of films made by Namibian filmmakers and films about Namibia. Nigerian Nollywood films are popular in Namibia, as they are in other African countries and beyond. There are a number of annual film festivals in Windhoek.

THE FUTURE OF THE ARTS IN NAMIBIA: BUILDING ON A USABLE PAST?

The government plays an active part in sponsoring the arts in Namibia, as do the consular offices of a number of countries, including France, Finland, Sweden, Germany, and the United States. One of the portfolios within the Ministry of Youth, National Service, Sport and Culture is the Directorate of National Heritage and Culture Programmes, whose task is to promote the country's rich and diverse cultures. Each of Namibia's 13 regions hosts an annual Regional Cultural Festival. Some officials and activists express a sense of urgency about the need to revive and maintain traditions that no longer exist or are seen as close to extinction. Naturally, this tension leads to debates and controversies about cultural identities, especially when coupled with the concerted effort to make culture appealing to tourists. So-called traditional dances, ordinarily performed as part of ceremonies such as weddings and initiation rites, nowadays are performed on demand for tourists. Domestic and international tourists travel to the Kalahari to attend the annual Kuru San Dance Festival, usually held in August, at which various San groups perform San healing dances. The impulse to preserve culture while marketing it to outsiders makes for a delicate and complicated journey.

For foreigners what is perhaps most striking about the arts in Namibia is the degree to which dance, music, and theater are employed as tools for social rehabilitation and to address social issues. This comes out of Namibia's recent revolutionary history but is also rooted in deep cultural patterns. The arts, like all aspects of culture, are dynamic and ever-changing. So-called traditional dance, music, and drama in Namibia have never been static, and were certainly not so in the period before European presence. Cultural habits and patterns change in response to internal as well as external forces. Namibia has long been open to a variety of external sources. Some of the external factors that impinge on Namibian expressions of culture in more recent times include migrant labor, forced migrations and the creation of Bantustans, the modern school calendar, improved communications, and AIDS.

NOTES

1. Voice of Namibia, set up in Tanzania and subsequently in Angola, was run by the South West Africa People's Organisation (SWAPO) to counter the propaganda of the government-controlled South West African Broadcasting Corporation (SWBC) and South African Broadcasting Corporation (SABC). SABC and SWBC both had programming in the main African languages, designed to serve the government's ideological purposes.

2. Minette Mans, *Music as an Instrument of Diversity and Unity: Notes on a Namibian Landscape* (Uppsala, Sweden: Nordiska Afrikainsitutet, 2003), p. 55.

3. Sidadi, Music Project in Namibia, http://hem.bredband.net/mbuende/Sidadi/Sidadi.htm.

9

Tourism and the Natural Environment

MANY AMERICANS FIRST heard of Namibia in 1995 when the Miss Universe contest, which has a huge audience in the United States and around the world, was held there. More recently, the decision by U.S. actors Angelina Jolie and Brad Pitt to have their baby in Namibia introduced the country to a new generation of Americans. Although Namibia remains relatively little-known, tourism plays a central role in the economy of the country. The tourism industry accounts for about 20 percent of the country's total work-force as well as about 20 percent of its gross domestic product (GDP); recent government figures indicate that in 2009 close to one million tourists visited Namibia. While mining remains the largest single contributor to Namibian coffers, tourism has replaced fishing as the number-two source of revenue. Mining accounts for more than half of the country's export earnings; tourism is almost as important as mining in terms of its share of the GDP, and tour-ism greatly outstrips mining in total numbers employed. Mining employs less than 5 percent of the population; agriculture is the chief area of labor but contributes relatively little—less than 10 percent—to the GDP.

Since independence, there has been a steady increase in the number of tourists visiting the country. In 1991, there were about 150,000 foreign visi-tors, and the following year that figure jumped to over 170,000. By 1994, close to 300,000 overseas visitors traveled to Namibia. Fifteen years later, Namibia hosted nearly one million visitors. A country of enormous natural beauty, Namibia attracts a notable percentage of repeat visitors who fall under

the spell of a place described with fondness by residents as the "land God created in a fit of anger." Nature enthusiasts, wildlife photographers, and trophy
hunters make up a significant portion of the visitors from overseas. Namibia
is rapidly emerging as a major ecotourism destination, with the government,
nongovernmental organizations, and private entrepreneurs vying to proclaim
their commitment to sustainable development. A huge country with a tiny
population, Namibia's vast open spaces and parks draw the largest number
of visitors; Namibia's towns, especially those with a marked German heritage, such as Windhoek, Swakopmund, Luderitz, and Keetmanshoop, are
also popular among visitors. Some visitors are attracted to Namibia by an
interest in "first peoples," and they tour Himba and San communities. Tours
to townships (for example, Katutura in Windhoek or Mondesa in Swakopmund) are also gaining in popularity.

The sand dunes of Sossusvlei are the country's most famous natural landmark so it comes as no surprise that the Namib Desert, where Sossusvlei
is located, is perhaps the single most popular tourist destination. The sand
dunes are in constant motion; shape and height are ever fluid. Many, however, insist the tallest dunes in the world are to be found in the Namib. The
dunes certainly reach a very high altitude: Dunes of more than 1,100 feet
(as high as 350 meters) have been recorded. The Namib stretches along the
entire coast of Namibia, extending north into Angola and south into South
Africa. Surprisingly perhaps, a large variety of animal life is found in the
Namib, including chameleons, ostriches, hyenas, and a number of smaller
animals. When the Benguela current hits the cold South Atlantic waters,
mists of water are produced that are carried into the desert, providing moisture that sustains a remarkable number of life-forms. While photographs of
the dramatic red and orange sand dunes of Sossusvlei have become iconic
images representing Namibia, the country's topography is varied. Namibia is
home to some impressive mountain ranges, and even forests.

Because of the country's unique ecosystems, Namibia holds great attraction for scientists in a variety of fields. The Namib Desert, after which the
country is named, is probably the most studied desert in the world. Geolo-
gists also have much to interest them in the country, from the millennia-old
rock formations along the coast to the world-famous Fish River Canyon and
other lesser-known natural formations. In the plant kingdom there are numerous plants endemic to the region; for example, scientists have recorded
more than 4,500 plant species in Namibia, and of these about 250 are found
only in Namibia and southern Angola. So, although the landscape is often
stark, Namibia has a diverse and rich plant and animal life, with many species
that are unique to the country or the region, such as the bottle and the quiver
trees. Both trees are very unusual-looking, with stout trunks. However, the

Canyon carved out of the desert by the Fish River in Namibia. (Jeremy Richards | Dreamstime.com)

oddest plant in the Namib is, without a doubt, the *Welwitschia mirabilis.* This is a plant with just two very long and tough leaves that sit atop the sand, with roots that penetrate deep below the surface. Botanists believe that some of these *Welwitschia mirabilis* plants are more than 1,000 years old. The *Welwitschia mirabilis* belongs to the conifer family of plants but is the only plant in its genus. Plants as well as animals have had to adapt to the harsh arid conditions in Namibia in order to survive. A good number of the country's wildlife have made remarkable adaptations to live in conditions where there may be no access to water for weeks, or even months, at a time. Some Namibian elephants, for example, can survive for months without water. Some animals burrow into the sand to reach moisture; other animals, which live along the coast and survive on the surface of the sand, are able to absorb moisture from the fog for which the Namib Desert is famous.

Tourism and environmental concerns are inextricably linked, even if the two are not often enough considered together; in Namibia, one cannot afford to ignore this connection. In Namibia a single government ministry is in charge of both tourism and the environment, the Ministry of the Environment and Tourism (MET). The government is eager to take advantage of Namibia's natural attractions and make the most of the tourism industry; at the same time, Namibia cannot sustain vast numbers of tourists because of its fragile ecosystem. So the only way forward is to encourage tourism while

Trackers examine sprawling, gargantuan leaves of a rare Welwitschia plant. (Volkmar K. Wentzel/National Geographic/Getty Images)

at the same time trying to ensure that tourists do not overtax an already-burdened natural environment. Apart from the MET, a host of other, private initiatives target specific aspects of environmental and conservation issues and also encourage visitors, for example, Save the Rhino Trust.

Namibia was the first country to include a statute for the protection of the environment in its constitution.[1] One of Namibia's game reserves and a site popular with tourists, Waterberg Plateau National Park, is known today as an important wildlife preserve that is home to a number of endangered species. Just 40 years ago, many of the wildlife that can be seen in the park today were almost extinct, and the government began a protection program, closing the park to safeguard the animals. Today, Waterberg supplies other national parks with protected animals such as the black and white rhinoceros.

Namibia has more than 20 national and game parks, accounting for about 15 percent of the country's land surface. The flora and fauna of these national parks offer spectacular variety to tourists, whether local or international, and it is this striking plant and animal world that attracts numerous visitors to Namibia. The most famous national park in the country is Etosha, located in the north of the country, about 300 miles from the capital; it is often the big draw for visitors from outside the continent. In the early 20th century, when Etosha was first established, it was the largest national park in the world; although the park is now less than one-quarter of its former size, it continues to enjoy success because it is home to a dazzling population of animal species, including lions, leopards, elephants, cheetahs, zebras, giraffes, gemsboks, and rhinoceroses. The terrain is usually dry, but during the rainy season (December–April), when rainfall tends to be short and heavy, water collects in the Etosha Pan.

Located in the midsection of the Namib Desert, the Namib-Naukluft Park, which covers an area of about 22,000 square miles (or roughly 55,000 square kilometers), is by far the country's largest national park; it is the largest conservation area in Africa and one of the largest in the world. The topography of the Namib Desert varies, and three of the country's major nature reserves are located in the desert: the Namib-Naukluft, Skelton Coast (in the north), and the Sperrgebiet (in the south) National Parks. Wild horses roam in the Sperrgebiet, and legends abound about the origins of these horses. Big Welwitschia, a *Welwitschia mirabilis* plant believed to be at least 1,500 years old and perhaps as old as 3,000 years, is located in the Namib-Naukluft Park, and many tourists trek the so-called Welwitschia Trail specifically to see this marvel. The baboons in this desert section of the park endure months without any water. The Namib-Naukluft Park is home to zebras, giraffes, gemsboks, springboks, and black rhinos. The latter were reintroduced to the park in 2007.

Etosha Salt Pan, Namibiathe. (Travel Pictures Gallery)

Wildlife at a busy waterhole in Etosha National Park in Namibia. (Steve Allen | Dreamstime.com)

Sandwich Harbour, in the northwestern corner of the Namib-Naukluft park, is considered one of the world's most important wetlands, providing a home to a diverse population of sometimes rare and endangered seabirds and other marine life. The park is mostly uninhabited today; however, a few hundred Topnaar Nama people live in a dozen villages near the Kuiseb River valley, maintaining livestock and cultivating a variety of plants, including the Nara melons, which belong to the cucumber family.[2] Sossusvlei, also part of the Namib-Naukluft Park, is located more than 350 miles (almost 600 kilometers) southwest of Windhoek and about 40 miles (70 kilometers) from the coast.

The Caprivi Strip in the northeastern corner of the country is singular in Namibia for its tropical climate, wetlands, and lush greenery. Whereas much of the rest of the country is extremely arid, Caprivi gets a plentiful supply of rainfall, often causing floods during the rainy season. Bwabwata National Park, located in the Caprivi Strip, is held up by the government as a model of how to marry wildlife conservation and sustainable development for the local community. However, tensions between the local residents' desires and needs and government policies remain intractable. For example, local communities often lose livestock and crops to wild animals, which, naturally, they do not always welcome. Just a generation ago, the area was an active war zone, and separatist sentiments still smolder in some quarters.

The government has invested heavily in developing tourism and highlighting ecotourism in the park. Stocks of game have been increased. In 1978, for example, there were only 35 elephants and 1 hippopotamus. By 2007, there were at least 340 resident elephants and about 350 hippos. Bwabwata National Park is divided into three core conservation areas and one multiple-use area. Local populations live in the latter, and there are schools, shops, clinics, and a variety of tourist provisions. Tourist facilities include campsites, lodges, and a spa resort. The best-known attractions in this park are the enormous baobab trees and the Cape buffalo. Elephants, leopards, hippos, crocodiles, and African wild dogs also live in the park, as well as some lions. Bwabwata National Park has more bird species than any other park in Namibia.

Other parks include the Khaudum National Park in the Kavango Region and the Sperrgebiet National Park, which was established in 2008, making it Namibia's youngest national park. The Sperrgebiet occupies part of the Succulent Karoo, an ecological zone that extends into the Republic of South Africa. The Succulent Karoo is regarded as the most diverse desert ecosystem (or hot spot) in the world; it is thus perhaps not too surprising to learn that the Sperrgebiet National Park is home to almost 20 percent of the entire flora of Namibia (some 1,000 species of plants) although it occupies less than 3 percent of the country's total land area. At least 10 percent of the plants in the Sperrgebiet are found nowhere else on earth. The park is home to several ghost towns, including Pomona, Elizabeth Bay, and Märchental, sites of diamond activity in the first decades of the 20th century. Remains of abandoned factories, houses, and train stations can be seen here; the government intends to allow these artifacts to remain. The word *Sperrgebiet* is German for "forbidden area," and this area was so named because in the early diamond-mining days, access was forbidden to all but those working in the diamond mines. Today, some of the area is open to outsiders, but much of it remains closed to the general public, as the operation of the park must coexist with the regulations and needs of the mining industry. Access to the park is, and likely will remain, controlled and restricted, with much of the area off-limits to the public, including tourists.

The vast majority of visitors to Namibia are from South Africa and Angola; between them these two countries account for more than half of all visitors to Namibia each year. Germany, with its strong historical ties to Namibia, sends the third-largest number of visitors. Many Namibian families have relatives in Germany or South Africa, or both. Tourists from the United States make up only a relatively small number. Groups involved with tourism are eager to increase the number of tourists to Namibia, especially those coming from Europe and North America, because, when they do travel to Namibia, these visitors are the biggest spenders.[3]

Domestic tourists often favor historical or holiday sites. The resort town of Swakopmund is very popular with Namibians as a weekend getaway spot. Situated as it is between the ocean and the desert, Swakopmund is an ideal location from which to admire some of the unique beauty of Namibia, from the man-made to the natural. Although the German population in Swakopmund is in the minority, the German element is still powerful, despite the loss of political power. Swakopmund is described frequently as "a little Bavaria in Africa." Heavily dependent on tourism, Swakopmund's political and business leaders understand the need to maintain the town's German heritage, a major magnet for tourists. Yet, because towns all over Namibia are expanding at an incredible pace, development is inevitable. Not surprisingly, battles have raged between politicians and local residents, as well as between local business owners, politicians, and conservationists, over how to marry development with historical preservation and a changing political climate. When some street names were changed recently, some residents of German descent forcefully voiced their discontent in the local media.

As well as Swakopmund, the towns of Luderitz, Bethanie, and Kolmanskop are popular with domestic as well as foreign visitors. Kolmanskop is an abandoned former diamond-mining town, now "overgrown" by sand. The interior of many houses in the town is almost completely filled with sand, and the town's epithet, ghost town, is well deserved. Bethanie, with its strong Nama heritage and presence, was the site of the home of the early-19th-century London Missionary Society." The harbor town Luderitz was purchased by the German merchant Adolph Luderitz in 1884; whether the transaction was understood in the same way by the two sides and, indeed, whether *kaptein* Josef Fredericks enjoyed the authority to make such a sale, remain contentious issues for historians. Luderitz is striking with its eclectic and colorful colonial-era buildings. Walvis Bay has had an interesting history. Acquired by the British government (through its representatives in the Cape Colony) in the late 1870s, it remained under British control for decades while all the land around it (i.e., the rest of what is today Namibia) was claimed by Germany. Walvis Bay remained a part of the Cape Colony, and when the Union of South Africa was declared in 1910, Walvis Bay was included in that union. In 1915 the rest of Namibia came under South African control and remained that way until 1990.[4] But even after Namibia was declared independent, the South African government held on to Walvis Bay. It was not until 1994 that Walvis Bay was officially incorporated (or reincorporated) into Namibia. Walvis Bay is the only deep harbor in Namibia, and along with the dozen nearby offshore islands, is rich in guano, a precious commodity. With its large population of flamingos, Walvis Bay is popular with photographers. *Walvis* (or *walfisch*) means "whale," and the bay used to be a major whaling port, attracting a large and steady number of whalers from North America and Europe from the 18th century until the 20th century.[5] Apart from the flamingos, other birds can be seen in Walvis Bay as well, including pelicans and cormorants.

Namibia's well-developed tourism industry is expanding rapidly, assisted by the combination of planning, stable government, and great natural beauty. An overwhelming percentage of tourists cite the landscape and wildlife of the country as their reason for visiting. The government has a proactive approach to the tourism industry, and a key goal for the future is to increase the numbers of foreign tourists, especially those coming from wealthy countries. It remains to be seen whether the desire to appeal more to high-spending tourists will be realized. At the moment, most of the tourists to Namibia are South African neighbors, and they spend significantly less than tourists from Europe (primarily Germany) and the United States.

In the long term, the biggest challenge to this industry, which the government seeks to make even more profitable, are continued political stability and the successful management of growing environmental challenges. It is difficult to disagree with experts who predict that the biggest challenge to Namibia's tourism industry—as well as to the country as a whole—is climate

Luderitz. (Harald Süpfle)

change. Namibia is one of the most arid countries in the world, and prospects of further rises in temperature, as many scientists predict, are alarming. Statistics show that in the 20th century temperatures rose in Namibia at a greater rate than the global average. If Namibia faces a future with even more severe water shortages and devastating floods than it currently experiences, this will not only affect, of course, the wildlife and the tourism that it attracts but also have devastating effects on the human populations, especially the poorest, who are always the most vulnerable. In the 30 years since independence, sections of the Namibian population have seen their quality of life, which was already low to begin with, remain unchanged or even deteriorate. The political stability for which the country is celebrated in the international arena may be in jeopardy if the numbers of Namibians who feel independence has brought neither a better life nor prospects for greater equity continue to grow.

NOTES

1. Many pro-environment legal theorists consider the Namibian law too vague; some point to Ecuador's 2004 amendment to its constitution as the first significant victory with regard to guaranteeing environmental protection.

2. Henno Martin, a German geologist who spent more than two years hiding in a canyon in the park during World War II, wrote of his experiences in *The Sheltering Desert* (Johannesburg, South Africa: A. D. Donker, 1983).

3. In 2003, 58,000 German tourists traveled to Namibia. That same year, over 222,000 South Africans and over 222,000 Angolans visited. In 2005 the corresponding numbers were 61,000 Germans, 281,000 Angolans, and 231,000 South Africans. By 2007 there were 336,000 Angolan visitors, 250,000 South Africans, and 80,000 Germans. Throughout this period the number of U.S. visitors remained between 11,000 and 20,000. These figures are from the *Official Namibian Tourism Directory for 2009* (Windhoek: Ministry of Environment and Tourism, 2009).

4. Under South African occupation, Walvis Bay was administered, as was the rest of Namibia, from Windhoek and not Pretoria, which many would later point to as indication that Walvis Bay was not South African but Namibian. In 1977, however, as the resistance and international calls for an end to South African occupation heightened, the South African government brought Walvis Bay under direct South African administration, clearly an attempt to establish its claims to Walvis Bay in any post-independence agreement.

5. There are now international agreements in place protecting whales. These have been signed by many countries, although not all (Japan, Denmark, Iceland, and Norway are notable exceptions). Namibia also has its own laws to control fishing, legal and illegal; nevertheless, fish piracy is a continuing concern in Namibia.

Glossary of Commonly Used Terms in Namibia

Baas   Afrikaans for "boss."

Bakkie   A truck or pickup.

Biltong   A dried meat snack, a type of beef jerky made of a variety of meats, including ostrich and kudu.

Bobotie   A casserole usually using ground beef or lamb and bread, eggs, and spices; fish may also be used. Of Cape Malay origin, it was introduced to Namibia by Nama and Afrikaner immigrants; usually served with yellow rice.

Boerwors   A type of dried sausage; literally, "farmer's sausage."

Born-frees   Those born after 1990, the year of independence.

Braai   Barbecue.

Broetchen   Bread roll.

Combie   Minibus that travels along fixed routes, stopping to drop off or to pick up passengers based on demand; also *kombi* or *combi*.

Cuca shop   Kiosk that sells some food and small household items such as soap as well as alcohol; neighborhood bar.

Dankie   Afrikaans for "thank you."

Droewors   A type of biltong made from sausage.

Eanda   Among the Herero, the matrilineal group to which an individual belongs; individuals trace their lineage through both their father and their mother.

Eewa   Okay.

Efundula   Initiation ceremony for Ovambo girls; also "traditional marriage." Also known as ohango in the OshiNdonga dialect.

Eish!   Goodness!

Epata   Among the Ovambo, a clan descended from a female ancestor.

Hostel school   The Namibian term for boarding school, common in Namibia where families often live in isolated rural settings.

Jol   Good time, often used as in "have a jol;" also used by young people to mean "kiss."

Kambashus   Structure (such as home, kiosk, etc.) constructed of cardboard, wood, and zinc or corrugated iron; shack; kiosk.

Kapana   Barbecued meat, usually eaten on-site with a variety of dry relishes.

Kaptein   Title for leader or chief in Nama communities; sometimes used to describe "headman" or chief in other communities.

Kashipembe   Name used to describe any number of extremely intoxicating home-brewed brandies made using different fruits.

Kraal   Fenced enclosure.

Kuku   Grandmother.

Learner   Student.

Lobola   Bridewealth, also brideprice.

Mahangu   Millet, a staple, especially in the north; used to refer to both the raw and the prepared dish.

Meme   Term of respect for a woman (literally "mother"), used for any older woman, for example, "Meme Mary."

Moffie   Derogatory term for homosexual or effeminate man.

Namlish   Popular with the young, a mix of English, Ovambo, Nama, Afrikaans, and other local languages.

Ohango   Initiation ritual for Ovambo girls; marriage. See Efundula.

Omaere   Sour milk (Ovambo).

Oom   Afrikaans for uncle, used as a term of respect for any older man.

Oruzo   Among the Herero, the patrilineal group to which an individual belongs; individuals trace their lineage through both their mother and their father.

Oshifima   Porridge made of corn usually, or of millet (*mahangu*) or sorghum; stiff porridge, typically served at every meal.

Oshikandela   Dairy drink, similar to a yogurt drink, sometimes described as "sour drinking yogurt," now also produced commercially.

Oshikundu   A fermented drink made with sorghum or millet, usually translated as "beer."

Oshitaka   A cultured yogurt drink with corn (maize) meal.

Oshiwali   Bean soup (Ovambo).

Potbrood   Literally, "pot bread" (Afrikaans); a bread dough "baked" outside in a cast iron pot; eaten mostly in southern and central Namibia and in Afrikaner communities.

Potjiekos   Any dish cooked in a three-legged pot over an open fire, literally "pot food."

Rand   South African currency, accepted throughout Namibia.

Red Line   Under German colonial rule, the Red Line divided the country into two, with the areas to the south of the line (central and southern Namibia) reserved for white settlement. The movement of cattle from north to south was forbidden, and the movement of Africans was also restricted. The "native" areas north of the Red Line (mostly Ovambo and Kavango areas and Caprivi) were ruled by "indirect rule," while south of this line—known as the Police Zone—the government ruled directly. This Red Line (also known as the veterinary fence) remains a feature of the Namibian economy and politics. Discussions are underway about whether to move the Red Line to the Angolan border (effectively eliminating it) and thus allow cattle from the north to be sold all over the country as well as overseas; the line was moved at various times in the past. As discussed in chapter 6, the Red Line plays a role in the way in which civil courts handle property matters in divorce.

Robot   Traffic light.

Samosas   Pastries stuffed with vegetables and/or meat, of Indian origin.

Shebeen   A spot for socializing and drinking, usually located in a township and often unlicensed.

Smiley   A delicacy made with whole goat head, sometimes sheep; also known as *skaapkop*.

Sosatie   Roasted meat on a stick; kebab.

Stoep   Porch.

Sundowner   Evening drinks with friends.

Tackie   Tennis shoes, also *takkie* or *takkies*.

Tannie   Afrikaans for "auntie," used as a term of respect for any older woman.

Tate   Father or grandfather, also term of respect for an older man.

Tombo   Locally made beer, usually made from sorghum.

Vetkoek   Dough that is stuffed with meat or jam and fried, sometimes sold by street vendors.

Bibliography

BOOKS AND ESSAYS

Amukugo, Elizabeth. *Education and Politics in Namibia*. Windhoek, Namibia: Gamsberg and Macmillan, 1995.

Bauer, Gretchen. *Labor and Democracy in Namibia, 1971–1996*. Athens: Ohio University Press, 1998.

Bauer, Gretchen. "Namibia: Losing Ground without Mandatory Quotas." In *Women in African Parliaments,* edited by Gretchen Bauer and Hannah E. Britton. Boulder, CO: Lynne Rienner, 2006.

Bauer, Gretchen. "Namibia in the First Decade of Independence: How Democratic?" *Journal of Southern African Studies* 27, no. 1 (March 2001).

Becker, Heike. "Making Tradition: A Historical Perspective on Gender in Namibia." In *Unravelling Taboos: Gender and Sexuality in Namibia,* edited by Suzanne LaFont and Dianne Hubbard. Windhoek, Namibia: Legal Assistance Centre, 2007.

Becker, Heike. "'New Things after Independence': Gender and Traditional Authorities in Postcolonial Namibia." *Journal of Southern African Studies* 32, no. 1 (March 2006).

Brautigam, Deborah. *The Dragon's Gift: The Real Story of China in Africa*. Oxford: Oxford University Press, 2009.

Buys, G. L., and S.V.V. Nambala. *History of the Church in Namibia: An Introduction*. Windhoek, Namibia: Gamsberg Macmillan, 2003.

Chanock, Martin. "Making Customary Law: Men, Women and the Courts in Colonial Rhodesia." In *African Women and the Law: Historical Perspectives,* edited by Margaret J. Hay and Marcia Wright. Boston: African Studies Center, Boston University, 1982.

Cleaver, Tessa, and Marion Wallace. *Namibia: Women in War.* London: Zed Books, 1990.

Cliffe, Lionel, Ray Bush, Jenna Lindsay and Brian Mokopakgosi. *The Transition to Independence in Namibia.* Boulder, CO: Lynne Rienner, 1994.

Cohen, Cynthia. "'The Natives Must First Become Good Workmen': Formal Educational Provision in German South West and East Africa Compared." *Journal of Southern African Studies* 19, no. 1 (March 1993).

Cooper, Allan D. *The Occupation of Namibia: Afrikanerdom's Attack on the British Empire.* Lanham, MD: University Press of America, 1991.

Dedering, Tilman. "The Prophet's 'War against Whites': Shepherd Stuurman in Namibia and South Africa, 1904–7." *Journal of African History* 40, no. 1 (1999).

Dierks, Klaus. *Chronology of Namibian History: From Pre-historical Times to Independent Namibia.* Windhoek: Namibia Scientific Society, 2002.

Dore, Isaak Ismail. *The International Mandate System and Namibia.* Boulder, CO: Westview Press, 1985.

Dreyer, Ronald. *Namibia and Southern Africa: Regional Dynamics of Decolonization 1945–90.* New York: Kegan Paul International, 1994.

Dyer, Geoff, and Jamil Anderlini. "China's Lending Hits New Heights." *Financial Times,* January 17, 2011.

Editions Revue Noire. *Namibia.* Paris: Editions Revue Noire, 1994.

Ekejiuba, Felicia I. "Down to Fundamentals: Women-Centred Hearthholds in Rural West Africa." In *Readings in Gender in Africa,* edited by Andrea Cornwall. Boulder, CO: Westview Press, 1995.

Epprecht, March. *Hungochani: The History of a Dissident Sexuality in Southern Africa.* Montreal, Canada: McGill-Queen's University Press, 2004.

Ezzell, Carol. "The Himba and the Dam." *Scientific American* 284, no. 6 (June 2001).

First, Ruth. *South West Africa.* Harmondsworth, UK: Penguin Books, 1963.

Gewald, Jan-Bart. "Flags, Funerals and Fanfares: Herero and Missionary Contestations of the Acceptable, 1900–1940." *Journal of African Cultural Studies* 15, no. 1 (June 2002).

Gewald, Jan-Bart. *Herero Heroes: A Socio-Political History of the Herero of Namibia, 1890–1923.* Athens: Ohio University Press, 1999.

Gewald, Jan-Bart. "Memory, Trauma and Redemption; Coming through Slaughter: The Herero of Namibia, 1904–1940." In *The Practice of War: Production, Reproduction and Communication of Armed Violence,* edited by Aparna Rao and Michael Bollig. New York: Berghahn Books, 2007.

Gordon, Robert J., and Stuart Sholto-Douglas. *The Bushman Myth: The Making of an Underclass.* Boulder, CO: Westview Press, 2000.

Green, Reginald H., Marija-Liisa Kiljvnen, and Kimmo Kiljven, eds. *Namibia: The Last Colony.* London: Longman, 1981.

Grotpeter, John J. *Historical Dictionary of Namibia*. Metuchen, NJ: Scarecrow Press, 1994.

Hailonga-van Dijk, Panduleni. "Adolescent Sexuality: Negotiating between Tradition and Modernity." In *Unravelling Taboos: Gender and Sexuality in Namibia*, edited by Suzanne LaFont and Dianne Hubbard. Windhoek, Namibia: Legal Assistance Center, 2007.

Hartmann, Wolfram, Jeremy Silvester and Patricia Hayes, eds. *The Colonising Camera: Photographs in the Making of Namibian History*. Athens: Ohio University Press, 1999.

Hayes, Patricia. "'Cocky' Hahn and the 'Black Venus': The Making of a Native Commissioner in South West Africa, 1915–1946." In *Gendered Colonialisms in African History*, edited by Nancy Rose Hunt, Tessie P. Liu, and Jean Quataert. London: Blackwell, 1997.

Hayes, Patricia. "Order Out of Chaos: Mandume Ya Ndemufayo and Oral History." *Journal of Southern African Studies* 19, no. 1 (March 1993).

Hayes, Patricia, Jeremy Sylvester, Marion Wallace, and Wolfram Hartmann, eds. *Namibia under South African Rule: Mobility and Containment 1915–46*. Athens: Ohio University Press, 1998.

Henderson, W. O. "Germany's Trade with Her Colonies, 1884–1914." *Economic History Review* 9, no. 1 (November 1938).

Hishongwa, Ndeutala Selma. *The Contract Labour System and Its Effects on Family and Social Life in Namibia: A Historical Perspective*. Windhoek, Namibia: Gamsberg Macmillan, 2000.

Jones, Brian T. B., Moses Makonjio Okello, and Bobby E. L. Wishitemi. "Pastoralists, Conservation and Livelihoods in East and Southern Africa: Reconciling Continuity and Change through the Protected Landscape Approach." In *The Protected Landscape Approach: Linking Nature, Culture and Community*, edited by Jessica Brown, Nora Mitchell, and Michael Beresford. Gland, Switzerland: World Conservation Union, 2005.

Journal of Southern African Studies. "Namibia: Africa's Youngest Nation." *Special issue*, vol. 19, no. 1 (March 1993).

Katjavivi, Peter. *Church and Liberation in Namibia*. London: Pluto Press, 1990.

Katjavivi, Peter. *A History of Resistance in Namibia*. Trenton, NJ: Africa World Press, 1990.

Kgobetsi, Siballi E. I. *Poets Against War, Violence, and Nuclear Weapons (PAWN): An Anthology of Contemporary African Poetry*. Windhoek, Namibia: Gamsberg Macmillan, 2000.

!Khaxas, Elizabeth, ed. *Between Yesterday and Tomorrow: Writings by Namibian Women*. Windhoek, Namibia: Women's Leadership Centre, 2005.

!Khaxas, Elizabeth, and Saskia Wieringa, eds. "Same-Sex Sexuality among Damara Women." In LaFont and Hubbard, *Unravelling Taboos: Gender and Sexual In Namibia*. Windhoek: Legal Assistance Centre, 2007.

Knappert, Jan. *Namibia: Land and Peoples, Myths and Fables*. Leiden: Brill, 1981.

LaFont, Suzanne, and Dianne Hubbard, eds. *Unravelling Taboos: Gender and Sexuality in Namibia.* Windhoek, Namibia: Legal Assistance Center, 2007.

Lau, Brigitte. *Namibia in Jonker Afrikaner's Time.* Windhoek: National Archives of Namibia, 1994.

Leacock, Eleanor Burke. *Myths of Male Dominance.* New York: Monthly Review Press, 1981.

LeBeau, Debie, Eunice Iipinge, and Michael Conteh. *Women's Property and Inheritance Rights in Namibia.* Windhoek, Namibia: Pollination Publishers/University of Namibia Gender Training and Research Programme, 2004.

Lee, Richard. *The Dobe !Kung.* New York: Holt, Rinehart and Winston, 1984.

Lenssen-Erz, Tilman, and Ralf Vogelsang. "Populating No-Man's Land—Rock Art in Northern Namibia." *South African Archaeological Society Goodwin Series* 9 (December 2005).

Lewis, I. M. *Ecstatic Religion: A Study of Shamanism and Spirit Possession.* New York: Routledge, 2003.

Lewis-Williams, Dowson. *Images of Power: Understanding San Rock-Art.* Cape Town, South Africa: Struik, 2000.

Lewis-Williams, J. D. "The Evolution of Theory, Method and Technique in Southern African Rock Art Research." *Journal of Archaeological Method and Theory* 13, no. 4 (December 2006).

Leys, Colin, and Susan Brown. *Histories of Namibia: Living through the Liberation Struggle.* London: Merlin Press, 2004.

Leys, Colin T., and John S. Saul. *Namibia's Liberation Struggle: The Two-Edged Sword.* Athens: Ohio University Press, 1995.

Lilienthal, Adelheid, and Annaleen Eins, eds. *Art in Namibia.* Windhoek: National Art Gallery of Namibia, 1997.

Lorway, Robert. "Breaking a Public Health Science: HIV Risk and Male-Male Sexual Practices in the Windhoek Urban Area." In LaFont and Hubbard, eds. *Unravelling Taboos: Gender and Sexual in Namibia.* Windhoek: Legal Assistance Centre, 2007.

Maddox, Gregory. *Sub-Saharan Africa: An Environmental History.* Santa Barbara, CA: ABC-CLIO, 2006.

Maho, J. E. *Few People, Many Tongues.* Windhoek, Namibia: Gamsberg Macmillan, 1998.

Malan, J. S. *Peoples of Namibia.* Pretoria, South Africa: Rhino, 1995.

Mans, Minette. *Music as Instrument of Diversity and Unity: Notes on a Namibian Landscape.* Uppsala, Sweden: Nordic Africa Institute, 2003.

Marshall, Lorna. *The !Kung of Nyae Nyae.* Cambridge, MA: Harvard University Press, 1976.

Martin, Henno. *The Sheltering Desert.* Johannesburg, South Africa: A. D. Donker, 1983.

Mazrui, Ali. "African Security: The Erosion of the State and the Decline of Race as a Basis for Human Relations." In *Globalization, Human Security and the African Experience,* edited by Caroline Thomas and Peter Wilkin. Boulder, CO: Lynne Rienner, 1999.

McKittrick, Meredith. *To Dwell Secure: Generation, Christianity and Colonialism in Ovamboland.* Portsmouth, NH: Heinemann, 2002.

Melber, Henning. "Colonialism, Culture and Resistance: The Case of Namibia." In Melber, *It Is No More a Cry: Namibian Poetry in Exile.* Basel, Switzerland: Basler Afrika Bibliographien, 2004.

Melber, Henning. *Namibia: A Decade of Independence, 1990–2000.* Windhoek: Namibian Economic Policy Research Unit, 2000.

Melber, Henning, ed. *Our Namibia: A Social Studies Textbook.* London: Zed Books, 1984.

Melber, Henning. *Re-examining Liberation in Namibia: Political Cultures since Independence.* Uppsala, Sweden: Nordic Africa Institute, 2003.

Melber, Henning. *Transitions in Namibia: Which Changes for Whom?* Uppsala, Sweden: Nordic Africa Institute, 2007.

Melber, Henning, ed. *It Is No More a Cry: Namibian Poetry in Exile.* Basel, Switzerland: Basler Afrika Bibliographien, 2004.

Minter, William. *King Solomon's Mines Revisited: Western Interests and the Burdened History of Southern Africa.* New York: Basic Books, 1986.

Müller-Friedman, Fatima. "'Just Build It Modern': Post-Apartheid Spaces on Namibia's Urban Frontier." In *African Urban Spaces,* edited by Toyin Falola and Steven Salm. Rochester, NY: University of Rochester Press, 2005.

Namhila, Ellen. *The Price of Freedom.* Windhoek: New Namibia Books, 1998.

Nampala, Lovisa, and Vilho Shigwedha. *Awambo Kingdoms, History and Cultural Change: Perspectives from Northern Namibia.* Basel, Switzerland: P. Schlettwein, 2006.

Nghidinwa, Maria Mboono. *Women Journalists in Namibia's Liberation Struggle, 1985–1990.* Basel, Switzerland: Basler Afrika Bibliographien, 2008.

Nujoma, Sam. *Where Others Wavered: The Autobiography of Sam Nujoma.* London: Panaf Books, 2001.

O'Callaghan, Marion. *Namibia: The Effects of Apartheid on Culture and Education.* Paris: UNESCO, 1977.

Orford, Margie, and Heike Becker. "Homes and Exiles: Ovambo Women's Literature." In *Contested Landscapes: Movement, Exile and Place,* edited by Barbara Bender and Margot Winer. Oxford: Berg, 2001.

Pendleton, Wade C. *Katutura: A Place Where We Stay: Life in a Post Apartheid Township in Namibia.* Athens: Ohio University Press, 1996.

Pool, Gerhard. *Samuel Maharero.* Windhoek, Namibia: Gamsberg Macmillan, 1991.

Shostak, Majorie. *Nisa: The Life and Words of a !Kung Woman.* Cambridge, MA: Harvard University Press, 2000.

Smith, Woodruff D. *The Ideological Origins of Nazi Imperialism.* Oxford: Oxford University Press, 1989.

South West Africa People's Organisation (SWAPO). *Namibia: Culture and the Liberation Struggle* [Pamphlet]. Luanda, Angola: SWAPO Department of Information and Publicity, 1986.

Sparks, Donald, and December Green. *Namibia after Independence.* Boulder, CO: Westview Press, 1992.

Stals, E.L.P. *The Afrikaners in Namibia: Who Are They?* Windhoek, Namibia: Macmillan, 2008.

Susser, Ida. *AIDS, Sex, and Culture: Global Politics and Survival in Southern Africa.* Oxford: Wiley-Blackwell, 2009.

Susser, Ida and Richard Lee. "Confounding Conventional Wisdom: The Ju'/hoansi and HIV/AIDS." In *Updating the San: Image and Reality of an African People in the 21st Century,* edited by R. Hitchcock. Osaka, Japan: National Museum of Ethnology, 2007.

Thomas, Elizabeth Marshall. *The Old Way: A Story of the First People.* New York: Farrar, Straus and Giroux, 2006.

Trüper, Ursula. *The Invisible Woman: Zara Schmelen: African Mission Assistant at the Cape and in Namaland.* Basel, Switzerland: Basler Afrika Bibliographien, 2006.

United Nations Environment Programme (UNEP). *Africa: Atlas of Our Changing Environment.* Nairobi, Kenya: UNEP, 2008.

Vale, Helen. "Namibian Poetry in English 1976–2006: Between Yesterday and Tomorrow—Unearthing the Past, Critiquing the Present and Envisioning the Future." *NAWA: Journal of Language and Communication* 2, no. 2 (December 2008), available at http://www.polytechnic.edu.na/academics/schools/comm_legal_secre/comm/nawa_journal/NAWA_2008/namibian-poetry-english-Vale.pdf.

Viljoen, Hercules. "Is Namibian Art (Still) Provincial + Regional + Untouched?" In *Transitions: Botswana, Namibia, Mozambique, Zambia, Zimbabwe, 1960–2004,* edited by Barbara Murray and John Picton. London: The Africa Centre, 2005.

Vogt, Andreas. *National Monuments in Namibia: An Inventory of Proclaimed National Monuments in the Republic of Namibia.* Windhoek, Namibia: Gamsberg Macmillan, 2004.

Wallace, Marion. "'Making Tradition': Healing, History and Ethnic Identity among Otjiherero-Speakers in Namibia, c. 1850–1950." *Journal of Southern African Studies* 29, no. 2 (June 2003).

Willcox, A. R. *The Rock Art of Africa.* New York: Holmes & Meier, 1984.

Williams, Christian A. "Student Political Consciousness: Lessons from a Namibian Mission School." *Journal of Southern African Studies* 30, no. 3 (September 2004).

Ya-Otto, John. *Battlefront Namibia: An Autobiography.* Westport, CT: L. Hill, 1981.

Zimmerer, Jurgen, and Joachim Zeller, eds. *Genocide in German South-West Africa: The Colonial War (1904–1908) in Namibia and Its Aftermath.* Translated by Edward J. Neather. Monmouth, Wales: Merlin Press, 2003.

REPORTS AND PAMPHLETS

Government of Republic of Namibia. *A Review of Poverty and Inequality in Namibia.* Central Bureau of Statistics, National Planning Commission. Windhoek, Namibia, 2008.

Government of the Republic of Namibia. *United Nations General Assembly Special Session (UNGASS) Country Report.* Reporting Period April 2006–March 2007. Report on AIDS/HIV. Produced by the Directorate of Special Programmes, Division Expanded National HIV/AIDS Coordination, Windhoek, Namibia.

Keulder, Theunis. *Catching the Voice of the Born-Free Generation of Namibia through Mobile Phones.* Namibia Institute for Democracy (NID), December 2009, http://www.nid.org.na/pdf/publications/UNICEF%20final%20report.pdf.

!Khaxas, Elizabeth, Liz Frank and A. Rimmer. "We Women and Girls of Namibia Claim Our Right to Survive HIV and AIDS by Challenging Poverty, Oppression, Cultural Practices and Violence." Published by the Women's Leadership Centre, Windhoek, 2007.

Ministry of Education, Government of the Republic of Namibia. *The Development of Education: National Report of Namibia.* Report prepared for the UNESCO 48th International Conference on Education, Geneva, November 2008.

"Understanding the Perpetrators of Violent Crimes Against Women and Girls in Namibia; Implications for Prevention and Treatment." Windhoek, Namibia, 2008. Available from the Konrad Adenauer Foundation, Windhoek.

World Bank. *Namibia: A Country Study.* Washington, DC: World Bank, 2009.

World Bank. "Ratio of Female to Male Enrollments in Tertiary Education around the World." The World Bank (WB) publishes these statistics annually; consult WB for most recent or previous data.

ENGLISH-LANGUAGE NEWSPAPERS

Informante! http://www.informante.web.na
Namibian Sun http://www.namibiansun.com
New Era http://www.newera.com.na
New Namibian http://www.namibian.com.na
The Southern Times http://www.southerntimesafrica.com

WEBSITES AND ORGANIZATIONS OF INTEREST

Joint United Nations Programme on HIV/AIDS http://www.UNAIDS.org
Ministry of Environment and Tourism http://www.met.gov.na
Parliament of Namibia http://www.parliament.gov.na
Sister Namibia http://www.sisternamibia.org

VIDEO

Téno, Jean-Marie. *Le Colonial Malentendu.* In English, French, German, with English subtitles. Available from California Newsreel, 2004.

Index

About the Author

ANENE EJIKEME, PhD, is associate professor in the Department of History at Trinity University, San Antonio, Texas. An expert in modern African history, Ejikeme previously taught at Barnard College in New York, New York, where she also served as the director of the Pan-African Studies Program.